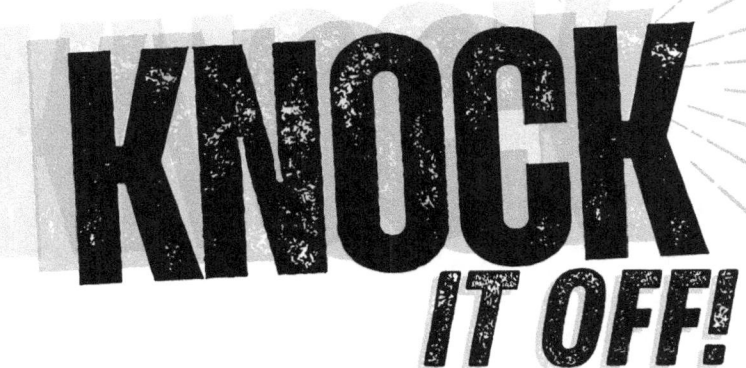

KNOCK IT OFF!

Imitation Isn't Flattering

CALLING OUT *the* **POSERS** *the* **ABUSERS** *the* **KNOCK-OFFS!**
(+ TIPS FOR *YOU* TO LIVE *YOUR* MOST AUTHENTIC LIFE!)

Alanna Zabel

KNOCK IT OFF!

Copyright © 2024 by Alanna Zabel

ISBN: 979-8-9893235-1-7

www.aziam.com

Dedicated to:

THE CREATORS, THE INNOVATORS, THE TRUTH SEEKERS,

and

MY FATHER, ALPHONSE: NO ONE HAS A SHARPER EYE THAN
YOU WHEN IT COMES TO SPOTTING A POSER OR A FAKE.

*"No matter what people tell you, words and ideas
can change the world."* **– Robin Williams**

TABLE OF CONTENTS

PREFACE

There's no clearer sign from the universe that you're amazing than witnessing some of the richest and most famous people on our planet try to pass off your creations, your business, and even your life as their own. But let's be real—while it's a backhanded compliment, they only pulled it off because I was too forgiving and vulnerable—shaped by developmental factors and exposed to cunning narcissists.

I've been sitting on the idea for this book for quite some time, and I'm even considering turning it into a podcast because I know there are countless others with similar stories who need a space to be heard. It's essential that we normalize these conversations—to bring the hidden realities of manipulation, deception, narcissism, and gaslighting into the open, while exposing the rampant theft of ideas and concepts from hardworking creatives and visionaries. This will empower people to speak up, heal, and learn how to avoid similarly damaging experiences, especially when these abuses come from the rich, famous, and powerful. You see, there is an unspoken code among the top 10% of the world's wealthiest—not unlike a gangster's code of silence. Naturally, they don't want to risk their good fortune and privilege, even if that means turning a blind eye to unethical behavior, exploitation, or deception.

While I have met some incredibly generous and kind individuals who happen to be vastly wealthy, some truly talented celebrities, and some inspiring influencers, the reality is that most worldly successful people got where they are through a mixture of luck, who they know, and ruthless drive. With the stakes and competition as high as they are, many will do whatever it takes to keep their place in line. It's a shark-infested pool, and the waters are far more dangerous than they appear on the surface.

To be honest, I have not been eager to publicly share the personal experiences in this book. They're painful and some are downright embarrassing. However, I recently witnessed the surreal spectacle of a social-climbing 'celebrity' (and former client) posturing my work as her own. The whole experience was so absurd, so brazen, so mind-blowing…it reminded me of the last time this happened!

That's when I not only recognized the pattern but knew it was finally time to tell my story. That selfish act solidified enough blatant proof to dissolve any lingering doubts from previous experiences that had held me back from confronting these kinds of abusers. I know that I am not alone in these experiences, and sharing my journey could offer guidance to others navigating similar waters. I hope to empower you to recognize manipulative dynamics, trust your instincts, and stay fiercely true to who you are.

I mean, we all know there's an epidemic of superficiality and fake-ness in the world right now. From influencers peddling nonsensical and wasteful products—caring more about their quick buck than how the product impacts their followers—to brands charging premium prices for low-quality, toxic goods, using your purchase dollars to pay celebrities millions to endorse the very products they don't actually use, in order to create the illusion of a luxury brand. In essence, you're paying to fool yourself.

Oh, and what about the celebrities accused of bullying and abuse, all while publicly touting kindness and positivity? It's time that the public wakes up to the fact that those are nothing more than manufactured PR campaigns, designed to gaslight the public to forget about their bad behaviors. These celebrities know that their status, favor, and financial wealth depend on keeping up with their appearances. Celebrities can usually buy their way out of any scandal, even when caught red-handed. To them, it's all a make-believe game, carefully orchestrated to protect their image—not to actually walk the walk they love to lecture you about.

And then, of course, there's that special breed of low talent celebrities who don't even bother creating anything original when they can simply steal business concepts, designs, and playbooks. I've experienced this more times than I can count, but I'll share some, just some, of the most outrageous examples in the pages that follow. I'll save the rest for another day.

I hope you come to recognize the power of your individual attention and praise—and how valuable these truly are. Don't waste them on the manufactured personas of celebrities desperately vying for public approval. Understand that they purchase their popularity, hire teams to manage and maintain that curated image, in order to leverage your manipulated belief in their fabricated facade, all so that they can profit from your fandom; you may as well be idolizing a fictional character created by artificial intelligence. It's time to stop glorifying make-believe idols and start appreciating real humanity.

They say that *imitation is the highest form of flattery*, but I am not flattered when my concepts and hard work are knocked off. However, at some point, you just have to laugh at the absurdity. I'm a yogi trying to live an honest, service-oriented life. I value the quality of my life over possessions and titles. Yet, I found myself surrounded by celebrities at the pinnacle of fame and wealth, and everything that comes with it—and somehow, they were envious of me?! That's when it became clear: this wasn't just about imitation—it was my uniquely authentic creative essence that they wanted. To them, it has priceless value, it is something they don't have and they can't buy. No amount of money in the universe can buy authenticity or creativity if someone doesn't have it! But I hadn't yet fully realized my own worth, and this put me in a danger zone—an open door for exploitation.

So here we are: this book, this slightly snarky, raw, call-it-as-it-is exposé to help you navigate the strange, poser-filled world we're all living in. This book was born out of a realization that in today's world, authenticity has become a rare and endangered species. Everywhere that you go today, you'll find someone who cares more about the appearance of success than the substance behind it. It's a copy and paste world, and if you have something of value, you had better learn how to protect it.

This book is also my way of clearing the air and making peace with these painful experiences as a pure-hearted celebrity yoga instructor who was used as a pawn by the rich and famous for their own gains; it's the same old Hollywood tale, but different. It's a call-out, a reflection, a healing, and a guide to recognizing—and rejecting—anything not aligned with truth. These narcissists may have clipped my wings, but miraculously, what I've organically achieved with broken wings soars far beyond anything they could ever dream of doing honestly on their own. Personally, I do not believe that the end justifies the means, at least in the worldly sense.

Through this journey, I hope you not only learn the tactics that these master manipulators use to deceive, but also reflect on how you might be attracting similar people in your own life—and most importantly, learn new ways to value your own unique authenticity.

I wrote this for the creatives who've been overlooked, for the entrepreneurs whose ideas have been hijacked, and for the visionary dreamers who still believe that authenticity matters in a world obsessed with templates, copies and shortcuts. This book is for those who've been silenced while someone else takes the credit. It's for the people who have put in the hard work, only to see it relabeled by someone who couldn't recognize real effort if it was sewn inside their Birkin bag.

Thank you for being part of this shared journey toward truth and authenticity.
~ Alanna

Introduction
The Yogi

People behave unethically all the time, but the rich and powerful tend to get away with it far more often than most. This book gets real about the inner workings of the privileged and famous, and what happens when a pure lamb lives amongst the wolves, which happens every day in Hollywood. Each chapter dives into a different character (with most names changed) who acted in ways so shockingly selfish and narcissistic, it'll leave you questioning how these people ever made it to the "top"—until you realize that is actually how they made it there.

We'll dive into the character flaws and personality disorders that drive people like them, how to deal with them, and maybe, just maybe, we all have traces of those traits that could use a little reflection. Each chapter will close with insightful lessons we can all learn from, because the real truth isn't just about exposing others; it's about recognizing the parts of ourselves that need growth too. I believe it's healthy to approach every lesson from both sides of the coin, so I'll get real on my end while calling out the posers on theirs. By the end, you'll have tips to navigate your life with clearer vision and a stronger sense of self.

Like many, I was born with very diverse and extraordinary talents —natural beauty, profound insight, exceptional creativity, effortless athleticism—while holding a heart of gold, and uniquely, an unshakable connection to organic spirituality—refusing to bow to the demands and absurdities of today's modern world; a world obsessed with superficiality, consumerism, and chasing empty promises. I was highly valued for being a refreshingly real person in a world full of posers and opportunists. But that shifted after I experienced a profoundly traumatic relationship—one so life-altering that my life and self-worth as I knew it crumbled, propelling me onto a path of deep inner healing, away from worldly pursuits and external validation. In that process, I inadvertently uncovered layers of unprocessed emotions from some early life traumas, dysfunctional developmental programs, and even traces of ancestral traumas I unknowingly carried.

Our personal journeys are a unique blend of our natural talents, desires, and insights intertwined with the impact of our development and past traumas—these powerful forces influencing and hindering each other throughout our lives. These contrasting energies shape our experiences, with moments of great expansion bumping up against unresolved resistance. Yet, there was another disruptive factor in my mix—a sociopath with a knack for manipulation and brainwashing. It only takes one toxic person in our lives to alter our life's course, or knock down all the carefully placed dominoes we've built. I'll illustrate how this happened in my life and share insights on what to watch for.

I view every scenario in my life from two perspectives. First, through the lens of the worldly chain of events—what occurred on the surface, in tangible actions and outcomes. This perspective helps me understand the relational, psychological and situational aspects of my experiences. Secondly: the universal energetics at play—the unseen forces that shape these events on a deeper level. This perspective considers how global trends, karmic cycles, and ancestral influences contribute to what manifests in our lives.

Metaphorically speaking, we humans are like a colony of ants, busily navigating our lives within the confines of our hive—which, for this analogy, is inside a freight train car. Unaware of the bigger picture, we go about our daily routines, oblivious to the fact that unseen moving forces are affecting us, taking us to unknown destinations beyond our awareness or control. We believe our tiny world is everything, yet in reality, other forces are constantly at work, shaping our experiences without us fully realizing it.

THE GOOD EGG

There was a time in my early adult life that felt organically powerful, as if all of my stars were aligned. It was a time when I was teaching private yoga sessions to some of the biggest names in Hollywood—celebrities, producers, directors, musicians, as well as politicians, designers and athletes—a lot of the movers and shakers in the world…AND let's not forget, a few wealthy and gossipy socialites.

I thrived in this work, not only because I was exceptionally skilled as a yoga instructor, but because I genuinely cared about each of my clients' well-being. They called me "a good egg," and I was. I often didn't even realize they were famous or influential people—I simply saw them for who they truly were. I had no ulterior motives nor did I ask any special favors. At least initially, this is (strike a gong for the ominous foreshadowing to *Chapter 1: The Sociopath*).

Originally, my easy-going and compassionate personality naturally aligned with a career as a yoga instructor. Teaching felt effortless and authentic. However, when our lives burn brightly, they tend to attract people drawn to that light—not always for the right reasons. Some are motivated by self-interest, hoping to take what they can for themselves. Knowing this, celebrities have layers of protection—teams of people to shield them from these opportunists. But as someone connected to high-profile individuals, I didn't have those same barriers or understanding. I was left exposed, and that vulnerability opened the door for someone highly experienced with manipulative intent.

I begin this book with *The Sociopath* in *Chapter 1* because it marked this pivotal moment when my life and personality shifted in ways I was unable to control. This person had studied and developed mind control tactics, using them to intentionally manipulate, and even though my experience was extreme, we all encounter similar, more subtle dynamics, whether with manipulative people in our personal lives or authoritarian and corporate influences on a larger scale. It felt like watching the train of my life's purpose—something I had spent years building—derail in slow motion, as someone else hijacked my controls, destroying the very thing he desired in the process.

As my personality changed, so did my relationships—most for the worse. I could no longer tolerate even the slightest toxic behavior from others, leaving me without the emotional bandwidth to care for others as I once had. In search of relief from the emotional discomfort and newfound insecurities that I was experiencing, I began saying yes to opportunities more impulsively, hoping for a quick way out of the pain and back to a sense of inner security, back to the life I had known before. That set the stage for the events in *Chapters 2* through *7*, as I navigated through a series of unethical experiences before finally finding the strength to take back control and begin the healing process.

It's important to make clear that, although I was compromised from The Sociopath's abuse, the subsequent characters in this book knowingly chose to take advantage of my vulnerability at that time, acting with unethical and selfish intent. Their actions were deliberate, and my compromised condition does not excuse or justify their behavior.

It has taken me fifteen years to get to this point, and the work is still ongoing. Healing is not a linear process but a continuous journey, full of twists and turns. Regaining control of my life and rediscovering my authentic self required patience, persistence, and a deep reconnection to the anchor of who I once knew myself to be. It wasn't about becoming someone new, but rather peeling back the layers of habitual brainwashing that had altered my life. However, with every step forward, I gained valuable insights—not just about myself, but also about how to help others on their paths to living most authentically.

Well before this sociopath entered my life, I approached everything I did with pure intentions, opting for an organic approach to life, trusting that the right paths and people would align in their own time. I've had an almost allergic reaction to anything superficial. Marketing? Ugh. The idea of using predictable, in-your-face tactics to sell something made my skin crawl. My philosophy has always been, if people want what I'm offering, they will find me. For one, I'm not about to beg for attention, and two, it feels selfish to yank people's focus away from their own lives just to get a spotlight on mine—what if they were like me, allowing their lives to unfold naturally, in the moment? Well, fat chance of that—I soon realized how very rare I was in this regard—even if I didn't fully understand the developmental reasons behind this easy going, surrendered way of life.

THE SUPERFICIAL

I believe that the forced, down our throats "popularity" of a specifiK reality show hijacked an entire generation. The rise of social media, combined with this family's superficial assault on the world, transformed this promising millennial generation into one with increasingly superficial tendencies.

The show became more like *Keeping Up With Narcissus*, staring at their filtered, photo-shopped, and surgically enhanced reflections in the river, where they began to believe the very delusions crafted by their own marketing teams, managers, producers and plastic surgeons. Then, they demanded that we believe it, too! The worst part? The fake, manufactured appearance of "success" sold their sham to the susceptible youth, who then took the same means, hoping for the same result. Boom: a superficial epidemic, just like that. It seems that people are far more determined to project their lies than they are to persuade others of their truths.

Superficial people tend to be starved for security, like plants without roots blown wherever the wind takes them. On the other hand, a person with depth is deeply rooted in their purpose and who they are. Staying grounded to my authenticity has always been my priority, even in a world filled with endless pop-ups teasing "the next big thing." Luckily, I had already seen first-hand that there truly is no "big thing," and that's my message to you. It's time to open the windows to let the smoke out, and break the mirrors that deceive you into believing otherwise. Your life is far more important than filtered, fake, gaslit celebrity life, and it's waiting for your attention.

For about ten years, I watched, and partook in from the sides, the glittering life of fame and fortune. During this time my passion for wellness had morphed into a brand, which was on trend, and this passion was aligned with my purpose. I starred in a nationally best-selling DVD in the fitness category, designed a gorgeous activewear line, I was writing inspirational books, leading retreats worldwide and had invented *The World's First Yoga Doll®* collections. The opportunities were rolling in: infomercials, reality show deals, licensing offers—all ready to slap my brand name on mass-produced garbage that I wouldn't touch with a ten-foot pole. So, after far too many negative experiences with the groomers, charlatans, posers, desperate housewives and puppet masters, I began to say "no" and do less.

I refused to compromise my authentic essence and business for the sake of fame and wealth. I turned down opportunities—even from some of the most influential people in the world—while working to forge a path that went against the mainstream direction society was pushing at a ferocious pace. One thing I can say with absolute certainty: I've lived true to who I am in every way that I have known, and in my opinion, at the end of our lives, that is what will matter most. In *Chapter 8*, I'll explore the healing work that led me through these experiences, back to who I truly am. It's never too late to be you.

I believe there is no more powerful act that we can take than to live true to who we are. This always reminds me of the powerful quote by Mohadesa Najumi: ***The woman who does not require validation from anyone is the most feared individual on the planet.*** *Energy is everything.*

INTEGRITY

Here's the thing: I am a bit stubborn about integrity. If it's not natural, I'm not interested. I can smell if a person has integrity, or if they don't, like a wolf in the wild. And let me tell you, it hasn't exactly made me the most popular person in the room. I've clashed with my own yoga community more times than I can count, mainly because I couldn't stomach their performative spirituality, ego fueled hypocrisy, conspiracy theory delusions, topped with empty buzzwords (so "love and light" of me, eh?). Turns out, being real makes some folks a little...uncomfortable. Especially in a world where image is everything.

Again, I could've sold out. I could've bought fake followers, fake likes, fake reviews—the whole fake package. I could've handed over my rights to publishers who would've reshaped my story into something more marketable, starred in the cheesy reality shows, and licensed my brand for more cheap, plastic garbage. No thanks. Instead, I stayed real, sticking to what I know is true, fumbles and all—no matter how slow or unglamorous the roads might have been, because I knew they were true.

You see, I am a deeply spiritual person navigating a vastly and increasingly superficial world. Can you relate? My life has been filled with extraordinary experiences, wrapped in rich synchronicity, which makes the mundane human experiences incomparable. My soul is of greatest value to me, not manufacturing nylon yoga leggings.

ORIGIN

I've illustrated that I am fascinated by truth and authenticity, but also by origins—by where things begin, how ideas are born, the spark that ignites creativity, as well as the subsequent evolution of that spark that follows. Inspiration is a natural part of being human, and we are all innocently influenced by the world around us. However, there's a vast difference between being inspired by something and claiming an origin that isn't ours—or worse, outright stealing someone else's innovations, which happens every day in our modern world.

As yogis, we are taught to honor the source of our teachings and inspiration, giving thanks to each teacher and guru that came before us. This practice instills a mindset of humility and accountability. For me, both origin and inspiration are sacred, reminding me that I am part of a much bigger, interconnected picture. Without this awareness, it becomes all too easy for individuals to fall into the ego-driven illusion that they alone are the source—that they themselves are God.

I often think of origin with the visual of a pebble striking the surface of a pond—the moment of impact is the origin, and every ripple that follows carries the intention and energy of that initial action, with its own inspiration and journey. But the ripples are not disconnected from the source. When, like ancient yogis, we respect the origin, we amplify its power, just like those ripples carrying the purpose of that first pebble across the surface of the water.

I believe that it is important to distinguish between organic action —those decisions and movements that arise naturally from within— and actions that are inspired or influenced by external sources. Inspiration from external sources requires discernment. We must pause and ask ourselves whether we are truly inspired, meaning the idea resonates deeply with our values and purpose, or if we are being subtly driven by ego or competition to replicate someone else's path.

This discernment requires honesty—checking in with ourselves to ensure our actions are aligned with who we are, rather than a reaction to someone else's influence, or wanting what someone else has. Knowing when to embrace inspiration and when to honor it, as it is, is key to maintaining integrity. When we act with truthfulness, whether the source is internally organic, or externally inspired, the result will feel more authentic.

THE EVOLUTION OF MORALITY

Since we're diving into "Bad Habits of the Rich and Powerful," it's helpful to zoom out for a moment and consider the bigger picture—the historical shifts and moral objectives that humankind has strived for over the millennia. We're trying to be good people, but truthfully, we're still very much a work in progress! It's only been around 2,500 years since the birth of democracy in Athens, and that's barely a blink in the short timeline of human history. We've made significant strides in governing systems and moral philosophy, but the ongoing struggles between power, wealth, and ethical responsibility show that humanity's collective moral compass is far from true north.

Many religious and philosophical traditions formalized moral principles, creating distinctions between right and wrong, or good and bad behavior. For example, Confucianism, Buddhism, Judaism, Yoga, and Greek philosophies, to name a few, each emphasized compassion, justice, and a collective good for all people.

Of course, you probably can't find a more iconic example of moral conduct than Moses' Ten Commandments—principles designed to govern the people he led through the desert for 40 years. I, too, would have created some rules if I were leading the same group around for that long! A few hundred years later, the Upanishads detail how to cultivate righteousness, which evolved into Yoga's eight-limbed path. However, around 900 AD, the vastly increasing spread of Christianity began to alter moral landscapes across Europe. In addition, our means of maintaining written records had advanced to advertise these concepts more easily to greater groups of people. Christian teachings encouraged kindness, humility, and service to others. Naturally, these teachings spread even further after the 1400s, thanks to the invention of the printing press.

So, why do some people feel compelled to act morally, and others do not? And why is it that the latter are the ones who seem to "win" the most worldly gains? This past year, I immersed myself into a series of documentaries examining pivotal moments in history when unethical forces seized power and control over the masses. These included Stalin's rise to power, Hitler's ascent and Nazi political tactics, Mayan spiritual practices, the blood-thirsty, ruthless conquests of the Vikings and Romans, and the political landscapes of ancient Egypt and Greece.

My curiosity was driven by a desire to understand the origins of fake news smear campaigns, as well as the evolution of morality in humankind - two opposing forces that gained momentum with the use of the printing press. If we aspire to live in a world where conscious morality and ethical leadership replace power-hungry dictators and harmful business practices, it is essential for each of us to cultivate the ability to discern truth from fiction.

You see, before this widespread popularity of Christianity, Buddhism and Yoga, moral conduct was mostly influenced by cultural beliefs—how groups and tribes lived amongst each other. Morality was rooted in honor and the appeasement of their particular gods. Human sacrifice, war and conquest, which hopefully seem barbaric to us today, were common practices for many of these cultures, especially Viking, Roman and Aztec. Murder was simply part of life, and it wasn't unusual for people to kill a family member to climb social ladders, take slaves, torture, or rob the poor without facing any consequences, or feeling any sense of guilt or wrong-doing.

Now, regardless of religion or personal beliefs, it's fascinating to trace these global shifts in morality with the popular rise of both Buddhism and Christianity, with the latter introducing a burden of guilt while creating an ethical bar for repentance. This transformed how societies recognized, and punished, right from wrong.

I bring this up because many prominent figures throughout history, past and present, even those, like Vladmir Putin (who proudly touts himself as Christian), have continued to act from barbaric and self-serving mindsets—driven by the same impulses to conquer and control, even when their faith outwardly rejects those acts. They lie, cheat, murder and steal, without batting an eyelid, let alone feel any remorse. Yet, hypocritically, they demand that the people act in accordance with their governance and laws, or be punished for their crimes.

The Vikings were barbaric, thriving on conquest and the glory of battle. To them, the most honorable death was one met in combat, securing a coveted place in Valhalla. Interestingly, we can see echoes of this deluded mindset in modern-day jihadist ideologies, where acts of terror are driven by a similarly distorted sense of honor and afterlife reward. Either, common men were brainwashed into believing these things so that their leaders could ensure strong armies for their personal objectives, or each individual justified their barbaric acts by convincing themselves they were serving a higher purpose.

In my opinion, the Vikings' impressive reputation for conquest may have contributed to the later, distorted Nazi ideal of their "Aryan" elitist race, which included similar physical features: tall, strong, fair hair, fair skin. Between the 8th and 11th centuries, the Scandanavians migrated into what is now modern-day Germany and Poland, crossing the southern shores of the Baltic Sea. This included the fierce and physically impressive Vikings. These settlements contributed to the development of Germanic ideals, which eventually fed into the very German Nationalism that inspired Nazism. Mind you, the original concept of an Aryan people actually stems from Indian and Iranian references to noblemen from the Middle East, having nothing to do with the fair hair and light skin traits that the Germans later adopted. But Hitler wasn't known for being an honest historian. He heavily distorted historical interpretations to serve his political agenda and conspiracy theories.

Follow along with my train of thought here, please—I believe that the influence of this fair-haired, new Aryan race may have played a role in shaping the later concept of being "all-American." I'm not taking any political stance whatsoever, I am simply trying to understand how we've arrived at where we are today, where specific appearances and superficial presentations have evolved into a massive advertising ideal—used to sell everything from lip gloss to blind adoration. It's fascinating (and a little unnerving) to see how deeply ingrained superficiality has become in shaping our desires, our identities, our beliefs, and even our sense of belonging in the world. *But can we trust the source of this ideal?*

The Nazi Party employed a sophisticated array of techniques to influence public opinion and cement control over Germany. They monopolized all media while cleverly using fake news and fear-mongering to exploit people's desperate hunger for change. They pioneered a form of branding that combined political objectives with elitist imagery, using a logo (the swastika) and short, memorable logans to leave a strong impression on the public's psyche.

Around the same time, brands like Coca-Cola were just beginning to explore celebrity endorsements and strategic branding. But the Nazis took it to another level, weaponizing the concept by promoting an image of an elite, fit, blonde-haired, blue-eyed ideal as the deceptive face of their ideology - hiding their monstrous intentions behind an alluring facade. They introduced the idea of a "supermodel" to sell their lies. And let's not forget, Hugo Boss designed the Nazi uniforms - talk about brand sponsorship!

Here is how I believe the racial elitism that defined the Nazi regime subtly influenced the "all-American" ideal, where fit, blonde-haired, blue-eyed individuals came to symbolize an aspirational standard of American nationalism. This bias is evident in many aspects of American society, including how missing blonde girls often dominate media coverage and public sympathy, while missing African American girls, sadly, receive far less attention. Even cultural icons like Beyoncé recognize that being blonde in America leads to greater popularity and broader appeal.

These same deceptive tactics set a dark precedent for how power can exploit perception, influencing not only politics but also the modern world's approach to branding, marketing, and media. Today, brand development includes all of these same elements: a mission statement, logo, slogan, desirable models, and attractive ads. These same tactics are used by corporations, celebrities and influencers today, using superficial facades to harness your attention, loyalty, and ultimately your purchase, like, or vote.

Throughout history, authoritarian leaders have used this image, as well as other specific strategies of misinformation, to harness power over the masses. Somehow, basic principles of 'service to the people' and 'lead by example' often get buried beneath personal agendas and a hunger for power, where the people of democracies are fed lies in order to ensure their compliance and support.

Since most people have an innate desire to belong, to be part of an "in" crowd, many feel safer aligning with a powerful figure, even if— and often because—that person is an unethical bully, because it provides an illusion of protection. I call this "mass Stockholm syndrome." The fear of losing perceived advantages to "lesser races" fuels blind allegiance to the bully, driving people to compromise their morals, all for the comfort of fitting into that deceptive, fear-mongered illusion of an elite class, and securing what they have been led to believe is rightfully theirs—again, turning a blind eye to the leader's actual intentions or behaviors, which rarely have anything to do with the people's well-being.

What I'm trying to convey is that these ruthless, self-serving, and gaslighting actions of the powerful have been entrenched in our societies since the dawn of humanity, stemming from our primal, animalistic instincts. Instead of pledging loyalty to the alpha male in our pack, or rallying behind victorious armies in ancient battle formations, we now channel these same primal passions, fears, and allegiances when cheering for the most dominant team at the Super Bowl or backing a candidate in a Presidential race. We feel safer aligning with the fiercest fighter, not necessarily the most ethical or democratic.

However, my stance and my belief is that we need to evolve beyond these primal tendencies if we are to survive as a species, if we ever want to see our communities living honestly, in peace amongst each other, and in harmony with nature. Truth is not subjective; it is the foundation upon which reality is built, and truth requires that each of us develop the courage to see things as they are, not as we wish them to be. Gaslight is the new green light for global manipulation, therefore more importantly than ever before, it is essential for each of us to cultivate the ability to discern truth from fiction.

So, without further ado, let's dive into the unethical behaviors of the everyday posers and predators running rampant in our societies today, using these same self-serving forces of ancient conquerors and the same greedy tactics for power, except now they are hidden behind computer screens, masked by polished images, and armed with manipulation and unethical schemes. How many of these posers preach environmentalism from their private jets, kindness after berating their own staff, or humanitarianism while stealing from their yoga teachers? It's time to get real and stop giving our attention to these posers. To do so, you and I have to be astute in seeing through their bullshit and illusions.

You see, these superficial, hypocritical posers, abusers and predators come in every form imaginable. They might be in your family, at work, on your dating app, or running for local office (including all parties). They could be business owners, neighbors, teachers, lawyers, priests, yoga teachers, or even police officers.

Immoral, selfish tendencies arise from a combination of our development and genetics. These egoistic tendencies have simply evolved into the narcissists and sociopaths of our modern world, and trust me—you're far wiser (and safer) knowing their tactics than staying in the dark!

Take a moment to examine who you "follow" and admire. Are you overlooking questionable behavior? If so, you're not alone. People often turn a blind eye to narcissistic behavior, buying into phony facades due to manufactured appeal and charisma, as well as individual self-doubt, social pressure to "fit in," fear of repercussions, denial, or even personal benefit from the association. What would happen if you started living true to what you genuinely feel is "right"—calling out the posers and abusers while choosing a life of conscious morality?

As we step into the dawn of AI-driven content dominating our world, it is equally wise to sharpen our ability to discern reality from deception. So, join me in this call to keep it real!

Future generations depend on us.

CHAPTER 1

The Sociopath

Gaslighting is a slow unconscious loss of reality.

TRIGGER WARNING

Situations described in this chapter include domestic violence. It may bring up painful feelings or memories, so please take care of yourself. If you, or someone you know, are experiencing domestic violence, help is available. You can call the **National Domestic Abuse Hotline at 1-800-799-7233**

THE SOCIOPATH

This is usually the point where I stop writing or walk away. I despise this chapter of my life—it's the most painful of all—but it lays the foundation for everything that followed. I haven't shared the details of this chapter with many people, not even my family. To this day, I refuse to speak the real name of The Sociopath. I've worked to erase him from my consciousness as much as possible, even though the scars of his abuse still remain, shaping me in ways I continue working to reverse. But now, it's finally time to share this story. For the purpose of this book, I'll call him Jack—short for jack-ass.

Earlier, I mentioned a precious time in my life when everything felt perfectly aligned. Imagine this with me: I'm in that golden moment, filled with joy, creativity, and purpose, the epitome of health and vitality. I was living the dream I had worked so hard to build—teaching yoga to celebrity clients, traveling the world leading empowering retreats, writing inspiring books, designing eco-conscious clothing, and developing my children's brand of yoga dolls and toys, *AZ I AM Kidz*.

I had complete control over my schedule, allowing me to live a life where work, creativity, and adventure blended into each other effortlessly. Each day felt like a fresh opportunity to dive deeper into my passions and share them with the world. In return, incredible opportunities seemed to pour in: TV shows, infomercials, headlining festivals, and product recognition on major networks.

Amidst this whirlwind of success and excitement, a woman who regularly attended my yoga classes approached me after class one day —let's call her Tina. She was a gossipy woman who always spoke in a whisper, as if she were the giver of everyone's secrets. She wanted to introduce me to a man who, according to her, could help me with business analytics if I wanted to open a yoga studio. Her enthusiasm was convincing, and I thought, *Why not?* I was open to new connections, especially if they could potentially benefit my growing business.

However, if I could change just one moment of my life, it would be that one; to never have met Jack that day, or ever. In hindsight, it's clear that this man's intentions were not as professional as I had been led to believe. He began attending my Thursday night yoga classes, asking to be a guest each week in exchange for his business analysis that, let me remind you, I never actually asked for. But I was generous by nature—especially back then—and I didn't mind letting him attend my classes for free; a bit of goodwill didn't feel like much of a sacrifice.

After attending my classes for a few weeks, he began inviting me to dinner afterward. At first, I thought it was just a friendly gesture, perhaps a way to discuss business in a more casual setting. But as the weeks went by, it became apparent that he was pursuing something more.

I wasn't attracted to him—not in a physical or emotional way. He wasn't unattractive by any means, but there was something off about him that I couldn't quite put my finger on. It wasn't anything overt or obvious; it was more of an intuitive feeling. There was a lack of soul, a lack of emotional depth that I couldn't ignore. He spoke in a measured, calculated way, and while his demeanor was polite and charming, there was something missing. It was as if he was performing rather than genuinely engaging in the moment.

Jack's energy, though calm, felt hollow. He was like a glass of water that looked refreshing but you're still left thirsty. Still, every time I tried to imply this incompatibility, he would counter with, "Still waters run deep," as if I was the one missing something unseen.

It was a strange defense for someone who seemed to lack the very depth he claimed to possess in some hidden box which he referred to as a means to seduce interest. Something about the way he carried

4

himself felt almost effeminate, but not in a typical or visible way—just a subtle undercurrent. I also felt that he mimicked my emotions rather than feeling his own; he seemed fascinated by how open and comfortable with my emotions that I was. Again, it was difficult to put my finger on at the time, but something wasn't right, at least for me.

I continued to brush things off. I wasn't interested in him anyways, so it didn't actually matter. I convinced myself that maybe he was just a different type of person, someone whose passions weren't as obvious as mine. I'd seen enough of the world to know that not everyone wears their heart on their sleeve.

Every Thursday, we'd have dinner, and I'd politely listen as he droned on about numbers, business models, and analytics. All the while, I kept thinking of a way to end this weekly habit without being offensive. But he was persistent, always showing up and inserting himself into my world. I allowed it, in part because I didn't want to appear ungrateful or rude. Plus, Tina had done a really good job of selling how amazing he was, and that he could help my business—she added an element of trust. I was also distracted by the many other exciting things happening in my life, which was spinning fast and I was having a lot of fun!

Looking back, I can see now that Jack's persistence wasn't about building a professional relationship—it was something else entirely. He was trying to weave himself into my life in a calculated way, under the guise of offering something that he was convincing me that I needed. Little did I know, this seemingly harmless connection was the beginning of a lesson that would destroy my boundaries, my trust, my sanity, and my ability to call out an abuser who doesn't have my best interests at heart. Again, I would do anything humanly possible to go back in time, and never meet this Jack.

My life was still moving at an exhilarating pace, and I had an upcoming Surf and Yoga retreat in Costa Rica that I was particularly excited about. I was co-leading it with my dear friend Chase, someone I had once dated, and though we had gone our separate ways romantically, I still adored him. He was one of those people who just brought joy into every room—kind, fun, spontaneous, and with an infectious love for life. We'd shared many, many laughs, danced ourselves deliriously many ecstatic nights, and his energy was magnetic. I often wondered if he was "the one who got away," but we had transitioned into great friends and business partners, running our retreats to Costa Rica several times a year.

Chase was everything that lights up your spirit, the kind of guy you couldn't help but love. Tall, with sun-kissed skin from years of surfing, he was the embodiment of adventure and positivity. Instead of holding onto regret, I cherished the friendship we had built. Our partnership on these retreats was effortless, filled with laughter, shared responsibilities, and a mutual love for yoga and the ocean.

But then, there was Jack. It's hard to say exactly how Jack and I ended up "dating." The truth is, I don't recall agreeing to it. One day, Jack simply started implying that we were together, and unfortunately my easy-going nature kind of went along with it, thinking that I would "see how it goes." I wasn't one to make waves, and I tended to believe that (try not to laugh), everything that happened in life was a gift from the universe, and well, "meant to be." I preferred to always go with the flow.

By the time the Costa Rica retreat rolled around, Jack had weaseled his way into the trip, too. He signed up to join us in Central America. Chase, of course, was as excited as ever for the retreat. We had a fun group of attendees, and the vibe was set for the perfect mix of surf, yoga, and laid-back tropical adventure. The contrast between Jack and Chase couldn't have been starker. While Chase was spontaneous, warm, and full of life, Jack was...well, Jack wasn't. Maybe it was his overly calm and controlled demeanor, or the way he carried himself with an air of entitlement, as if he was always assessing things or calculating something in the background. But then, just when you thought he was stale toast, he'd blurt out a hilarious joke, sending the room into stitches; just really unpredictable.

At this point, I still didn't know Jack was a multi-millionaire—not that it mattered much, but I wouldn't have been giving out as many freebies and discounts had I known. I was comping his classes, picking up checks, and paying for things here and there because that's who I am, and he had a way of waiting for me to do so. I had no idea he was someone who definitely didn't need to be comped, and in hindsight, it was pretty uncool of him to expect me to work for free and give more, but that is more ominous foreshadowing. His wealth wasn't something he flaunted overtly, and it hadn't yet dawned on me that his persistent presence in my life might have more to do with control than with any genuine connection.

As the retreat drew closer, I felt a strange unease about Jack joining us. It wasn't a gut-wrenching feeling, more like a persistent whisper that something wasn't right; I didn't want to tarnish how special my retreats with Chase were, and worried that Jack would sour that. But again, I brushed it off. I figured, "What's the worst that could happen? It's just a retreat, and there are plenty of other people on our trip that he can hang out with. It'll be fine."

I warned Jack in advance that I would be "working," and that was my priority, so that he didn't expect me to be on vacation. Little did I know, this retreat would be the beginning of something far more complicated than I could have imagined, and it was only a matter of time before that balance would tip.

TAMARINDO TICO

It was the fourth night of our retreat in Tamarindo, Costa Rica. Everything had been going smoothly—morning surf, afternoon yoga, and the golden sunsets that made us all feel like we were living a dream. Chase, with his infectious, hilarious energy, was the perfect co-host. He kept everyone in high spirits, making sure the retreat had the right balance of fun and relaxation.

That night, most everyone in our group decided to head out to a local bar, which was just a five-minute walk from our hotel. The night was buzzing with the kind of tropical energy that makes everything feel alive, even after the sun goes down. But Jack and I decided to stay in. I wasn't feeling the pull to go out, and honestly, I wanted a little quiet time. At least, that's what I thought.

A little after 2 a.m., something very strange occurred. Something that had only happened to me two other times in my entire life. I woke up abruptly, fully alert. Without any real thought or consideration, I began to get dressed. It was as if I was being pulled by an invisible force, moving with a purpose that wasn't entirely my own. I was in an altered state, as if on autopilot, watching myself as I moved—conscious, but not in control. Robotic, yet deliberate. It was eerie and unsettling.

Jack stirred from his sleep after hearing me getting dressed. He asked, "What are you doing?" His voice was filled with confusion, understandably so—it was the middle of the night, after all.

Without missing a beat, I replied, "I'm going out." The words came out so matter-of-factly, so detached, that even I barely registered them. "It's 2:20 in the morning," he pointed out, clearly baffled by my behavior. But I wasn't interested in explaining. I pulled a skirt up my body and started searching for my shoes, entirely focused on my task, again, as if I were running on some unknown script. Jack, still trying to make sense of the situation, asked, "Do you want me to come with you?"

I paused, but only for a second. "If you want to come, come. If you don't, don't." My voice was void of any emotion or care, as if I was indifferent to whether he followed me or not. That seemed to be enough of an invitation for him because he started getting dressed as well, trying to catch up to me. I didn't think much of it. In my strange, detached state, it didn't really matter to me either way. As we were about to leave the suite, I grabbed the keys to the rental car that were on the kitchen table, without even thinking about it. Something was pulling me—and I was just acting it out.

"Why are you driving?" Jack asked, his voice tinged with concern. He could sense that something was strange, but he was also strangely following along. Again, my response was robotic. "If you want to come, come. If you don't, don't." There was no discussion, no negotiation. I didn't even look him in the eyes. I was on a mission, but I didn't even know what that mission was.

So Jack followed.

I drove the car for the short forty-two second drive from the hotel to the bar, where our group had gone earlier that night. It was a very small town, and it was still bustling with energy—locals, or "ticos" as they're known, filled the streets, their laughter and Spanish chatter spilling out into the warm night air. The bar was alive with music and movement, but our group was nowhere to be seen.

I stood there, just outside the bar, scanning the crowd, who were completely oblivious to the out of body experience that brought me there. We walked into the bar, sitting down at a small, open bistro table. Jack went on to order a beer, asking if I wanted anything to drink.

I didn't even answer him as I was too busy scanning the bar, looking for any sign of my group.

The crowd swirled around us, the music thumping in the background. I had no real reason to be there, no logical explanation for why I had felt the need to leave the comfort of sleep and venture into the night. All I knew was that I wasn't myself—not entirely, anyway. Jack, too, was confused.

All of a sudden I locked eyes on a tico standing in the corner of the bar, drinking a bottle of beer. He had one foot on a chair, while laughing loudly and obnoxiously. Something about him immediately triggered me. I felt my skin and blood turn hot. My jaw clenched. My eyes squinted, overcome with anger at the sight of him. As the heat of anger spread through my body, I became hyper-aware of how I was acting. My entire body language was tense and aggressive, completely out of character for me. For the first time since waking up at 2 a.m., I became fully conscious of my behavior. I was embarrassed—mortified, even—by how out of control I had been acting without even realizing it. In my periphery I could see Jack watching me, and I grew even more embarrassed by my behavior, enough to snap out of this trance and regain control of myself.

Whatever force had drawn me out was now loosening its hold, and suddenly, the weight of what had just happened came crashing down. I turned to Jack and said, "Let's go." He seemed slightly annoyed, holding up his unfinished, half drunk beer bottle, but he didn't argue with me.

And just like that, we got up to leave, heading towards the exit door. I felt a strange mix of relief and confusion. The spell had broken, but the lingering sense of something unresolved stayed with me.

As we walked through the small, sandy parking lot toward the car, yet another something unexpected happened. Right on cue, the rest of my group from the retreat was walking by us, from the street, cutting through the parking lot towards the beach. I was instantly relieved, elated actually, very happy to see them. I offered them a ride back to the hotel. The group, however, was in high spirits and wanted to walk back along the beach instead, as it was a bright full moon. Everyone except for the one and only man in the group, who agreed to take the ride with us.

And here's where the oddities began again. Even though I'm not the "mother hen" type by any means, I felt a sudden and intense urge to insist that the whole group either drive back with me, or that the man who opted for a ride should walk the group back along the beach. I didn't feel comfortable leaving them to walk back alone, even though it was irrational. At that time Tamarindo, Costa Rica was very safe. We walked around town at night often, without fear for our safety. However, my offer was non-negotiable. After some back-and-forth, the man agreed to walk with the rest of the group back along the beach—it was a 7 minute walk, so not a big deal. I drove Jack and myself the *blink of an eye* car ride back to the hotel.

When we arrived at our hotel, Jack began heading toward the steps leading to our suite, which was just to the left of the lobby, directly upon entering the hotel. But something in me resisted. I wasn't ready to go back to the room. Instead, I was steadfast as I walked towards the back of the hotel, towards the beach. Jack was clearly annoyed. "Come on!" he whined, his patience running thin. But I ignored him. Once again, that robotic state took over, something deeper was driving me. "I am not going to sleep until I see them return," I said, my voice focused and resolute.

Jack sighed, frustrated by my insistence, but he followed along, likely realizing by now that arguing with me when I was in this state was pointless. I made my way back toward the beach, determined to see the group's safe return.

I walked toward the shore, the warm night air brushing against my skin, and a bright, full moon painting the ocean's surface. The sound of the crashing ocean grew louder, soothing but also foreboding. I sat on top of a concrete table, calm and alert; waiting. Jack caught up to me, and stood to my right, beside the table. He didn't say a word.

Suddenly, the silence of the night was shattered by the most blood-curdling scream I had ever heard. I sat up taller, frozen in place, listening. Both of us were completely still, looking towards the direction of the screams, the shrill and terrifying sounds. My heart pounded in my chest as I listened, straining to make sense of what I had just heard. The peaceful night air suddenly felt thick with tension, as if something dark and dangerous had entered the scene.

Hotel workers began running towards the back of the hotel, where we were, responding to the screams. Moments later, a group of five or six people came running up towards us, their hands on their heads, all of them were bleeding. Their faces were pale, their expressions panicked. They had been jumped, beaten, and robbed as they walked along the beach back from the bar. My stomach clenched at the sight of them—their wounds, the fear in their eyes. It was like watching a nightmare unfold in real life. I was now deeply concerned about my group and made my way towards the ocean.

Two minutes later, my group appeared in my view, perfectly safe. The relief that washed over me was almost overwhelming. They were laughing, talking, completely unaware of the danger that had been lurking just minutes ahead of them on the very path they'd been walking. If they had left the bar just a few minutes earlier, they may have been the ones attacked. They had no idea how close they had come to being part of that horrible scene.

Jack, standing beside me, was no longer confused or annoyed by my strange behavior from earlier that night. Now, he was looking at me as if I were some kind of sorcerer. He couldn't hide it—his expression was one of awe and fear, totally fixated. Somehow, by having the inhibition to follow that strange pull to go out in the middle of the night, by insisting on seeing my group safely return, I had delayed them just enough to avoid such a vicious attack. Had we not gone to the bar, had I not insisted on seeing them return safely, they very well could have been the ones beaten and robbed on that beach. Jack silently recognized this as well, having been a witness to it all.

But the story doesn't end there. What made the entire situation even more chilling was what we learned later: the person who led the attack was none other than the very tico I had become transfixed on at the bar earlier in the night. The man who had triggered my inexplicable anger, the man whose presence had made me feel on edge, was the same person who had orchestrated the brutal attack on that beach.

Jack's energy made a dramatic and obvious shift after that. He was now looking at me with a kind of reverence, as if I had tapped into some hidden power that he didn't understand. For a man who had always been emotionally guarded, he suddenly became energetically intense, alive, almost worshipful. It was unsettling, and it turned from awe into a desperate need to possess me. This is where an abusive and dysfunctional seed was planted in our relationship. He saw me not just as a spiritual woman with heightened intuition, but as something otherworldly, something beyond his comprehension. Someone who could be of valuable service to him, who could protect his children, even though I was clear in never wanting that.

When we returned to our room, the atmosphere shifted. Jack's energy now turned dark. As soon as we were inside our room, he pinned me down on the bed with a force that took my breath away. His face contorted into something almost demonic, his eyes burning with a strange, possessive intensity I had never seen before. He held me down, his weight pressing into me, his grip too strong for me to break free from.

"You are mine," he grunted, his voice low and chilling. I tried to wiggle out from under him, but his strength was overpowering, and the look on his face made me feel nauseous. I was scared, not just of his physical strength but of the darkness I saw in his eyes. I don't wear seat belts, I don't wear leashes on my surfboard, and my dog doesn't wear a collar. I do not like to be restrained.

I don't know how long he held me there, but eventually, he let go, and I pulled myself away, feeling shaken. There was something profoundly disturbed with him. The man who had been emotionless and detached for so long was now obsessed and possessive in a way that terrified me, but I didn't address it.

The next morning, around 5am I got out of bed very quietly, so as to sneak out of my room without Jack's attention. I walked down to the ocean to take a morning dip during the sunrise, followed by meditation. When I came back up to our suite, I found a quiet moment alone with Chase while we were setting up for breakfast. He had always been my confidant, the one person I felt completely safe around. I told him what had happened with Jack the night before—how concerned I was about him, how his behavior had shifted in a way that left me feeling uneasy and afraid.

Chase was immediately concerned for me, too. His protective nature kicked in, but I didn't want to make a big deal out of it, especially since Jack was there and I didn't want to stir up drama during the retreat or involve anyone else. I reassured him that I'd be okay, but deep down, I knew things weren't right.

"Are you going to break up with him?" Chase asked. I sighed and replied, "Honestly, it's not like I even realized we were a couple—it just sort of happened, I swear. I can't explain it. He's planned this road trip up the California coast for my birthday in October, which is coming up. I'll see how things go in the next few weeks, but if he pulls that behavior again, it's over. After my birthday, I'll work to shift things back to a friendship. He's not the one for me."

From that night, I started to pull back, distancing myself from Jack as subtly as possible to avoid making a scene. But the more I withdrew, the more his obsession intensified. He was always watching, always trying to draw me back into his orbit. Yet, instead of being openly aggressive, he became overly helpful and attentive, which made walking away feel less urgent and more complicated.

HOW TO MAKE A WOMAN FALL IN LOVE WITH YOU

A few weeks after that unsettling night in Costa Rica, I found myself at Jack's place one morning, making the bed after he had left for work. I was still living in San Diego half of the week, and in LA from Sundays til Thursday. I would often spend the night at Jack's on Thursday nights if it was too late to drive back to San Diego after dinner. At first I would stay in his guest room. He had relaxed a bit since Costa Rica, so we found our weekly habit back in full swing. As I straightened the sheets and fluffed the pillows, something on his side of the bed caught my eye —a book, face down on the nightstand, clearly recently read.

Curious, I picked it up and glanced at the cover. The title made me laugh out loud, *How to Make a Woman Fall in Love with You*. Was this a joke? Jack, the emotionally guarded, calculated and confidently controlling man who never showed his hand, thought he could make me fall in love with him? The idea was so absurd that I couldn't help but chuckle to myself.

I sat on the edge of the bed and flipped open the book, turning to the page where he had apparently left off reading. My eyes skimmed over the bold, manipulative advice: "Ask her to do things for you. The more energy she invests into you with her actions, the more she will begin to feel invested in the relationship, believing that she is in love with *you*."

I let out another laugh. Was this seriously his strategy? Did he think that by asking me to run a few errands or do favors, I'd suddenly become emotionally invested in him? Please. I was far too kind and generous of a person to be manipulated by something as petty as doing favors. I would happily do these things for any of my friends—kindness was my nature, not a sign of my romantic investment.

Later that afternoon, Jack called me from work, his voice smooth and casual as ever. "Hey," he said, "I have these shorts that Diane bought me for my birthday, and I need to return them to a store on Rodeo Drive. There is a receipt in the bag." I laughed to myself, and laughed at myself laughing at myself in the mirror as I spoke to him. Oh, here we go. Was this his way of testing the waters? Did he think this little errand would somehow pull me deeper into his hypnotic web? I was almost amused at how transparent the whole thing felt after reading that ridiculous book. But, in my usual easy-going way, I agreed. "Sure," I said, thinking, *Get over yourself, Jack. This doesn't mean what you think it means.*

So I returned the shorts for him. It was a simple enough task. As I said already, I would have done it for any friend. But as the weeks went by, I noticed that Jack had begun to develop a pattern—a list, really, of things he would ask me to do for him. Small favors here and there. He was in the process of building a house nearby, and suddenly I was helping him manage little errands, making calls, running around town, even paying for his services (he always said that he would pay me back, however that never happened). He was trying to tip the scales of power in his direction. I, sadly, was not previously aware of these kinds of manipulative mental and emotional games, and I had walked directly into a very dangerous trap.

Jack began to dangle the idea of a future together, like some shiny lure, even though it was not even what I wanted! I was starting to lose control of what I wanted, but I wasn't aware of it yet. These new behaviors weren't unpleasant yet, simply atypical habits and new experiences, so my internal alarms were not sounding. However, this was only the beginning.

The cat was officially out of the bag—Jack was a multi-millionaire. He had been hiding it well at first, but now that I knew, he wasn't shy about suggesting a life filled with luxury: extravagant trips, endless opportunities, investing in my business, even the idea of marriage. He dropped these hints casually, as if trying to nudge me closer and closer to a life with him, that I wasn't sure I wanted.

The problem was, I started to feel as if I was an outsider *watching myself* growing invested in the relationship. Yes, Jack was handsome, successful, adventurous, and yes, he had wealth, but there was something missing—something essential that I still couldn't put my finger on. His lack of passion was different than what I was used to. It was as though Jack was playing a game, and in hindsight I can tell you 100% that he was. I had become a reluctant participant without even realizing it, and before I knew it I was becoming Pavlov's dog.

I can see the strategy now, the way he was trying to build a sense of obligation, of emotional investment, through small, seemingly innocuous requests. But when I questioned it, he turned into Mr. Nice Guy, sweet and kind, which dismissed and distracted my concerns.

Jack's tactics were working, but I didn't realize it soon enough. I initially stayed because I was trying to find the right time to break things off without losing a friendship, which I enjoyed. I was now staying out of habit and mind control. I wasn't the woman Jack thought he could mold into the perfectly submissive partner. I was strong and I had a fiercely independent spirit. I wasn't falling in love with him because of love, I was led to believe that I was falling in love with him through his carefully calculated tactics.

Each time I returned home to San Diego, I would slowly slip back into my natural rhythm and habits, but the mind games were taking their toll. In the bigger picture, I was losing ground, even with those brief moments of recovery. Jack thought he could make me fall in love with him, but what he didn't realize was that love isn't something you can manufacture through manipulation or favors. It's something deeper, something real—Jack was a sociopath, so he could not understand this. He also didn't realize that he was about to unleash the strongest force in our universe through his manipulation, and I do not advise anyone to incite love if their intentions are not loving.

There was a man named Jay who I really liked in Encinitas, where I lived. We met at a weekly drum circle on the beach, where he played two large djembes. I danced. He was cool, sexy, kind, and very handsome. Our feelings towards each other were growing mutual, which was exciting. Jack, sensing my growing distance and connection with Jay when I was away, started to up the ante, and quickly. This is when the emotional abuse began.

After a loving and wonderful visit with Jack, filled with warmth and kindness, we would say our goodbyes for a few days. But just hours later, he would fabricate an extreme issue out of nowhere. For example, we'd be on the phone discussing something completely mundane when, suddenly, Jack would erupt in fury. His anger seemed to come from thin air—he'd half accuse me of something absurd, without ever explaining what it was, but it was always something I had supposedly done. Then, he'd abruptly hang up, leaving me stunned and reeling. I'd sit there, confused and upset, struggling to make sense of what had just happened. When I tried calling him back, he'd ignore me.

You see, Jack found my weakness: I cared about people—often too much. I had a deep instinct to uplift others, paired with a strong sensitivity to what they were going through, oftentimes before they found the words to express it.

These instincts and behaviors served me well in my career as a yoga instructor and were part of why I was so valued by the rich and famous. However, their origin was rooted in unconscious conditioning from my early development. Jack was about to exploit my core programming.

THE CRACK OF ENTRY

Growing up in an emotionally explosive family—with a mother who is a Leo sun and Leo rising, a Scorpio father, and a brother with Aries sun and Aries moon. And then there was me, a peace-seeking and sensitive Libra. My parents are both highly creative and passionate individuals who didn't have the same opportunities that my brother and I did. I can only imagine the frustration of setting aside personal dreams for a lackluster 9-5 job, just to provide for a growing family. Yet, I starved for closure to each outburst that occurred, but those never came. My family simply moved on from each one, repeating the same dysfunctional patterns over and over again. I was expected to simply cope, accept it as it was.

My mother had a traumatic upbringing as the eldest of six kids, with an abusive stepfather after losing her own father tragically at just five years old. She learned to survive through defensive coping mechanisms—always prepared to fight at the slightest sign of a threat. Her defenses were often tinged with a simmering resentment, which she managed through her deeply reverent and devout Catholic faith.

Her reactivity, however, combined with my father's post-traumatic stress disorder from his time in the Vietnam War, created an atmosphere where I constantly walked on eggshells. We never knew what might set my father off, so it felt safest to stay in line and out of the way. As a result, I developed a heightened ability to read energy, always prepared to either diffuse a threat as it emerged, or confront it head on, if need be —as well as a lingering sense of being a burden, or in the way. I felt a constant need to make things better.

Despite all of this, deep down, a true and powerful love connected us all. We were good people who wanted the best for each other, but each person's individual traumas often prevented this love from being expressed in healthier, more functional ways. Without consciousness, love can feel overwhelming, which can lead to a need for control. Like many families, we simply needed more space for consciousness.

I wanted to ease my parent's burdens, often making efforts to lift everyone's spirits. Alongside these family dynamics, I excelled greatly in athletics and music—I became 1st violin when only in 4th grade, I played Varsity soccer while only in junior high, I became captain of both the tennis and soccer teams, and was exceptionally gifted in dance and performance. I grew accustomed to praise, to entertaining and pleasing others. And so, with all of this, a textbook *people-pleaser* was born.

In hindsight, it is clear that Jack picked up on this particular vulnerability that I had unconsciously built my career on. I would spend hours, sometimes all night, agonizing over what I'd done wrong when he threw his unexpected tantrums. I'd replay the conversation in my head, over and over, trying to find the mistake, the moment where I had somehow triggered his anger. I wanted to fix it, to make it right. But Jack wouldn't answer my calls, he wouldn't respond. He'd shut me out completely after his bizarre and false accusations, and I'd sit there, worried sick, wondering if he was okay.

Eventually, I couldn't take the silence anymore. I'd get in my car, sometimes at midnight, and drive two hours to Santa Monica just to check on him—often after just getting back from the two hour drive—just to make sure he was okay. It was crazy, but at the time, it didn't feel crazy. It felt necessary. I wanted resolution to the insanity, some kind of closure to the conflict he had created out of nowhere, but he would never give that to me, using a tactic called withholding. I was soon overcome with a persistent anxiety that was affecting my ability to focus or work.

When I arrived at his door after these episodes, Jack would greet me with open arms, acting as if nothing had happened. "There you are," he'd say happily, giving me a huge hug, playing the part of the loving boyfriend, inviting me inside while I stood there emotionally distraught, drained, and utterly confused. He was wearing me down.

The morning after one of these incidents, I was descending the stairs when he asked me, with a smile on his face, "Have I fucked with your head enough?" I was confused and insulted. I asked him what he meant. He quickly deflected afterwards, denying having said what I knew that I had heard, instead jokingly and playfully blaming me for daring to ask something so ridiculous. The gaslighting had now begun, but again, I was too confused, too kind, and too uninformed to know how dangerous this situation was.

If I was in my right mind, and if Jack wasn't playing Mr. Loving 90% of the time, mixed with Mr. Gaslighting Abuser 10% of the time, I would not have been so misled. I promise you that I would have walked away, however there is a pattern to this kind of intentional abuse. I was getting programmed to stay, programmed to not abandon him, and programmed to believe that I loved him. I was under the influence of his mental and emotional manipulation, and there is absolutely no way for me to explain this to someone else, as only experiencing it for yourself would suffice (which I don't wish upon anyone).

I know that I sound weak and gullible, and this is one of the reasons that I have not spoken to anyone about what happened during this time in my life, or about Jack; people just think that I changed, that I had a "bad break-up" and didn't recover, but they don't know why, or the extent of the abuse I endured. I'll be honest—if I had witnessed someone else in the same situation I was in, I probably would have thought, *Why didn't they just leave?* But believe me when I say, it's not that simple.

Looking back now, it's hard to believe how I got sucked into Jack's twisted web. On the surface, I had always believed that I was a strong, independent woman, and a natural leader. Somehow, well we know how, Jack had begun to carefully dismantle everything I thought I knew about myself. Soon, I became the caged canary, dependent on Jack for all aspects of survival—once the strong, beautiful, wild, free bird he desired for its untamed, pure spirit, now trapped, weak and broken. To add insult to injury, with my newfound needy change of character, I was growing less desirable, and easier to abuse.

At first, it was subtle—so subtle that I didn't even notice the shift. The emotional conditioning and abuse intensified. Jack would withdraw suddenly, right after our most loving moments, when I was the most vulnerable. When he did this, it felt as if the oxygen was taken out of the atmosphere. I couldn't breathe. This time, he was clear in what he wanted, "Move to Los Angeles, or I will withdraw from you," he said. If only I had realized that threat would have saved my life, my sanity, my spirit. It was such an insidious ultimatum. He wasn't asking me to move to LA because he loved me or wanted to build a future together—he was using it as a weapon, a threat. And somehow, he had habituated himself in my life so deeply that the idea of him withdrawing—of losing him— felt like the ultimate punishment.

I'm sure it's not surprising that I gave up my beautiful home and abundant life in San Diego to move in with Jack in Los Angeles, placing me not only in deeper dependency, but deeper danger.

The stress of this relationship began to take a serious toll on me. I was losing weight, and without realizing it, I was slowly becoming a version of myself I didn't even recognize—a subservient woman catering to the whims of a man who seemed to oscillate between affection and cruelty.

At one point when we had first met, I had told Jack about how special my birthdays had always been. They were spiritual, magical, and often filled with profound synchronicities. I usually traveled on a solo trip during this time. But in Jack's domineering fashion, he insisted on controlling this year's birthday festivities. I had also shared with him that on two past birthday trips, I experienced thunderstorms and lightning at the exact minute of my birth—1:30 a.m.—which felt magical given the unique circumstances of where and how they happened. He prodded me in a derogatory fashion, "I want to see the thunderstorms."

THE COAST OF KALI

Jack was insinuating that he thought I was a little *crazy*, but the idea clearly piqued his interest at the same time, especially after what had happened in Costa Rica. I asked him not to put energy into what I had shared with him—I didn't want to tarnish any previously special occurrences. He brushed it off, smugly reminding me that he had checked the weather reports and there was absolutely no chance of rain during our trip. *Whatever*, I thought. I wasn't expecting it to happen again; I was just sharing something that had happened in my past, there was no need to hold me to it, let alone mock my spiritual experiences.

My birthday trip up the coast of California included a few days in San Luis Obispo, two nights at Esalen, and a couple of nights in Monterey. It should have been idyllic. The scenery was beautiful, the air was fresh, and on the surface, the trip seemed like the perfect way to celebrate another year of life. But the emotional roller coaster never seemed to end. His personality shifted constantly—from being a gentleman, kind and attentive, to being withdrawn and then cruel. The swings were exhausting, leaving me in a constant state of confusion. But he had figured out that this was how I was motivated in my primary relationships with my parents, and worse yet, that it pulled me in— because I felt compelled to fix things. I now know that his abuse was intentional, and it was on this trip that I fully lost myself. I actually began to believe—although I know now that it was brainwashing—that I was head over heels in love with him.

The first day of the trip was beautiful, leading up to my birthday night. We went for a hike, soaked in mineral hot springs, had massages, and had reservations for dinner at the hotel restaurant. Everything was lovely, and for once, Jack seemed genuinely engaged and warm. Maybe the relationship was finally past all of the bumps in the road, I hoped.

At dinner, our waiter's name was Paul. He took good care of us throughout the evening. As we finished the main course, Jack started asking me serious questions about marriage, what kind of life I wanted, and the type of staff I'd like at our home—housekeepers, nannies, chefs. It was very real and very serious. The conversation was so loving, I almost allowed myself to believe in the dream he was painting.

And just then, as I was feeling safe and wrapped in the warmth of the moment, Paul returned to our table, asking, "May I get you anything else?" Without batting an eyelid, Jack answered, point blank, "How about a blonde? I'm done with her," while motioning towards me. Time seemed to stop. I stared at him, the words hanging in the air like a slap. Paul looked visibly flustered and quickly walked away, clearly unsure of how to respond. I turned to Jack, appalled. "What did you just say?" I asked him. He feigned complete innocence, not missing a beat, responding in the sweetest, kindest and most concerned voice, "What, Honey? What's wrong? Would you like some more wine?" I then repeated to him what he had just said to the waiter, to which he acted deeply offended, "What are you talking about? Are you OK? Why would you say something so absurd?!"

I was losing my grip on reality, beginning to question everything—my memory, my sanity, my sense of self. Each time I tried to stand up for myself, to call out his manipulation, he'd twist the truth until I didn't know what to believe anymore, and instead I was wrongly accused of the conflict, which led me down the rabbit hole to fix the situation.

That night, after dinner, I was tipsy and emotionally drained from the day of hot springs, massages, and, of course, Jack's psychological games. I fell into a deep sleep, trying to shake off the strangeness of the evening. But something wouldn't let me rest. I was jolted awake by the sudden, violent crack of thunder. Lightning lit up the sky outside our window, bright and powerful. I glanced at the clock—1:30 a.m. It was the exact time of my birth. *Happy Birthday*, I thought to myself. I turned to look at Jack. He lay next to me, his eyes were wide open, staring ahead. He knew. He had heard it too. The storm that wasn't supposed to happen, the thunder and lightning that had twice before graced my birthday, had arrived. Neither of us ever spoke a word of it. We both lay there in silence. If only it could have woken me up from the nightmare I didn't yet know I was living.

With my life unraveling at the seams, my relationships also began fraying. Jack was pulling me deeper into his manipulative web. He began asking me to leverage my connections, to request favors from my celebrity clients—putting my work and reputation on the line, for him. And of course, I complied, because by then I was conditioned to please him, to never leave him, even when it went against my better judgment. Meanwhile, I was losing patience with everyone and everything in my life. The easy-going, service-oriented person I once was had morphed into someone I barely recognized—needy, anxious, and silently screaming for someone to please help me.

Even my daily habits were paralyzed. I used to work out early every morning without fail, but soon I became afraid to leave the house, even for a quick run, afraid to leave before Jack did because I had to make sure he was OK first, programmed never to abandon him. I will never forgive this monster for intentionally manipulating me for his benefit—that he was too insecure to be able to woo me honestly, so he resorted to mind control games, regardless of my life and my intentions.

In hindsight it is clear that Jack was continually trying to get me to do things that the 'sound of mind' Alanna would never do, because when you betray yourself, you no longer know who you are and you will become easier to control and manipulate.

It was now clear that I had to get out. I had to end this toxic relationship before it consumed me entirely. I spoke to some of my friends about what was happening, helping my brain start to reference the situation more clearly. But even as I made that decision, I could feel the weight of his control pulling me back, making me doubt whether I had the strength to walk away. Anyone who has ever experienced a deeply abusive relationship knows that it is not a straight line.

Jack could sense when I was disappointed with the relationship, and knew how and when to act like Prince Charming again, albeit momentarily, and this charm always preceded more mental abuse.

THE ROCK STAR

During this time, I was training a very well known rock star, Aaron, and his band. The connection with Aaron was instant, natural and fast. We had a lot of fun. He asked me to travel with the band during their tours, because he and his band felt comfortable with me around. We never crossed any lines, sexually, but late-night and early morning calls and texts from him were not uncommon.

Yes, Aaron was very flirtatious, but I was used to that. He had a girlfriend, and I was with Jack. Aaron practiced yoga in his skivvies, and we often sat in a sauna together before yoga, so there was a relaxed, comfortable, familial vibe between us, but again, we were never sexual. My main focus was helping with his back issues and increasing his flexibility. I share more about this relationship in my book *As I Am: Where Spirituality Meets Reality*, but for now, I bring him up for a different reason—more related to Jack and the perfect storm that was brewing in my life. Things were about to get even more complicated.

Jack became more abusive, ironically enough. There were two reasons for this: 1) He was jealous of my relationship with Aaron, and 2) he finally had me—so now what? With his prize in hand, he couldn't hide his emotions anymore. He felt completely out of control. When we finally get what we think we want, we don't always react in the ways we'd expect. His emotions overwhelmed him, spiraling from confusion to frustration, and quickly into anger. And let's not forget, Jack was a sociopath; emotions are not their strong suit whatsoever, control is. In fact, emotions are a threat to sociopaths. I had unwittingly entered the most dangerous zone of all—the point where desire turns to resentment.

JEALOUS JACK

Note: For the sake of telling this story more smoothly, I've condensed the dialogue in the next section into one instance, even though some occurred over separate incidents.

One afternoon, I was soaking in a bath, trying to unwind and relax. My phone was just outside the bathroom, in the master bedroom on a night table. This was back when we didn't have passwords or face ID, so I left it out without a second thought. An old Motorola flip phone, to be precise. At one point, I heard the notification of a text come in, but I didn't think much of it—I was relaxing, after all, and I didn't have anything to hide. However, Jack didn't ignore it, unbeknownst to me.

He opened my phone and read the incoming message, and only God knows what else. By the time I got out of the bath, dressed, and checked my phone, I saw that the text was from Aaron. It was flirtatious, mentioning spending the day together, and immediately I assumed he'd sent it by accident, thinking he was texting his girlfriend. So, I replied to Aaron, asking if that message was meant for her instead. Again, I didn't think twice about it, and I went downstairs.

When I reached the living room, I was hit by an entirely different scene. Jack was pacing, face red, seething with rage. Before I could get a word in, he exploded, screaming about the text, about Aaron, and then spiraling into random, hurtful attacks. "Why did you go to such a shitty school?" he yelled, as if that had anything to do with the current situation. He went on and on, increasing in nonsensical rage, comparing me to other yoga teachers, "Suzy went to Vanderbilt, and Katie's from the Kennedy family..." It was like he was pulling out every insecurity he could find to make me feel small, to make me feel worthless; to hurt me.

I tried to explain, telling him that the text was clearly a mistake, that it wasn't meant for me, and I showed him my text to Aaron asking if it was in error, but he didn't care, and Aaron didn't respond to that clarification text, which would have deescalated the incident. Instead, Aaron's lack of response only exasperated it. In fact, Aaron never responded to that text.

Jack kept coming at me, louder, more furious with every word. As he screamed, I raised my hands defensively in front of my face, pleading for him to stop. But that only enraged him further. He grabbed my wrists, forcefully snapping them outward with so much force that I felt my left wrist snap.

The pain shot through me like a lightning bolt, and I cried out, crumpling to the floor. The realization hit me all at once: this wasn't just a fight. This wasn't just Jack's anger getting the better of him. He had hurt me—physically hurt me—and in that moment, something broke inside me along with my wrist. I was in shock and started to cry.

Jack ran out of the house, leaving me with a throbbing, swollen wrist. I went straight to the freezer and grabbed some ice to wrap around it. My mind was spinning, but one thought was clear—I needed to get out, and NOW. I couldn't stay any longer. I went upstairs and began packing, moving very quickly, trying to gather the essentials: my computer, jewelry, personal items. I debated calling the police but felt too scared, too uncertain, as well as emotionally confused due to the mind fucking I had endured the past 18 months. I figured my first move was to leave, to get out before anything else happened.

In my rush, I began looking for an envelope to pack some important papers, so that they wouldn't get soiled in my bag. There was a loft upstairs, above the master bedroom, that Jack used as his office, so I went up to search for some envelopes. That's when I stumbled across some things that shook me to my core. Inside a lower cabinet, tucked among some ordinary envelopes, was a large, disturbing stack of documents.

At first, I thought it was just some old paperwork, but then I saw what was inside. An entire envelope full of pamphlets—pamphlets about mind control, how to hypnotize someone, and a receipt from an actual mind control course! My heart started racing, and I could feel the blood drain from my face and a chill take over my body. What was this? Next to the pamphlets were about thirty thick stacks of cash—$30,000, neatly stacked in $100 bills, labeled.

But it didn't end there.

I found another envelope, and inside were black-and-white photos

—topless women, dozens of them. Each photo had a resume attached, and stapled to each was a printout of a Craigslist ad. The ads were for a supposed "acting gig with a major television network," auditioning for topless actresses. My hands shook as I pieced together the sickening reality: Jack had been using these fake ads to solicit topless photos. *Was he a psychopath?!* My mind screamed.

And still, it didn't stop there.

On his desk was another stack of papers, with post-it notes on them —this time, profiles of several other female yoga teachers in town. These weren't just names. They included their schedules, home addresses, and their zodiac signs. These were women I knew, women I'd worked with. It felt like something straight out of a twisted movie. I couldn't believe what I was seeing, and I simply couldn't process all of the emotions overtaking me at that time. Overwhelming is an understatement.

This wasn't just emotional abuse anymore. This was something far darker, more sinister. My stomach turned as I realized the depth of Jack's deception, and fear gripped me like never before. I had to get out —now.

Fuck, my heart skipped a beat as I heard the garage door opening. Jack was back. Fear electrified every cell in my body, sending a deeper cold wave through me. My hands fumbled as I hurried to gather the disturbing materials I had just found—pamphlets, photos, cash—I wrapped them up quickly, shoving everything back where I'd found them. I didn't have time to fully process what I'd seen, or even to take photos; my priority was to get out without Jack realizing what I had discovered.

I threw my personal items into my bags and quietly stashed them in the guest room, hoping he wouldn't notice. My pulse was racing, and my thoughts were spinning. The door would open any second.

I sprinted back into the bedroom, barely breathing as I jumped into bed. I pulled the covers up to my chin, turning towards the outside edge of the bed, forcing myself to lie still, pretending to be asleep. My heart pounded in my ears as I heard his footsteps. The air was thick with tension, and I braced myself for whatever was coming next, praying he would just leave me alone until the morning when I could get out.

About an hour later, Jack finally came upstairs. I could feel his presence before I even heard him. He crawled into bed next to me, and drifted off to sleep. I, on the other hand, didn't sleep a wink. I lay there, perfectly still, eyes wide open, paralyzed with fear, staring at the window in front of me, waiting for the first light of dawn. My mind raced. My body was tense, every muscle bracing itself. My wrist throbbed with agonizing pain, but I couldn't risk moving.

As the minutes crawled by, all I could think about was that I was sleeping next to a psychopath. At that time, I don't believe that I really understood what a sociopath was, but I will fast forward just a little bit for you. I was soon to discover that Jack was the absolute epitome of a very dangerous sociopath; not the benign, extreme narcissist, but a true and through sociopath. At that moment, however, all I could imagine was getting out—how close I was to escaping, while being hit with a cascade of emotions, including guilt and believe it or not, *worrying about him!*

Every time Jack shifted in his sleep, I held my breath, praying he wouldn't wake up. The room felt suffocating, but I forced myself to stay still. Finally, after what felt like an eternity, the sun began to rise, casting a pale glow through the window curtain. It was enough. I had my excuse. Slowly, carefully, I slid out of bed, keeping my movements quiet and deliberate. The pain in my wrist was unbearable, but I pushed it aside. My only focus was getting out of that house, and getting to a doctor.

GETTING OUT, BEFORE LONG

I made three slow, tiptoeing trips up and down the stairs, carefully retrieving my bags from the guest room, loading whatever I could into my car. On my last pass through the kitchen, I noticed the bouquet of roses that Jack had bought me the night before, along with a pack of my favorite ginger kombucha. As if that could magically erase what he'd done! Please don't judge me, but I'll embarrassingly confess, seeing those gestures of kindness weakened my hatred for a moment, leaving me with a small, dangerous hope that maybe—just maybe—he'd acknowledge how he had hurt me and to apologize. Looking back, I realize how disturbingly high my tolerance for abuse was, and how I could still find compassion for people who hurt me. It was like an uncontrollable, twisted reflex.

The morning air was cold and misty, and I locked the car doors as soon as I was safely inside. I don't think I exhaled until I was several blocks away. My first stop was St. John's emergency room to get my wrist checked out. The x-ray confirmed what I already suspected—it was broken.

The nurse and doctor both asked me how this happened. I could feel their eyes on me, waiting for an explanation, but I just stared back at them, frozen, unable to speak. They understood the silence and gently told me they could call the police if I needed help. But I was paralyzed, unsure of what to do, caught in that suffocating space between fear, confusion, and the faint hope that things might somehow get better.

I had given up my home in San Diego, moved to Los Angeles, and now I found myself as the victim of domestic violence with nowhere to go. It was a brutal reality to face. I've never been good at sharing the burdens I carry, so in true fashion, I just kept going.

My yoga practice was severely impacted by the injury (no handstands for awhile!), but I could hide the wrist brace under a long sweatshirt and continue teaching classes and seeing my private clients, focusing on them and pretending that nothing was wrong.

One morning, not long after the incident, I was teaching a yoga session to Linda and Judy at Linda's house. Linda and I had known each other the longest, and she knew more about me than anyone else. For whatever reason, I finally told her a little bit about my situation and what had happened. She looked over at Judy and asked, "Is your pool house available?"

Judy was a lifesaver, no doubt about it, allowing me to stay in her pool house. We both assumed my stay would be brief, since the following month I was set to leave for a national tour with Aaron's rock band, working as their yoga instructor while on the road. It seemed like the perfect escape where I could heal, write, travel, hear great music—a fresh start away from this chaos. At that moment, it felt like everything was lining up for me to step away from the wreckage and jump into something new. Little did I know, it wasn't going to be as simple as that.

For anyone out there navigating a similar experience as mine, here is some advice: When you're carrying the emotional baggage from trauma, it's no different than lugging around multiple overstuffed suitcases on your journey—constantly slowing you down, forcing unnecessary delays, and making every step feel harder than it should. Lightening your load, prioritizing your healing, and letting go of what's weighing you down will allow you to move forward more freely, while minimizing further damage. Take the necessary time to heal before you embark on the next chapter of your life—you'll travel much lighter and faster when you do. However, I didn't.

The next week, I saw Aaron for the first time since Jack broke my wrist. I told him how the whole fight had started after his text—the flirtatious one he sent to my phone. I expected at least some kind of reaction, maybe an explanation, apology, or even a simple acknowledgment. But instead, Aaron just changed the subject, like it was nothing. Sigh. It was like there was no escape from this constant gnawing anxiety that now plagued my every waking hour.

I've always wondered, if my job hadn't been as a yoga instructor, would I have faced these emotions head-on much sooner? Because I would have felt the discomfort and devastation sooner? Or to the contrary: maybe, just maybe, I was healing all along, little by little, through the very practices of yoga that I was teaching. It's interesting how the very thing meant to help others can end up being a lifeline for yourself, even when you don't realize it at the time.

A week later, however, Aaron called me—just three weeks before we were set to leave for the three-month national tour that he had asked me to join. He started the conversation by saying that his girlfriend had been having "nightmares" that he and I would "hook up on the tour." I sat there in silence for a moment, wondering where this was going. It seemed absurd that her dreams, of all things, would now be an issue, considering he had been the one who asked me to join the tour.

He said that it would probably be better if he brought a male instructor on the tour instead of me. I could feel my heart sink, the frustration and disappointment building up inside me. After everything I had already been through—the emotional manipulation, the betrayal, the abuse, and now this—I was being cast aside because of someone else's insecurities. I wasn't even attracted to Aaron in a sexual way, there wasn't anything to worry about.

I tried to be understanding, even though the disappointment was devastating, for personal reasons. I told him, "If she's 'the one' and you feel like me being there might complicate things, then do what you need to do. But if it's just her insecurities, I hope you can stick to our agreement, because I was really depending on this to get away." Even as I said it, I could feel my world shifting under my feet, again.

LIFE SAVING POOL HOUSE

Judy had worked in the music industry for most of her career, and every month she organized these incredible living room live music events, featuring iconic acts performing right there in her home. It was surreal—legendary musicians, intimate setting. I had the chance to meet some of the greats, including Mick Jagger. One event, after bonding with the band, I ended up practicing some yoga poses on the piano while Boys II Men serenaded the room. The experiences I had while living in Judy's pool house were nothing short of epic, and a welcome reminder of the magic that still existed, even in the midst of my personal chaos and pain. However, it kept me from fully digesting what had occurred. I was still partially brainwashed, thinking Jack would apologize and things would get better with him. I would still drive by his place out of habit and programming, but at least I was now able to recognize those thoughts and actions as being brainwashed when they occurred.

When I wasn't caught up in distractions, I crumbled into a weepy, desperate shell of who I once was. I'll admit that I would send Jack long, emotional texts—begging for an apology, for some kind of closure, for healing, for clarity. I pleaded with him not to let my life be destroyed by the twisted situations he had orchestrated, yet I couldn't seem to break free from the grip of it, from him. All I wanted was for him to acknowledge the pain he had caused, to fix what he had shattered inside me, to release me. Other people advised me that begging someone like him for anything was a losing game, but I just couldn't hear anyone, unfortunately, as right as they were. I was still programmed to protect him, even if my emotions were twisted inside out.

TIME TO CALL OUT THE ABUSE, MAYBE...

Since the tour with Aaron and the band was off, I decided to get my massage table back from Jack so I could start earning some money. He had given all my remaining belongings to his housekeeper, but the table had been my gift to the house, and after everything that happened, I wanted it back. Jack, being the prick he is, refused to drop it off anywhere. Every time I asked, he insisted I come to pick it up myself, which I did not want to do. I told him to drop it at a local yoga studio where I worked, but again, he wouldn't budge. Every conversation ended the same—him refusing to cooperate, and me left annoyed.

One morning, after a morning hike with my friend Lizzie, where I hashed out my feelings for two hours (bless her heart), she encouraged me to report the domestic violence incident to the police. I finally felt clear and empowered enough to take action and report it.

Around 8 a.m. the same morning, after our hike, I called the police to file the report. It was a nerve-wracking call, and I hung up twice before following through, but I knew it had to be done. I explained my situation to the officer, and then asked him what would happen next. He calmly explained that they would send someone to talk to Jack about the incident and that I would need to come to the station to give a full report. I hung up feeling a strange mix of relief, embarrassment and anxiety, not knowing what would unfold from there, but I made my way to the station shortly after.

When I finally got the chance to speak with a detective, I presented valid evidence clearly showing the abuse from Jack. As we continued to talk, more sinister details about Jack's past began to unravel. It turned out Jack wasn't just your average guy with anger and control issues—he was a convicted felon. He had spent four years in federal prison for masterminding one of the country's most notorious fraud scams. Jack was arrested for manufacturing fake ATM cards, stealing hundreds of thousands of dollars from unsuspecting people's accounts at ATMs across the country. This wasn't some run-of-the-mill crime either; this was a high-level, calculated operation of white-collar fraud. *How the hell was he getting loans approved for his home-building business?!* I thought. Here was a guy who had stolen millions through ATM card fraud, yet somehow he'd managed to rebuild his life, gain trust from financial institutions, and secure substantial loans to fund his luxurious construction projects.

It boggled my mind. Clearly, Jack was a master manipulator, not just in his personal life, but professionally as well. All of his manipulative tendencies suddenly made sense. This was someone who thrived on fraud, control, and creating illusions—whether it was with millions of dollars or with people's emotions. He knew how to play the system, how to put on a front that made him look trustworthy—maybe even charming—to bankers, contractors, and investors alike.

The shock of learning that I had been entangled with someone who had already been convicted of a federal crime hit me like a ton of bricks. The fact that I had been so close to someone capable of such criminal behavior made me question everything I thought I knew about everyone around me.

I told the detective everything I had uncovered in Jack's office: the stacks of cash—$30,000 neatly piled in hundred-dollar bills—the bizarre pamphlets on mind control, the receipts from hypnosis courses, and the most disturbing of all, an entire folder filled with topless photos of women gathered by Jack as he posed as a film producer looking for actresses willing to do topless scenes. My stomach churned as I recounted it all.

But that wasn't the end of it. I also told the detective about the files I had found on local yoga teachers—women I personally knew. There were detailed notes on their schedules, home addresses, even their zodiac signs, as if he was systematically gathering information for, only God knows what. Jack must be stalking them, obsessing over their routines, just as he had done with me! It was fucking creepy!

The detective listened intently, occasionally nodding, but I could tell that the gravity of what I was sharing didn't seem to faze him. His expression remained calm, as if this was just another day at the office. After I finished, he looked at me with a blend of mild belief and routine professionalism.

"Do you know where most of the domestic violence reports in Santa Monica come from?" he asked.

I took a guess. "Maybe Ocean Park? 90405?"

"90403," he corrected, naming the wealthiest area in Santa Monica. "Wealthy, white men are our top demographic for domestic violence. Unfortunately, I'm not shocked by any of this. Now get out of here and get your life back together," he said.

His response landed hard. It was a bitter reminder that this wasn't some anomaly or exception. It was part of a much larger, disturbing pattern hidden beneath layers of wealth and privilege.

How have I gotten here? How was this happening? I didn't even like this guy, remember?! And yet, here I was, my life in tatters, unable to recognize the person I'd become. That's when the full weight of it hit me—Jack never cared. Not one bit. He didn't care that he had systematically torn apart my life in his attempt to mold me into his version of the "perfect little woman." He saw my vulnerabilities, my traumas, and instead of nurturing or respecting me, he exploited them.

I was trapped in a reality that I rarely had compassion for in other women, and I couldn't expect others to have any for me. I firmly believe that only those who've been victims of a narcissist or sociopath can quickly recognize them in others, even when no one else can. It's like having experienced a vampire, I suppose—once you've been bitten by one, you see them everywhere.

Naturally, once I was no longer considered perfect, selflessly attentive to everyone else's needs, and beginning to have bigger personal issues, I became of little use to the people in my life. The moment I needed support, everyone disappeared. No one seemed to care about what I was going through. I was a people-pleaser, not a pleased-by-people. So, to protect my job and livelihood, I buried those feelings deep inside. But, as the saying goes: *what you resist, persists*. Eventually, those suppressed traumas surfaced with such force that they spiraled out of my control and even made international news headlines (*Chapter 7: The 22*).

These few stories barely scratch the surface to the abuse I endured from Jack's deliberate emotional and mental hijacking, and the dismantling of my self-protective mechanisms. His calculated tactics tore down the emotional defenses we all need to protect ourselves, leaving me vulnerable in ways I never imagined possible. Maybe someday I will have the courage to tell some of the worst events, but not today.

Since those incidents with Jack, I've made it a point never to speak his name again or allow him any space in my mind—except for writing this chapter. Oh, before I move on to the next social outcast, I should mention that I did eventually call that waiter in San Luis Obispo—years after Jack had asked him for "a blonde" during our dinner, only to deny it to me right after. I knew it was a long shot—wondering if he still worked there, if I even remembered his name correctly, or if he would recall that moment. But making that call turned out to be one of the most pivotal steps in my healing journey.

As fate would have it, Paul was still working there, and, yes, I had remembered his name correctly. Not only that, he vividly remembered the incident. He admitted that he had thought about me many times over the years, feeling sorry for what Jack had said.

Paul even confirmed that I hadn't imagined any of it, as well as apologizing for my experience with empathy. That validation felt like the missing piece I needed to finally trust my reality again after so much gaslighting and psychological abuse. The fog was lifting, and I was determined to see clearly once more. But the lingering question remained: *how do you explain this to people who can only see the surface?*

THE NEXT VICTIM

About a year later, I received a call from another yoga instructor in Santa Monica named Samantha. She was very, *very* distraught, and as she put it, suicidal. She had been dating Jack for the past nine months, and in just that brief conversation, she described the same emotional and mental abuse I had endured. It was eerie hearing someone else recount the exact manipulation tactics I knew all too well—confirming that Jack hadn't changed and was continuing to wreak havoc on people's emotions and mental states of mind.

For three months I called Samantha, nearly every morning, trying to keep her spirits up, as I was concerned about her, and I knew all too well how challenging it was for people to believe what we had been through. She wasn't as strong as I was, and it was clear she was emotionally unraveling under the weight of Jack's manipulation. But I made one condition clear to her: if we were to communicate, she had to promise never to mention anything about me—where I was, what I shared, or any part of my life—to Jack. She agreed, and I believed she understood how important this boundary was to me.

However, at the three-month mark, Samantha betrayed my trust, and told Jack things that I had shared with her. What followed was both bizarre and unsettling. In retaliation for my communication with her, Jack—who had always projected a carefully controlled, albeit toxic, persona—revealed a side of himself I wouldn't have anticipated. He contacted the detective involved in our previous issue and, in what can only be described as absurd and petty, claimed that I had "adopted a puppy intentionally to hurt him," because I "knew how badly he had always wanted a dog." I mean, *seriously*?! That just screams insanity.

After that, I knew I couldn't trust Samantha. I told her that I needed to protect my peace, asking her to respect my boundaries as I wished her well. She moved out of town shortly afterward, and to this day, I have no idea where she is or how she's doing mentally. I hope she found healing, but I had to prioritize my own safety and well-being.

This experience not only confirmed how abusive Jack was but also confirmed the concerning pattern I had suspected when I found the notes about other teachers—he specifically sought out yoga instructors. Knowing this gave me a clearer picture of his predatory nature. I was not wrong in how I responded to him, I was just emotionally distraught. People often dismiss those who express emotions, labeling them as irrational or overreacting, while giving more credibility to calm, composed voices—even if those voices belong to the abuser. This tendency is known as "emotional dismissal" or "tone policing." Unfortunately, it can lead to dangerous outcomes, especially in cases of abuse, because abusers are often skilled at presenting themselves as reasonable and trustworthy, using charm and confidence to manipulate others. Meanwhile, the victim, overwhelmed by fear, frustration, or trauma, may come across as distressed, making them easier to discredit.

It's also worth noting that not everyone responds to warnings of impending danger with gratitude. Shortly after I discovered the post-it notes on Jack's desk containing the schedules and addresses of other yoga instructors, I reached out to warn each of them. My intention was simple: to give them a heads-up about what I had uncovered related to their safety. Most of the instructors were grateful and thanked me, assuring they would keep an eye on Jack's behavior moving forward. Almost all responded with gratitude, but there was one exception—an entitled snob, to be blunt—who reacted with insulted hostility.

Rather than seeing the warning for what it was, she was personally offended that I would suggest anyone's interest in her was anything but pure, deserved adoration. Her response was unnecessarily hostile, cc'ing not only the CEO of the studio where we both worked (and where I was preparing to launch a children's program), but also her lawyer. She warned me to cease all communication with her, making it abundantly clear that she was not interested in my warning.

This incident was a tough but valuable reminder: not everyone will understand or appreciate your intentions, and not all women support one another in the ways we'd hope. Unfortunately, women often compete with each other instead of supporting each other. Society has conditioned many women to seek status and security through relationships, which can therefore foster competition rather than mutual support. This can make it harder for women to genuinely uplift and support each other.

Additionally, not everyone will understand your efforts when you attempt to reveal hidden truths, especially if those truths challenge their beliefs. This resistance can be disheartening, but it's essential not to let it deter you.

When faced with this kind of rejection or disbelief, shift your focus to finding other ways to communicate the message. Maybe you'll write a book to describe your experiences, as I have. Your role isn't always to make others see the truth immediately but to plant the seed and trust that clarity will come when they are ready to receive it.

It took thirteen years for Jeffrey Dahmer to be arrested, during which time he encountered police on multiple occasions in situations where they were alarmingly close to uncovering his crimes.

Listen to victims. Have compassion for victims. Trauma often silences survivors, trapping them in fear, shame, or the belief that their experiences will be dismissed or disbelieved. However, as society becomes more aware of how manipulative predators operate, we can create healing environments for victims to speak up and feel heard, making it easier for survivors to share their stories without fear of judgment, wrongful accusations, or retaliation.

THE LESSONS:

The Sociopath

"A sociopath will do anything to win. Anything." - Denzel Washington

REFLECTIONS:

Please do not make the same mistakes that I did. I ignored the early signs, brushing them off, believing I was too strong and too smart to be fooled or manipulated by Jack. Mind control and brainwashing are easier than most people realize, and if we are not firm in our own mental programming while avoiding manipulative people, we are susceptible to being taken advantage of. Subtle and deliberate tactics of psychological manipulation, emotional abuse, and control mirror techniques used in mind control to rewire how people think and perceive their world.

Never assume you're immune to manipulation—sociopaths are incredibly skilled at twisting even the strongest people into their webs. Trust me, no amount of intelligence or strength can protect you if you disregard those red flags. Recognize them, take action, and don't hesitate to walk away before you get pulled in too deep.

Be aware of the personal vulnerabilities shaped by your upbringing and development—don't feel any shame, we all have them! Understanding these areas helps you recognize when someone may be taking advantage of your goodwill or even manipulating your conditioned emotional responses.

RED FLAGS
- **Listen to your intuition:** Pay attention to your gut feelings, even when everything appears *perfect* on the surface.

- **Watch for inconsistencies:** Sociopaths often contradict themselves, or deny things they previously said or did. *Gaslighting* is a huge red flag—trust your version of reality, and seek witnesses to support you. You cannot risk losing your sense of reality.
- **Control tactics:** If someone is using guilt, shame, fear or withholding to manipulate your emotions, that's not love or support—that's control. Notice when their words or actions cause you to doubt yourself.
- **Don't Rationalize or Make Excuses for Bad Behavior:** Abusive or manipulative behavior should never be excused or ignored. A pattern of disrespect or manipulation is unlikely to change, no matter how sincere an apology may seem. Even more concerning, if someone refuses to apologize or take accountability for their actions, it's a serious red flag that should not be ignored.
- **Parental or Caregiver Relationships:** It is well-documented that sociopathic tendencies often develop in response to a lack of emotional bonding, affection, or consistent care from a primary caregiver during early childhood. Observe their caregiver relationships, or find out what their early childhood relationships were like.

KEEP TRUTHFUL FRIENDS

- **Keep trusted allies close:** Have at least one or two people in your life who knows the truth of your experience, someone you can turn to for an honest perspective. Often sociopaths try to isolate you from others, but don't let them succeed.

- **Seek professional support**, if possible: A therapist or counselor experienced in narcissistic or sociopathic abuse can be instrumental in guiding you through the healing process as well as recognizing patterns early on.

EDUCATE YOURSELF ON TACTICS

- **Know the tools of manipulation:** Understanding gaslighting, love bombing, and other manipulative tactics will help you see the signs early. Sociopaths often follow a predictable pattern, and once you learn it, you can spot it before you become emotionally invested.

- **Recognize love-bombing:** Sociopaths may start off showering you with compliments, gifts, vacations, and affection, but it's a tactic to reel you in. Watch for this pattern followed by devaluation.

- **The blame game:** They'll always make you feel like the problem, but stay strong and don't buy into it. You can't fix them, and you're not responsible for their behavior.

RUN RUN RUN

- **Have an exit strategy:** If you're in a relationship with a sociopath and it becomes clear you need to leave, plan your exit carefully. Sociopaths don't let go easily, and may likely retaliate. The more prepared you are, the better.

THE YOGI'S LESSONS:

LOVE YOURSELF

- **Be kind to yourself:** I was targeted because of my kindness, empathy, easy going nature, and open-heartedness—not because of weakness. Forgive yourself for falling prey to manipulation, and celebrate the strength it took to get out.

- **Empower your future self:** Each time you recognize these patterns and remove yourself from toxic people, you're empowering a future where you can still be open and kind, but with the wisdom to avoid those who would harm you.

- **Never change who you are for someone else:** Any changes that you make to your mind, body and life should be made for you, and you alone.

PRIORITIZE YOUR HEALING

- **Healing is not linear:** Understand that recovery from a relationship with a sociopath takes time. Be gentle with yourself and give yourself permission to feel what you need to feel.
- **Rebuild your sense of self:** Sociopaths tear down your identity. Focus on rediscovering what makes you, you. Reconnect with hobbies, passions, and parts of your life that may have been buried or lost.

Healing from a sociopathic relationship doesn't mean you have to harden your heart—just the opposite. You can learn to love yourself more deeply, honor your intuition, and open your heart to people who truly deserve to be in your life. Today, I maintain strong boundaries which have helped me avoid unnecessary mistakes and setbacks.

THE SOCIOPATH'S LESSONS:

If you're a sociopath—or suspect you have traits of one—acknowledging it is a huge first step. The challenge is recognizing that while manipulation and control might give you a temporary sense of power, they ultimately damage your relationships, your well-being, and your long-term happiness. Real connections require empathy, respect, and mutual trust.

Here's some advice: seek professional help, because you deserve a life with genuine human connections. Learn about the impact your actions have on others. Manipulating people may offer short-term gratification, but over time it isolates you and creates a false sense of control. It's not easy to change, but it's possible to cultivate healthier interactions without resorting to manipulation or deceit.

Understanding yourself more deeply, how your development may have led to your emotional manipulation, and learning to cultivate empathy might be the most challenging, but most rewarding journey you can undertake.

PROMPTS & POSITIVE ACTIONS

Define clear emotional, mental, and physical boundaries that you can implement to protect your energy from toxic people?

....

....

....

....

....

....

Grounding activities, like deep breathing, yoga, meditation, and visualization are helpful ways to keep you from feeling stress. Describe how you can implement these into your life:

....

....

....

....

....

....

Toxic people often use gaslighting to make you doubt yourself. Use positive affirmations below to remind yourself of your truth and worth. Having different opinions than other people does not make you *crazy*.

....

....

....

....

....

....

DON'T BE A JACK ASS!

CHAPTER 2

The Socialite

"A woman is most dangerous to herself when she is desperate to be loved." **– Vanessa Evelyn**

THE SOCIALITE

Adamant to heal and move on from the negative experiences with Jack, I threw myself into writing, manufacturing, inventing my yoga dolls—you name it, anything creative and inspiring! The excitement of my life, the deep sense of purpose in my work, and the many blessings I enjoyed still far outweighed the pain of those experiences. But abuse is sneaky, and it takes time to leave its mark. It's like chipping away at a concrete wall; with enough persistent force, it will eventually crumble.

One beautiful, sunny day in Southern California while I was going about my day, minding my own yoga-filled business, I received an email from *Hamptons Magazine*, asking me to call them to fact check an article for an upcoming issue. I think to myself, *Amazing, maybe they're writing a piece about yoga trends or wellness, in general.* Nope. Not even close.

When I spoke to the editor, he had some questions about "the founder of AZ I AM Yoga, Jill Monroe."

"I'm sorry, what? Who?!" I asked. The editor asked me to verify some facts about a woman—let's call her Jill— who was one of my private yoga clients in Los Angeles, meaning that I teach her yoga privately in her home versus a class setting at a studio or gym. The editor referred to her as "the founder of AZ I AM Yoga," which was my company, but I was the only executive and the only employee at that time.

There I was, phone in hand, completely baffled. I mean, borrowing ideas is one thing, but borrowing an entire company? That was a new one for me. And keep in mind, I was still green at this time, looking at the world through rainbow-colored glasses. So, I politely told the magazine editor they might want to double-check their source. His response? "Jill herself was the source." Uhhh... double whammy. (*Reality check:* she's lying. R*ainbow-colored optimism:* maybe it's just a mistake). Spoiler alert: it only got more weird.

First, a little backstory. Twice a week, I taught yoga to a group of women in Beverly Hills, at Rachel's house. It was an interesting mix of personalities to say the least. Alongside Rachel, who was kind, innately competitive and always up for some gossip, her husband—a super down-to-earth, funny newscaster—also joined in the sessions. Then there was Camila, the wife of a famous actor; Heidi, a well-known TV actress and entrepreneur; and Lisa, my very first private client whom I'd known for about 15 years. A few others rotated in from time to time, keeping the group dynamic, but these were the main characters in this little yoga soap opera.

Jill was a new addition to the group. She had recently relocated from NYC to LA with her husband, and they were in the process of house-hunting. In the meantime, they were staying at a former U.S. president's Beverly Hills home, which was conveniently close to Rachel's place. Turns out, Jill's husband and the former president were close friends.

Jill quickly hired me for private yoga sessions. One day, I remember casually asking Jill how she knew Rachel. She nonchalantly responded, "I have no idea. She thinks we're best friends. I was even her maid of honor at her wedding, but honestly, I don't even know her." Classic Beverly Hills, right?

How is this even possible? I thought. That just sounded so absurd. Do these women have arranged friendships? Here was Rachel, constantly acting like Jill was her best friend, when Jill had just admitted she barely knew her. And this wasn't an isolated thing. Soon, the same pattern started to unfold in our group sessions: they'd hug each other, gush over their supposed "bestie" status, and then, almost like clockwork, trash-talk each other behind the scenes. It was utterly confusing. The fake camaraderie followed by biting gossip was so toxic that every time I left those sessions, I felt gross—like I needed to cleanse myself from all the negativity. It wasn't just exhausting; you can't help but wonder if they're doing the same thing behind your back—talking about you the way they talk about each other. It plants a seed of distrust and paranoia that's hard to shake.

Now, back to Jill telling *Hamptons Magazine* that she's the founder of my company when I'd only taught her a handful of yoga sessions. Fast-forward to the following week, after I corrected the editor. There I am, setting up for a trunk show in Beverly Hills to showcase my AZ I AM clothing line. I've spent a couple of hours making sure everything's just right—a rolling rack on one side, a side table with neatly folded tanks and accessories on the other. I'm feeling great, ready to rock, and several of my private clients confirmed that they were planning to attend. This should've been my moment. But, of course, life had other plans.

Suddenly, I see Jill show up. I wave, excitedly, when seeing her. She's not alone. She's brought a whole entourage—a group of six other women, to be exact. *Amazing, how kind of her to bring friends!* I think to myself. However, the energy was a little strange, but I couldn't put my finger on it, until things took a turn. Jill's friends bee-lined for my rack of clothes and began touching the fabrics as if they'd just discovered silk for the first time. I was excited! Then they began to *ooh* and *ahh*, practically swooning over the clothes. This is a designer and entrepreneur's dream. The satisfaction was percolating!

And then it happens.

One of the women in the group turns to Jill, and she says, "Jill, this is a-mazing! You are AMAZING!" And the others chime in, showering

Jill with compliments about *her* brilliant clothing line. While I am standing right there. Jill even smiles at me, sheepishly at that.

At this point, I'm there, right next to the rack, blinking in confusion like I've somehow wandered into an alternate universe. Meanwhile, Jill is soaking up the praise like she invented yoga itself. I pulled her aside, quietly, trying not to make a scene.

"Jill," I say, "what's going on? Did you tell your friends that my activewear line is yours?!!" Jill looks at me, then she looks down towards the floor. She rolls her lips together, and then, completely serious, says, "You handled that so well, thank you. I'm just really insecure about moving to LA without having some kind of accomplishment to show for myself."

I stare at her, still trying to piece together how we got here. "So...you told your friends that my company, AZ I AM, was yours?"

"Yeah," she replies, as if it's the most casual thing in the world. "Do you think I could be part of AZ I AM with you? I'm really hardworking, I promise."

Now, I'm all for collaboration and helping people, but let's get one thing straight: telling people you're the founder of someone else's company is not how you do it. I mean, who just casually adopts someone else's business as their own like it's no big deal? And then tries to wiggle themselves into it without proper due diligence and progressive conversations? High wealth, socialite women who have lost the value of hard work, that's who.

Part of me was interested, as I was hoping to find a good partner to expand my business and brand, but I hardly knew her. I told her earnestly, "It really devalues all of my hard work when you tell people that my business is yours, do you get that?" To which she responded in word and gesture as understanding and being apologetic. So I let it go.

But I was still there, caught in the middle of the most awkward trunk show of my life, trying to process the fact that one of my own clients had not only hijacked my company's story, and assumed my hard work and creativity, but had done so with such confidence that she even convinced a magazine to run with a story. This wasn't my world, this was not how I operated, so I just didn't realize the danger that I was in.

So, after the whole "Jill taking credit for my company" fiasco, you'd think things couldn't get more bizarre. But Jill, being Jill, had more tricks up her sleeve. In what felt like an attempt to smooth things over—or maybe just buy her way in with legitimacy—she asked if she could invest in my company. At this point, I was juggling confusion, frustration, with a sprinkle of curiosity and a dappling of excitement, so I said, "Sure, let's talk." Next thing I know, she's dropping just a little under $150k into my company. Given that her husband is a billionaire, it was not a lot to her, but it would definitely help to expand the product line.

Now, we were compatible in our love for yoga, but incompatible in our work ethic. I built things from the ground up, sweat and tears from original innovation. She bought whatever she wanted and assumed all of the work and creativity that went into it. Admittedly, she was just in it for the appearance.

Within two weeks of being partners, and sharing a joint business bank account, Jill wrote a check for $23,000 to a PR powerhouse in New York City, with the primary objective of "getting her on the cover of Town & Country magazine as the founder of AZ I AM Yoga." That's right—she invested in my company, and then used that very money to rewrite the story where she was the star and founder. Talk about twisted ambition and blatant disregard.

What followed were ten months that can only be described as me babysitting a socialite who isn't used to building something from the ground up. How can one possibly find time to build a brand in between Botox appointments, facials, massages, lunches, workouts, hikes, and therapy? It was both frustrating and exhausting. I think this is when I started to feel the seeds of becoming jaded; the rainbow colored lens I had worn for years had now become black and white.

We had moments of alignment and hope, and she used her connections to sell some of the inventory, and to host trunk shows, but there was simply an impasse as to how to get the business operational without socialite problems.

You can't ever say that I didn't try to make this work, though. One day, I brought Jill along to meet my dye house rep—an important meeting, mind you. Before we head over, Jill tells me, "Oh, by the way, I've got a dermatology appointment after this, so we can't take too long." *No problem*, I thought, we'll make it quick. Famous last words.

We arrive at the dye house, and instead of discussing, I don't know, dye colors, or the dye process, or even anything related to the business, Jill spends the entire time talking to the rep about whether or not she should get a facelift. I wish I were joking. She hijacked the meeting, turning it into a consultation on her future cosmetic procedures. I couldn't get a word in edgewise to steer back on track. And of course, by the time she's finished curbing her unbearable insecurities for the afternoon, she's now late for her dermatology appointment—and guess who gets blamed? Me. Obviously. Because clearly, I was the one who held us up talking about facelifts during a business meeting.

But the madness didn't stop there. The following week, I took Jill to my clothing sample maker, to try on some new pieces for our upcoming collection. I'm in the zone, focusing on the important stuff

—fit, fabric, you know, the things that actually matter. I slip into a new sports top and turn to the mirror, checking how the side seams are sitting. Meanwhile, a few feet away, Jill is sitting at a table, absolutely laser-focused—but not on the collection, oh no. She's zeroed in on my breasts, practically in a trance. There it was, that same look of insecurity creeping over her face, the one that screams *I feel less-than*, even though she's trying to keep it together. You can probably guess what happened next. She breaks the silence with the inevitable: "Do you think I should get a boob job?" Classic Jill.

"I'm in LA now, I guess I should get a boob job!" she transgresses into another self-absorbed monologue, all the while I am trying to decide if I take 1/8" off the strap length. The entire time we're supposed to be talking business, she's stuck in some world of complete self absorption. So there I was, trying to keep things professional while my "business partner" had a full-on existential crisis over cosmetic surgery, AGAIN. I was slowly losing my patience.

But then she said it, and I'll never, ever forget this. While gritting her teeth, unable to hold back her feelings: **"My next lifetime, I am coming back as you!"** she said. Now this was just getting really uncomfortable. *What the fuck kind of teenage nightmare did I step into?!*

That comment really unsettled me; it's a strong statement! I can't even imagine the internal agony she must have been feeling, living the life of a Stepford wife—married to a man she wasn't passionate about, while keeping up appearances around the clock. Sure, it might look glamorous from the outside, but I promise you, most of these women are miserable inside. And then I came along: free-spirited, beautiful, passionate, spiritual, creative, making my own schedule, dating whoever I wanted. She wanted my life, and that made her not only dangerous but it also made our partnership far more complicated.

This behavior wasn't unusual for women like Jill, in my experiences. I used to teach private yoga sessions to the wife of one of the biggest A-list actors in the world, and she acted similarly. If I wore a sports top that showed a hint of my natural cleavage, she'd mumble comments about "going too large" with her breast implants, her gaze fixated on my chest with a deer-in-the-headlights look. She couldn't even close her eyes during savasana, unable to let go of her internal dilemma. It made teaching a practice meant for presence and self-acceptance very, very challenging.

It is not uncommon for the wives of rich and famous celebrities to avoid hiring staff who are more good-looking than they are, fearing that attractive employees might become a threat to their relationships. In these high-profile circles, insecurities often run high, and even though I never approached my work or presence in any way that was threatening or competitive—quite the opposite, in fact—I could still feel the push-pull dynamic from these women and the artificial pressure they were under. It left me feeling both sad for them and deeply misunderstood.

Like many other celebrity fitness instructors, I imagine, I had to navigate a delicate balance—we can't be too attractive or too fit, yet we still have to be impressive. It's a slippery slope filled with emotional insecurities and assumptions flying around, unrelated to us. The absolute irony of it all is that my goal was simply to bring a bit of spirituality and wellness into their days and lives. That's it.

At the ten month marker, Jill had now become friendly with enough women in LA that she no longer needed to hide behind my business to feel secure. I was now disposable and just another person for her to gossip about.

I doubt that Jill will ever look at herself or her actions, especially if she maintains the same desire for status and wealth as she did back then. I doubt that she will ever take any accountability for how her selfish acts affected my life and my business, let alone my reputation and business objectives.

I, however, decided to grow from this experience, end the partnership and to move on. I called Jill to tell her that I would buy her out of her shares, that our partnership just was not working. She refused to talk to me about it, or reply to any of my emails, completely putting her head into the sand as a show of avoidance. Eventually, after a month or so, she responded, asking if she could stay on the board of my company as an advisor. I was hurt by how challenging communication was with her, therefore I turned that down, to her dismay.

After waiting another month for her to come around, I finally had no choice but to contact her husband to find a solution. In the end, I lost far more than I gained—financially, emotionally, energetically, and reputationally. But I was able to buy her out of my company and get back to where I had left off before being further used as a pawn in a socialite's ploy for relevancy in the LA social circles.

However, this wouldn't be the last time I found myself in such an outrageous situation again. I believe it was Stephen King who contributed this doozy of a quote: "Fool me once, shame on you; fool me twice, shame on me; fool me three times, shame on both of us." If I ever had the urge to get a tattoo, this quote might just make the top ten list.

THE LESSONS:

The Socialite

"I think we are all insecure, and there is nothing wrong in accepting that. But the problem arises when we try to counter this insecurity by cultivating an illusion of control, and we start taking ourselves and everything we know too seriously." - **Sushant Rajput**

People like Jill prey on others because, deep down, they feel powerless. Don't be deceived by the glitz or wealth—it's merely a facade, a distraction from their own insecurities. Those who are extremely wealthy, especially those who married into wealth, often lose appreciation for material things. To them, everything—and everyone— becomes just another accessory to serve their needs, feeding the endless pursuit of status and control. It's a way to maintain the addictive high of avoiding the deeper, uncomfortable truths they don't want to face within themselves.

Your time, energy, and talents are precious—don't waste them on someone who sees you as a tool rather than a whole person, who's time and intentions matter. Stand firm in your boundaries, don't sell yourself short, and never forget that true power comes from within.

In this example, the character can vary from person to person, and may not necessarily be a real socialite, as in my experience. Essentially, it is a person who's entire existence is based on outward appearances and who is deeply invested in protecting that facade. If you find yourself in a situation with someone like The Socialite, consider finding solutions to cut your ties and walk away. If someone is bold enough to posture your work or business as their own, they are far more dangerous than you might realize.

THE YOGI'S LESSONS:

Early on, Jill's behavior presented subtle but significant red flags—like when she started claiming to be the founder of my company after only five yoga classes together; I liked her, but I didn't really know her. While it's tempting to brush off these early incidents as misunderstandings or insecurity (as she later claimed), they often signal something deeper and more nefarious. People who are willing to lie to a major publication about ownership of a business without hesitation or guilt tend to have larger, more self-serving agendas. This is classic manipulation: gaining trust, and then slowly inching toward taking control.

With time, as Jill's behaviors escalated—her true intentions became increasingly clear. The entitlement, the need for validation, and the expectation that I would tolerate it all while she took credit—these were glaring signs of her ulterior motives.

I have had to ask myself all of these years, "Why did I allow it?!" That has been my inner work. Yes, there are a high percentage of narcissists in the world, hunting for sweet, easy prey, but I also wanted to dive deeper into my own wounds to see where I could improve myself.

KNOW YOUR VALUE

It has taken me a lifetime to realize that my early childhood development had affected my self worth, distorting my own value. I had a bleeding heart, wanting to help others because it fed my people pleasing complex. You may not even realize that your history is affecting your future, but it likely is. In my situation, everyone else saw my brilliance, but they also recognized my vulnerabilities and used those against me to take advantage of my gifts, but here's the truth: their manipulation doesn't reflect your weakness, it reflects theirs.

DO NOT BE SWAYED BY MONEY OR STATUS

Jill threw money around as a way to gain my trust and buy legitimacy. While good investments are every entrepreneur's dream, don't let someone's financial contributions overshadow their behavior, because you will lose more time (which in my opinion, is far more valuable) trying to dissolve partnerships that are misaligned than having stayed the course on your own. From my experience, money and status can bring far greater dangers when they aren't tied to clear, contractual, and mutually respectful financial investments. Similar to marriage, the moment personal ego, power dynamics, and hidden agendas get involved, things quickly become messy—and even toxic.

THE SOCIALITE'S LESSONS:

People like Jill often compensate for their insecurity by trying to boost their image through superficial means—whether it's aligning themselves with successful people or buying their way into situations that make them feel important. Her attempts to be on magazine covers and present herself as the founder of my company were about creating the illusion of success during a time that she felt unimportant, rather than being confident with who she was or actually achieving her own successes through her own efforts. She didn't stop to consider the damage she would cause me, because her entire life revolved around high-stakes image protection at all costs. In her world, maintaining appearances was paramount, and anything—or anyone—was expendable in that pursuit.

VALIDATION SEEKING

Using power, wealth, or influence to project an image of success may temporarily mask insecurities, but it will never fill the void left by a lack of authentic self-esteem. Eventually, the truth catches up with everyone. In the end, all the posturing does is create a deeper sense of emptiness. Life is far too short to live behind a facade.

HEALING INSECURITIES

If you found yourself nodding along to any of Jill's antics, don't panic—nobody's expecting perfection here. Remember that authenticity is way more attractive than pretending to be flawless. Lean into your quirks and imperfections—they're what make you, well, you. And if you're in a social circle that expects everyone to be a walking airbrushed Instagram post, maybe it's time to find new friends.

If social insecurities are running the show in your life, seeing a therapist might be a game-changer. Cognitive-behavioral therapy (CBT), for example, works specifically at tackling social anxiety and insecurities.

Make changes to your habits and activities. Take an art or writing class. Watch your progress unfold, and marvel at what you can create when you let your mind wander and your hands get messy in a creative project. You don't need designer labels to prove that you belong anywhere, and you definitely don't need a nose worthy of a Greek statue to feel valuable. Your self-worth? That's an inside job. There are no shortcuts, no amount of followers, just you finding it within yourself.

Take this experience as a lesson in boundaries, and remember that just because you have a kind heart, doesn't mean you need to say *yes* to everyone. The world needs your light, but it also needs you to stand firmly in your worth. Reclaim your power, not by hardening your heart, but by recognizing that you don't need validation from anyone else, especially anyone who doesn't respect your value and time.

PROMPTS & POSITIVE ACTIONS

What specific situations trigger feelings of insecurity?
What do you believe about yourself in these moments?

....

....

....

....

....

....

Are there people in your life who you feel do not have your true best
interest in mind? How can you begin to lessen your ties to them?

....

....

....

....

....

....

Write this statement repeatedly in the space below using all
of the lines, and repeating to yourself:
I am enough as I am, and I trust my journey.

....

....

....

....

....

....

**DON'T POSTURE SOMEONE
ELSE'S LIFE OR BUSINESS!**

CHAPTER 3

The Social Climber

"I don't care that they stole my idea … I care that they don't have any of their own." **– Nikola Tesla**

THE SOCIAL CLIMBER

Let me tell you a little bit more about Camila, who I mentioned in *Chapter 2* as having been part of the Beverly Hills circle of women who I taught yoga to on a regular basis. These were women who needed a little light, a little spirituality, in their chaotic, fame-obsessed lives. I thought I could be the breath of fresh air, the calming voice amidst all the noise of their celebrity-driven worlds.

Oh, Camila. She was one of those larger-than-life types, with a personality that could fill a room. At first, I thought, *Wow, this woman has energy*, and I mean the kind of energy that buzzes around like she just downed six shots of espresso and is just waking up. Her smile? Infectious. Her laugh? Hearty. The whole package seemed magnetic—except that the target of her magnetism changed on the drop of a dime, depending on what she wanted or needed, or who she thought she could get the most from. And her duplicitous nature made gaslighting look like a kiddie theme park ride.

I quickly realized her high-energy charm was just a well-crafted part of 1) her innate ability to make people feel like the center of the world when she wanted something from them, and 2) her serious case of insecurities. Man, the kind of ADD that made me question how she ever sat still long enough to let her finger nails dry. Conversations with Camila? Never really finished. She would bounce from topic to topic, gossiping about this plastic surgery disaster or that celebrity scandal, while I was left wondering how we got from discussing her neck pain to the size of someone's lips. And speaking of lips, Camila had quite the obsession with them—hers, to be specific. Plastic surgery was her favorite topic, like a weird mix of self-help and hobby.

Camila really liked me. I am very grounded, present, I am generous with my attention and I give great advice. At first, I took it as a compliment, you know, until it became clear that her affection was fueled by an undercurrent of envy that she couldn't quite hide. She'd blurt out things like, "Jesus, you are 100% sex appeal!" in the middle of a downward dog, which, let me tell you, is as awkward as it sounds, not only because it was a little distracting, but because Camila was programmed to position herself as the hottest woman in the room —and she was not happy if she wasn't, even in a yoga session! If someone else was hot, or even hotter, she had to be their best friend. *Keep your friends close, and the hotties even closer*, was her motto. It was a slow build of backhanded compliments, gossip sessions, interests in fitness, and a friendship sparked with not only an interest to work together, but to party after hours. Yoga in Beverly Hills, yoga in Malibu, discuss a project, and then, hey, maybe drinks after?

Camila's husband, Peter, was kind and patient, in the way only a man married to a whirlwind like Camila could be. He didn't bat an eyelid to pay me when I showed up for a session while Camila was dealing with a botched filler or whatever was the plastic surgeon's special for that week, and therefore wasn't answering her phone.

I, just doing my job, became yet another object of her external fixations. And when she wants something from you, she wants you everywhere and all the time. In the beginning, I loved our friendship, I loved trying to help her, and it was exciting, she was exciting.

One day, however, after a session at her Malibu home, I realized that I had left my brand-new, $400 Gucci sunglasses on her patio table. Now, let me just say, that was a big splurge for me at the time to buy such expensive sunglasses, so the moment that I realized that I left them at her house, I called her immediately—it had only been ten minutes or so since I left her house, so she had to see them.

"Oh nooo, let me check," she said in that too-sweet tone, stating that she was looking for them. A few minutes later, she came back on the line and said, "Nope, they're not here!" Strange. I knew I left them there. My gut told me something was off, but I shrugged it off—after all, who steals sunglasses when they can afford to buy ten pairs of the same style? You'd be surprised, actually. Years earlier, I worked as a concierge at a popular day spa in LA. We frequently had expensive silver platters and cups go missing from the waiting and treatment rooms. I still remember my manager telling me, with complete conviction, "I promise you, it's not the staff stealing from us—it's the richest women in the world who we catch on our security cameras!"

Stealing is not about money; it's about the act of taking. It's rooted in control, power, and the need to fill a void that money or possessions can't touch. When someone steals, they're often trying to claim something they feel is missing within themselves—whether it's validation, worth, or a momentary suppression of their insecurities. It is a desperate need to possess what they believe they lack internally.

Two days later, I showed up for another yoga session with Camila, and there she was, opening the door of the house, wearing my sunglasses on her face. My Gucci sunglasses. In the same location where I left them. The ones she claimed "weren't there." She smiled at me as if nothing was wrong, like the whole situation wasn't the definition of ridiculous. I thought, of course, that's Camila.

I told her that those were my missing sunglasses. She feigned innocence, handed them back to me and made an abrupt distraction by saying how happy she was to see me. I don't know if this incident was intentional or not, but that's just the kind of woman she was— always grabbing at what she didn't have, whether it was a pair of overpriced shades or someone else's vibe. And when she is called out for her behavior, she quickly deflects and runs away. And me? I was just another accessory to her, right next to those Gucci sunglasses.

Hollywood, as we all know, is brutal on women. The constant

pressure to look perfect, to act perfectly, to stay youthful in a world that celebrates youth and discards age, especially for women in the public eye? It's a recipe for disaster, particularly in the social media age, where every imperfection is magnified and the online bullies are relentless. It eats away at the soul.

But as the years passed, I started to see another side of this glamorous world—one I could no longer tolerate. What began as spirited conversations about life inevitably turned into toxic gossip sessions. Their obsession with plastic surgery became nauseating, the inappropriate sharing of private details about each other—details that I had no business knowing. It was increasingly uncomfortable, duplicitous, frenzied energy.

Some of their husbands openly cheated on them, and over the years those women grew increasingly mean-spirited and competitive as a result, understandably. I just didn't see how I was helping them, because they didn't want my help—they just wanted me around, and to check off the workout box on their schedules. My breaking point came right after one of Camila's birthday parties.

Now, I genuinely cared about Camila. I'd even say she's one of the most infectious personalities I've ever met. People are drawn to her like moths to a flame, and it's easy to see why—on the surface, at least. Her personality is addictive, but here's the thing: it's addictive because it's elusive. It's built on a foundation of insecurity, masked by this confident, carefree persona that keeps everyone's focus distracted while she assesses what she can gain from them. She's the real Wizard of Oz, pulling all the strings, making sure no one ever gets close enough to see who's truly behind the curtain.

And the thing is, I get why men fall for her. Sure, she's beautiful, but it's more than that. She has this joie de vivre, this energy that makes you feel special, like you're the only person in the room—when she's paying attention to you. But here's the catch: when Camila's focused on you, it's not because she's genuinely interested in you. It's because she wants something from you, or she wants you to perceive her in a certain light.

Like Jill, Camila spoke about partnering with me with my business and stand-alone projects, like developing a fitness program together. However, even though I was interested, and I felt that I had more compatibility with Camila than I did with Jill, I had learned that lesson already. I made sure to properly discuss these endeavors with Camila, and be sure that she signed a non-disclosure agreement. She was fine with all of that, and introduced me to her manager at the time to continue these discussions around partnership opportunities.

However, things turned for the worse, very quickly. Camila's birthday party was an absolute spectacle. A live performance from a globally iconic musical artist, A-list celebrities—because of who her husband was at the time—and everyone living it up like they were at the Oscars after-party. At some point, the DJ started playing the song *Boom Boom POW*, and Camila, in her usual over-the-top way, shouted, "Alanna! Come dance with me!" So, of course, I joined her on the dance floor. It was just the two of us at first.

Now, I don't toot my own horn unnecessarily, but if you know me, you know, *I can dance*. I've got rhythm, I've got moves, I've got soul—it's just one of those natural gifts I've always been super grateful for. So there I was, dancing, having a great time, and everyone's eyes were on us. Well, apparently that didn't sit too well with Camila. The second she realized I was getting attention—maybe a little more than her—that infectious smile turned into a full-on scowl. She dismissively brushed me away and turned her back, leaving me standing there, completely humiliated.

Someone recently told me that there is a similar scene involving a yoga teacher, in a popular TV show that was produced by several people who were at that party. I wouldn't be surprised if that moment inspired that scene. Anyways, I felt like a total ass. Thoroughly embarrassed, I walked towards my date, telling him that it was time to leave, and we left immediately.

The next morning, I drove to Camila's house, with a check in hand for the three remaining yoga sessions she'd prepaid for in a package of ten sessions. I told her, flat out, that I was done. I didn't dedicate my life to yoga and wellness to become part of the toxic, gossipy, backstabbing world of Beverly Hills housewives. I quit. I deserved better. And that was that.

After the abusive relationship with Jack, my tolerance for toxic behavior dropped significantly. I became more sensitive and no longer allowed people to mistreat me. Maybe I should have been more compassionate, and considered that she was likely very drunk, high, and celebrating her birthday—she rightfully expected to be the center of attention. But again, I now had a knee-jerk reaction to any sort of mistreatment—I simply wouldn't allow it anymore. Perhaps this was the beginning of a lifelong journey toward finding the strength to speak the truth and stand up for myself.

YEARS LATER

The years went by. I had opened my own yoga studio in Brentwood, I was selling my yoga dolls at major retailers, and I was consumed with building my brand. I ran into Camila a few times over those years, after our private yoga days and friendship, including when she came to my yoga studio for classes. While things were always cordial, they were also, as per usual, scattered and fake—but not unpleasant. We exchanged the usual pleasantries, she commented on my books, but the heart and soul connection had long faded.

Then, Camila made headlines—not for anything admirable, but for having an affair with a prominent and well known businessman, Dan. But Dan wasn't your typical celebrity, or the typical guy Camila was attracted to. He was more of a business nerd, the kind of guy who probably spent more time analyzing spreadsheets than hanging out on red carpets. So, the hyper-sexualized aspect of their relationship? That was like hitting the jackpot for him.

It was an atypical match made in Beverly Hills—her wrapped in layers of faux confidence and camouflage make up, and him, well... basking in the excitement of it all, as if the captain of the cheerleading squad actually said *yes* to attend Senior Prom with him.

However, she did look happy, at least from what I saw in the press. Yet, even more surprising, her publicly stated intentions seemed to have taken a turn for the positive. She seemed to be aligning herself with more uplifting causes, initiatives that were actually helping people. It was as if she had evolved from that superficial person I knew into someone more in line with the work I'd spent my life dedicated to —uplifting others and making a real difference.

So, as I was finalizing the details of a new book that I was writing, I felt compelled to reach out to her, for two reasons: First, I wanted to genuinely congratulate her on her new relationship. She seemed happy, and honestly, I was truly happy for her. Second, I shared my excitement about my new book project that I'd been working on—and knowing that we had excitedly discussed partnership opportunities years earlier, including a book, it seemed appropriate to see if there was room for a collaboration with this one; that maybe our stars would finally align with an uplifting endeavor. Maybe we both had grown up and sobered up a bit since that birthday party of hers.

Also, given Dan's enthusiastic public interests in the topic of my book, and his public commitment to children's causes, I thought it was a natural outreach, one that would benefit her, Dan's initiatives, and, of course, the work I had poured my heart into. One of my doll character's, Niyama, is focused on environmentalism, in particular conserving the Amazon rainforest in Brazil, and I had an upcoming release of my character Pratya, who has aspirations to become an astronaut and fly to space; both of these have empowering themes for kids to be inspired by.

Again, whether the stars would actually align with Camila or not? Well, that's a different story. She didn't respond to my email, so I sent a private text as well as multiple Instagram messages, about this specific book project and the themes of mutual interest.

Within the months that followed, I decided to reach out directly to Dan, through his company. I emailed him twice, sharing the exciting details of my yoga dolls, children's brand, and upcoming book. Again, it seemed like such a natural fit, given his passions and his involvement in initiatives for children. Or so it seemed.

I have learned the hard way, more times than once or even sixty times...what celebrities posture to the public is rarely true. The media is driven by clickbait and sound bites, while celebrities need to maintain public interest and adoration. Together, they manufacture press and appearances to feed the media's demand for content, creating narratives that support a public image that they can monetize for their own benefit, and always at your cost. That's it. Otherwise, we'd have solved social issues of homelessness, hunger, child safety, the environment, and so many other issues, a long time ago.

Those who gain power often can't resist the seduction of it, and if they came into power without a disciplined intention to serve others, they will be consumed with an insatiable hunger to feed themselves, and only themselves, ensuring they keep their place at the top. This is when they begin to take from lower- and middle-class creatives when an opportunity arises, prioritizing their own image over supporting others. Also, keep in mind that donating 20% of billions of dollars is nothing sacrificial to them. Generosity and integrity are measured when we have little and no one is watching, not the other way around.

Yet, to my great surprise and delight, I received an email back from Dan's office. The message was polite, professional—the kind of reply you get when your email gets through but deferred to an assistant to respond. His assistant confirmed that Dan had received my email, as well as providing links where I could propose publishing my work with his publishing companies, and submit my consumer goods and media projects to other departments. It wasn't exactly the response I had hoped for, but at least it was something—a thread to pull on, perhaps.

I had always had great respect for Dan, who built his company from the ground up, with what seemed like sheer hard work. I admired that, and I felt that was why he cared to read my email and have it responded to; that he recognized kindred grit and spirit. Whether that was true, or if it would lead to anything more? Only time would tell.

Well, are you ready for this knock off? Have a seat, because about six months later, Camila—who I had shared my book details with—made an announcement that hit me like a ton of bricks. She announced that she was writing a book—get this—with the exact same premise I'd proposed, but twisted into an older, unrelated concept we had discussed collaborating on years ago. She essentially forced my storyline and concept into a previous, separate idea, making it appear as though the concept was hers all along. Coincidence? If I didn't know her personally, minutely potentially, and only if during a rare blue moon. But I knew her modus operandi. If I hadn't emailed her, sharing the details of my book with the same theme, plot line, unique characteristics, and objective. Hell no, this was blatant concept theft.

I did know her. And I did know she had read my emails and

messages. I had been open, generous, and excited to share my work with her. I believed that she had evolved and changed for the better, that maybe she was more aligned with the values she seemed to be promoting publicly. But I guess it's true that cheetahs never lose their spots. Why I would have believed someone so manipulative and narcissistic in the past could change so dramatically, is a far more far fetched fictional story than the one she knocked off from me.

So why would someone with her level of power, wealth, and influence knock off the idea, concept, or work of an artist, an activist, or—let's be real—even their former yoga instructor? Why would they steal from someone who is truly doing the work with heart, with purpose, with authenticity? I'll tell you; because rich people do it all the time. They want to appear as if they care. They want to don the cloak of compassion or creativity, not because they believe in the work, but because it helps them maintain their status, their wealth, their public image, and their power. Period.

And then, let's add another layer. What happens when someone is not only trying to look like a philanthropist or creative but is also desperately trying to maintain an image as a perfect Madonna, a public servant, an untouchable duchess in order to maintain her relationship with the source of all that wealth and power? Well, that's the most dangerous of them all. They'll take whatever they need to keep that illusion intact. And apparently, if that means stealing someone else's idea and turning it into their next big project, so be it.

Camila's announcement was just that—another strategic move in a long game of phony appearances. And I knew it for what it was. Because when you know the person behind the mask, you see right through the illusion.

CEASE AND DESIST

Flash forward a few months, and there it was—Camila splashed across the press, orchestrating articles about her "charity work" and her focus on children, blah blah blah, all while hyping up *her* new book. It hit me that she hadn't changed at all; if anything, she'd gotten worse, more desperate. The stakes were higher and she was ruthless. So, I did what I had to do: I issued a cease and desist letter to both Camila, and her publisher.

Camila's lawyers responded to my cease and desist letter, stating that she was not infringing on my copyrights since there are other stories with similar plot lines. My lawyer advised me to wait until she actually published the book; to see how similar the book will be to mine. I was extremely doubtful that she would continue with a similar story, had she continued to blatantly knock off my now-published story—beyond just the concept—after receiving the cease and desist letters. But... Holy smokes! Get another bag of popcorn!

Six months later, Camila's book was published. I mean it was never academics that advanced her career, but this was next-level shocking. It was basically the same story, except she swapped the main characters. The only other change? She flipped the idea of my studious and smart main character to one who had trouble in school. Well, ya think?! Who else would take someone's concept and then have the added nerve to knock off the same person's storyline, after being served a cease and desist?

I was incredibly hurt. Infuriated, really. There she was, prancing around the world, as if she actually cared about helping the underprivileged, championing humanitarian causes, *blah blah blahhhhh*, handing out hundreds of millions of dollars to her already rich "friends" at gratuitous awards ceremonies, all while Camila had just knocked off a hard working creative and pure-hearted yogi trying to make a positive difference for children today. I mean, what hypocrisy? It's just wrong, and she landed in a sticky web that she will have a hard time disentangling from.

What Camila feared most was the public realizing that I was the original source for her idea, that I was the unique creative infusing realness and sincerity in my branding, products, and stories that she felt entitled to borrow from. The idea of me receiving praise for my work stirred a jealousy that I personally experienced from her, when I worked as her yoga instructor.

Camila was working very hard at this time to reinvent her poor public image, and I can see how my work, my brand, and who I am—authentic, creative, sincere, and sacrificially driven to make a real difference—have not only inspired her, but enticed her. And honestly, being someone's inspiration is not a bad thing. But what's not okay is taking someone's work, voice, and message and using it for personal gain without credit or permission. That's exactly what copyright laws are meant to protect against.

I experienced a clear pattern of Camila mimicking what I worked hard to create, using both my concepts and manifest work, in attempts to harness public admiration while concealing from the public where these ideas really came from. I've worked without any outside funding—spending nearly two decades passionately building my brand and crafting my stories, on the salary of a yoga instructor, to create positive programs and write books to inspire younger generations. I know that this reality becoming publicly known threatens the illusion that she is trying to posture. With a single phone call, using her newfound influence and access to endless funds, she could easily and carelessly replicate my work, presenting it as their own.

I believe it was Pablo Picasso who famously said, "Good artists copy. Great artists steal." But that was back in the mid-1900s, before technology made it so easy to track intellectual property theft. Honestly, I don't think Picasso would be quite so bold with that statement today. In the age of the internet, where everything is documented and traceable, it would be a lot more embarrassing to be exposed as a fraud or a copycat. Let's face it, getting caught red-handed with someone else's ideas and work doesn't exactly scream *greatness*—it just looks desperate.

THE LESSONS:

The Social Climber

"Wanting to be someone else is a waste of who you are."
- Kurt Cobain

Dealing with someone like Camila is about safeguarding your integrity and energy, trusting your instincts, protecting your intellectual properties, and being prepared to fight back when wronged. Stay grounded in your truth, and remember that people who cling to superficiality will always crumble when faced with real, authentic confidence. Regardless of how wealthy they are, they will copy and steal from other people when given an opportunity, whether that is a pair of sunglasses, a silver tray, a book concept, a creative playbook or business objectives, all the while without taking any accountability or feeling any remorse.

Camila's behavior reveals deep-rooted insecurities and a constant craving for external validation. Her hyper-sexualized displays and need to align herself with others' success are signs that she feels unworthy on her own. But no amount of mimicry or attention-seeking can substitute for real self-assurance. Keep in mind that people like her will always be searching for genuine self-worth and creative authenticity, so if you're like me and overflowing with these attributes, be sure to watch your back and be careful what you share.

THE YOGI'S LESSONS:

BE WARY OF PR CAMPAIGNS

I was proud of myself for walking away from teaching yoga to Camila. After what happened with Jill, I lost my tolerance for these insecure, fake women. However, I wasn't expecting her betrayal to come back around, ten years later, in such a delayed, unexpected, and unsettling jab. It was a reminder to me, to trust my instincts. People rarely change, and I should have known better than to blindly believe that Camila had evolved just because of what I saw in the press. Public figures use managers, agents, filtered photos, and manicured press relations to impress a desired image to the public. The signs were there all along.

BE CAUTIOUS WITH FLATTERY:

When compliments are over the top or laced with envy, be wary. People like Camila will often use flattery as a way to get closer, only to take what they want once they've gained your trust. Pay attention to the subtle signs that someone may be more interested in what they can gain from you than in a genuine connection. Sociopaths are masters of manipulation and charm.

PROTECT YOUR WORK:

Whether it's an idea, a project, or a creation, be mindful of how and with whom you share your work. Do not throw pearls to swine. Especially with people who have a track record of being competitive or taking credit for others' efforts. Put protections in place—document your ideas, copyright them, make it clear they belong to you, and always leave a paper trail. Take legal action if you need to.

THE SOCIAL CLIMBER'S LESSONS:

INSECURITY AND LACK OF SELF WORTH:

Camila's infectious personality and desire for attention mask a deep sense of insecurity. People like her often thrive on external validation because they don't feel secure in their own worth. The compliments, the attention from others, the glamorous lifestyle—they're all distractions from an inner void. She's hiding from her own feelings of inadequacy, and instead of working on herself, she fills that emptiness with social status, materialism, and external praise.

ENVY AND COMPARISON:

Camila's behavior, especially towards me—inviting me into her world, then becoming visibly envious if and when I seemed to shine brighter—reveals her tendency to compare herself to others. Her choice to be around what she ultimately desires to be comes from a deep-seated belief that she's not enough. Can you genuinely feel happy for someone else's successes, beauty, and happiness? If not, take a moment to reflect on what might be holding you back. Jealousy often arises from a sense of lack within ourselves, but true joy is found in celebrating others' achievements as sources of inspiration rather than competition. By shifting your perspective, you can transform jealousy into abundance, discovering that rooting for others also unlocks the door to your own happiness, without being blocked by envy or anger.

SUPERFICIALITY AS A DEFENSE MECHANISM:

Camila's obsession with plastic surgery, status, and celebrity culture suggests that she may be using superficiality to protect herself from confronting deeper emotional issues. Her fixation on maintaining her image reflects a fear of losing relevance or becoming invisible. It's easier for her to chase perfection externally than to face the imperfections within. And, plastic surgery is very costly, which likely fuels interest in wealthy romantic partners.

DEPENDENCY ON EXTERNAL POWER & RELATIONSHIPS:

Her relationships may also reflect an underlying dependency on external power, and using relationships to gain relevancy. This likely offers her a sense of security, but it also highlights her fear of losing significance if she's not connected to someone influential. She's hiding from the reality that her self-worth is tethered to and dependent on someone else's wealth or status.

REFLECTIONS:

We all deserve relationships that not only respect our work and properties, but also celebrate our talents and contributions. We shouldn't have to feel guarded about sharing confidential and private business ideas with people, especially people that we know personally. The problem lies in the lack of integrity in how some people choose to behave, not in our openness or willingness to share.

Surround yourself with people who value who you are, as you are —not what you look like, or who you know. Your friends should appreciate your authenticity and honor your efforts without competing with you or trying to take advantage of who you are.

In *Chapter 6: The Posers*, I describe a time when I dressed down intentionally to avoid jealous reactions from my peers. What started as a simple strategy quickly turned into an extreme endeavor. Without skimping on self-care, I wore baggy clothes, a hat, skipped the makeup, and stopped focusing on my outward appearance. This may sound straightforward, but in today's image-driven world, it's one of the most challenging things to do, and I honestly wouldn't recommend it without proper support and guidance.

In this process, I not only learned to appreciate myself for who I am rather than how I look, but I also began seeing others for who they truly are, identifying those who were still consumed by the image-based world of delusions. I felt liberated, undeterred by outward appearances, but again, this is very challenging because this could easily lead to an identity crisis. For that reason, I'd recommend anyone considering this path to be mindful and have proper support.

For someone like Camila to truly evolve, the first step is self-awareness, then honesty. Real evolution starts from within, and it takes humility, patience, accountability, and a willingness to let go of the illusions that she is clinging to.

PROMPTS & POSITIVE ACTIONS

When you see something inspiring that someone else has created, are you tempted to replicate it without giving them credit? Do your actions honor the original creator's effort and originality?

··
··
··
··
··
··

How did it feel when someone else took your idea, work, or style without credit or acknowledgment?

··
··
··
··
··
··

Are you willing to collaborate when presented an idea from someone, or do you view shared concepts as fair game for the taking?

··
··
··
··
··
··

**FLATTERY IS NOT IMITATION,
NOR IS BLATANT THIEVERY!**

CHAPTER 4

The Charlatan

"The man who craves disciples and followers is always more or less of a charlatan. The man of genuine worth and insight wants to be himself; and he wants others to be themselves, also.
- Elbert Hubbard

THE CHARLATAN

After my experiences with Jill and Camila, I looked to invest my time and energy into more spiritual communities, and stay clear of the desperate housewives. So when the opportunity to move to San Diego for half of each week arose, I jumped on it!

MISS SEX.COM

One of my private clients turned friends, Gary, was involved in what became a globally recognized, landmark lawsuit—the Roe v. Wade of internet law, in many ways. Fifteen years earlier, as the internet was just blossoming, Gary had the foresight to purchase several valuable one-word domain names that each had the potential to anchor successful businesses. While he was busy building match.com, someone illegally transferred one of his other domains— sex.com—to himself. That someone, Stephen Cohen, then used the domain to create a billion-dollar porn site, unbeknownst to Gary.

When Gary discovered this, he sued Cohen and VeriSign (now Network Solutions), ultimately winning a $65 million judgment. However, Cohen fled to Mexico after trashing his lavish home in Rancho Santa Fe, San Diego, which Gary ended up acquiring as part of the outstanding lawsuit judgment. With the house gutted and in pursuit of finding Cohen, Gary asked if I wanted to help fix up the place, while helping him to get fit and healthy, when he was in town. He allowed me to live in the guest house for half the week, while I spent the other half in Los Angeles teaching my clients. Since my favorite yoga teacher, Tim Miller, was based in San Diego, this was an excellent opportunity that allowed me to balance both my yoga practice and my work between two cities.

This was a time—before reality shows were even a thing—that could outdo any reality show on air today. Living in Gary's house was wild. There was Gary's neurotic sister, a photographer embroiled in an affair with Mark, the studly handyman; Mandy, Gary's enigmatic, deeply insightful lesbian private investigator; Gary himself, the global matchmaker turned accidental porn mogul who was battling substance abuse, and well *finding himself*; and then there was me, the celibate, spiritually focused, yet wild and crazy yoga teacher. You just can't make this stuff up!

Between the Jammy Jam parties, the nightly hot tub sessions, and the party where I jumped out of a massive cake for Gary's birthday, dressed as Miss Sex.com, with Mandy by my side in a huge afro wig, as my assistant, Aphro (disiac), it was the absolute best of times—wild, unpredictable, raw, and full of the most colorful, motley crew imaginable. Forget scripted drama—this was life in the most surreal and unfiltered way!

While looking for things to do in San Diego, I landed a job at a local resort, running the Yoga and Pilates offerings at their athletic club. On the property was a wellness center, *The Sharma Center*, run by the world-famous physician, speaker, and author, Dr. Daarun Sharma. At the time, I had just published my first children's book, *A Chair In The Air*, and figured I'd meander over to The Center to see if they might be interested in selling my children's book in their store. It felt like the perfect place to share my work, so why not give it a shot?

THE SHARMA CENTER

I entered the lobby of The Sharma Center, carrying a copy of my children's book under my arm. Behind the front desk was a woman working as the receptionist, talking to a man, who was standing behind her. That man was heavier set, full, long white hair and a full white beard. They stopped their conversation as I approached.

"Hello!" I introduced myself. "I teach yoga next door. I was wondering if I could speak to your buyer to see if there is interest in selling my new children's book," I said while holding up the book to them.

The man behind the counter, Williamji, snapped his head towards me as I spoke, as if I had just delivered some newly unearthed Dead Sea scroll, unlocking the mysteries of humanity's past.

"You teach yoga?" he asked with his eyes wide with curiosity. I nodded, unsure where this was headed. "And you write children's books?!!" His interest was almost unsettling in its intensity. Again, I nodded, a little taken aback by his enthusiasm, but intrigued nonetheless. He quickly asked me to join him in his office for a meeting, saying, "You'll never believe what I'm going to tell you."

So I followed Williamji down a hallway behind the front desk, into a small room cluttered with yoga equipment and a modest desk. He leaned in, repeating, "You're not going to believe this, but just *last night*, our entire team of staff and teachers held hands in a circle, asking the Universe for a yoga teacher to manifest to our Center—one who also has an interest in teaching children." Now as I write this, in hindsight, I wonder if this, too, was part of the charlatanry that I was about to experience, as a cunning means to pull me in...or if that really did occur, as I have believed all of these years.

Wow, I thought. If you've read my book, *Meaningful Coincidence*, you'll understand why hearing this was like candy to a child. At that time, in particular, I lived for synchronicity. I surrendered my life to divine will, and I leaned into situations that felt meaningful and serendipitous. Plus, he sure made me feel very special, which didn't hurt my interest to hear more. Little did I know at the time, these were likely tactics to lure spiritually minded people like me to work for free, which as you may have already guessed, was coming down the tube.

As I look back on my life, I can't help but wonder if my early childhood development nudged me toward a spiritual path. Why did I always feel more comfortable saying 'yes' to everything? Was it driven by a fear of doing something wrong, a fear of rejection, or a desire to be given before I asked? Or maybe it was the fear of making the wrong decision. Did all of this stem from my upbringing? Maybe, but the result uniquely lined up a spiritual life, so I wasn't complaining.

As I mentioned in *Chapter 1*, I grew up in a household where we were constantly walking on pins and needles. My father, a Vietnam War veteran, was left with unaddressed post war PTSD. He worked nights, which meant we had to be quiet during the day while he slept. My mother, a survivor of childhood abuse, never sought professional help for her trauma either. She was drawn to the mystical, miraculous and unexplainable as a means to justify the unnecessary and unexplained loss of her father. This ignited my perceptive and scientific interest in spirituality.

So, despite all this—or maybe because of it—my past shaped me in ways that led to incredible spiritual insights and even experiencing the miraculous. So, while my upbringing was far from typical, I can thank those experiences for helping forge a unique and authentic spiritual life.

For several years, I "worked for" The Sharma Center, and by "worked for," I mean I taught weekly yoga classes for visitors and members, helped create training programs, and even taught classes during Daarun's large seminars. My encounters with Dr. Sharma were bizarre. He inquired with me as to why my yoga classes were the most popular, and not in a complimentary, "glad you're on board here at The Sharma Center," kind of way; more with a resentful, competitive tone. He often stared at my chest instead of my eyes while speaking to me, unless it was during the several even stranger encounters where he whispered into my ear, "We have karma," in some ritualistic form of spiritual seduction. I was starting to wonder who was serving the Kool-Aid at this place! But, I was clearly still sipping on some, myself.

Now, regarding being paid for my work. Frequently, whenever anyone on our team started to inquire about payment, a new mandatory "training course" or "requirement" conveniently emerged, turning our work into yet another required "trade for service." My requests for actual payment were always met with vague assurances that it was "coming," yet somehow, the follow-through never materialized, even though I did begin to receive small payments for my weekly yoga classes to the community.

Due to Daarun's popularity as a lecturer and author, the Center thrived off people like me—those eager to deepen their spiritual practice and broaden their work experience. But behind the scenes, they were exploiting that eagerness, continually pushing the goalposts further away whenever the conversation veered toward compensation. It became clear that while the Center claimed to be focused on enlightenment and spiritual growth, they were using that very desire against us, turning it into an unpaid workforce that lined their pockets while we kept "paying" in service, time, and energy.

About a year after volunteering and working for The Sharma Center, I had finished writing a new book, titled: *As I Am: Where Spirituality Meets Reality*. I reached out to Williamji, who was the COO of The Center, with an idea for a collaboration. I thought, this is it —the moment where my work, my ideas, and my vision would finally be taken seriously. The Center wouldn't be unethical if I share my ideas; we're all yogis, after all...aren't we?! Yogis don't steal...

I still reread those emails with Willamji today, long past the statute of limitations for any legal action, but as a reminder of just how overflowing with creativity I've always been—and how my unfortunate tendency to share golden ideas with unscrupulous sharks has been a destructive character flaw.

Williamji responded with excitement to hear my idea, and arranged for the Board to meet with me at The Center in two weeks time. I drove down from LA, brimming with excitement, ready to pitch this idea that I knew was going to change lives. I sat down with Williamji and several other executives on The Sharma Center Board.

My idea? A FREE Yoga + Meditation program for the public. Yep, free—because in my mind, spirituality and wellness should be accessible to everyone, not just the people who can afford overpriced retreats and seminars. Now, mind you, this was before free YouTube videos were an everyday expectation.

I explained that I had already developed a 21-day program, which I called *The Dharma Zone*, that was included in my new book, *As I Am*. I thought it would be wonderful to partner with The Center, since I already created trainings and programs for them, as well as teaching yoga there. I told them, "I'll provide the free yoga classes, and The Sharma Center can offer the free meditations. Free for 21 days!" I was so excited.

Williamji? He laughed. Not a chuckle, mind you—he heartily laughed out loud, and then, as if on cue, the entire room followed suit. They literally laughed at me. Williamji looked at me and said, with a grin that still haunts me, "We are a for-profit company, Alanna. WHY would we offer something for FREE?!"

I left that meeting with my tail between my legs, feeling utterly humiliated and defeated. I had come in with a pure intention, only to be laughed out of the room. But life has a way of teaching you lessons, right? I've never been dry of some humble pie, followed by some homemade lemonade!

However, six months later, guess what popped up? The Sharma Center launched their FREE Meditation Challenge—partnering with none other than Odessa Whitmore, a global influencer. Starting to see a pattern here? I offer up a golden idea to influential, powerful people, and they run with it, executing it successfully on a global scale without even a measly "thank you."

Meanwhile, there's little, old me—still working through my low self-worth and early life trauma issues—initiating positive global waves that go unseen as the source by everyone else. I wasn't motivated enough for fame and profit. I wanted to be told that I was worthy. Unfortunately the people I was asking loved that I felt unworthy, because it made me easy prey to steal from. Even the yogis!

The very same idea I had proposed, now wrapped in a glossy package and being praised as a groundbreaking initiative. As I mentioned above, by the time I found the strength and self-respect to consider legal action, the statute of limitations had already expired. I was too late. I had spent too long believing in the flawed idea that if I just told the people who wronged me what they had done, they would apologize, self-correct, and make amends. Spoiler alert: they don't! *Ever!* They just take what they want and move on, leaving you in the dust. And if you call them out, they'll double down that you are the one at fault.

I was absolutely incensed inside—not with frankincense, mind you, but with the kind of astonished fury that hits you when you realize that your trusted accountant has been pocketing your tax returns. Betrayal. Yet, despite how angry I was, I clearly wasn't confident enough to blow the kettle lid completely, and if I did, who would care?! Instead, I did what any semi-rational person would do: I shared my frustrations with my trusted private investigator friend, Mandy. True to her nature, she didn't just listen; she offered to help.

And help she did. A little digging into Dr. Sharma, and—*HOLY YOGI*—the guy had skeletons named Karma! First, there were multiple accusations of plagiarism. Several authors had shared their manuscripts with him, including an esteemed professor from Stanford and psychotherapist from Newport Beach. Lo and behold, their ideas, content and programs magically reappeared in Daarun's published works after they shared them with him. Apparently, he settled with them out of court, quietly handing over chunks of his royalties to keep things hush-hush. But that was just the tip of the iceberg. The good doctor also had credit card fraud allegations on his record, and to really spice things up—prostitution charges.

My mind was officially blown. The self-proclaimed spiritual guru had a scandalous past. The problem is, and he would even admit to this, people have a tough time seeing beyond surface presentations. He knew exactly how to play into their expectations, so as to profit from it. Because he was foreign, spoke with a seductive accent, was a remarkable speaker (as most actors and frauds tend to be), and effortlessly tossed around spiritual buzzwords like *enlightenment*, *consciousness*, and lest we forget, *karma*, he seduced the public into believing he was some enlightened sage instead of the snake oil salesman that he was.

Beneath that carefully constructed exterior, he was a cigarette-smoking, soda-slugging womanizer with a knack for plagiarism. Yet, no one questioned it. The accent, the seduction, the facade—it all worked like a snake charm. People wanted to believe in the image, not the man behind it. And that's how he got away with it for so long, pulling the wool over the eyes of those eager for a spiritual leader, when in fact, he was far from the enlightened soul they thought he was. However, I will add, since it has been ten years or so since these experiences, I do believe that he, unlike most charlatan frauds, has tried to fit into the shoes he initially and falsely claimed to walk in.

Aside from these very poor character choices, there are qualities in Daarun that I have admired. For one, he has a knack for making good choices about what content his sticky rice fingers postured as his own. This leads me to believe that he does have a profound capacity for comprehension of these matters, much like a brilliant fashion buyer who knows a great fit and upcoming trend, even if they aren't the ones actually designing the clothing. Daarun was simply thrown into the idea of being a guru before he was fully actualized as one, or behaving like one behind the scenes. Maybe we're equally to blame for expecting him to be something that he wasn't.

DR. SAYS

It doesn't stop here. After enduring this entire, deeply disappointing ordeal, I finally mustered up the nerve to ask about getting paid for all the work I had contributed to The Sharma Center over the years. You know, for all those training programs they were now scaling and replicating for profit. It was time to test just how *enlightened* and *peace-love* this world-famous doctor truly was when it came to fair compensation.

I sat down in the office of Daarun's partner at the time, Dr. Says, thinking I could have a professional, fair conversation with him. I mean, surely this medical doctor would be logical and reasonable, right? Well, guess again. I was wrong. So very, very wrong.

There I was, sitting in the left-hand chair of two chairs facing his desk. The wall was about six inches from my left shoulder—close enough to feel boxed in already. Then, out of nowhere, Dr. Says walked around his desk toward me, and before I could even process what was happening, he slammed his right foot against the wall directly in front of me, effectively trapping me in that tiny space. I didn't even have time to react to that before his spiritual lap dance started. I didn't even get any music or fancy beverage offers.

As if physically boxing me in weren't bad enough, he began to gyrate his pelvis in my face while lecturing me about how I "had too much ego" for daring to ask for payment. Oh, and for wanting to understand what the hell specific mantras meant in a training they were requiring teachers to repeat in classes. Yep, you read that right—I was being sexually harassed, demeaned, and insulted for simply requesting fair compensation for my work and for wanting clarity on the phrases we were being forced to parrot. Damn to that statute of limitations!

Let that sink in for a second: a supposedly enlightened, world-renowned doctor telling me I was in the wrong for wanting to be paid for my time and energy—while literally pelvic thrusting in my face. It was absurd and disgusting on every level, and in that moment, any remaining faith I had in the integrity of this place was shattered.

It infuriates me to this day, thinking about how differently things could have turned out if I had known my legal rights back then. But the truth is, I didn't. And now, I'm finally strong enough to admit what I couldn't at the time: I was a victim, masking my wounds as spiritual virtues. I convinced myself that my sufferings were just part of my higher path and process; and in some ways, I do still believe this.

Instead of standing up for myself, I walked away—from the job, from the credit, from the compensation I should have earned, and from the multiple legal actions I could've taken. However, if there is one certain thing that I've learned, over and over and over again (still learning it!), it's that staying quiet, hoping for people to *do the right thing* on their own, is a losing game. People like that don't apologize. They don't correct themselves. They just keep taking. They thrive on it. Because let's be honest, it's not easy to fight the system, to call out an abuser, or to demand credit for ideas shared with greedy and unethical people. They're the modern-day Vikings—pillaging, taking whatever they want without a second thought. And why? Because they know most people don't have the resources or strength to stand up to them. It's far easier for them to keep plundering, to bulldoze over boundaries, deny the truth, refuse to apologize, and to leave behind a trail of people like me—people who, at the time, didn't know how to fight back.

THE LESSONS:

The Charlatan

"The only real way to make money is to start a religion!"
- L. Ron Hubbard

The desire to pose as a charlatan, particularly in the realm of spirituality or wellness, often comes from a mix of needing to control others, craving for validation, and the allure of power and wealth. Charlatans prey on those who don't fully recognize their own value.

The fact that my ideas and creativity were exploited is a testament to their power. However, the real lesson for me was recognizing that I didn't fully value my own worth. When I encountered their hurtful, deflective rejections, I allowed their dismissal to diminish my belief in my vision and its purpose. This kept me from exploring other ways to bring it to life and following through with the conviction it deserved.

I also didn't take legal action when I was wronged, or criminal charges when I experienced sexual harassment. This is not unlike other forms of abuse, and it's crucial to remember that victims don't always respond in ways onlookers expect. Their reactions can confuse witnesses, prosecutors, and juries because of the deep-seated fear of confronting an abuser or the shame of having been taken advantage of.

Driven by a true and deep desire to see the world become more unified, kind, honest, and just—and fueled by an urgent, eleventh-hour concern for humanity—I readily shared my ideas with people of influence, hoping they might help bring these visions to life. I didn't expect most of them to use it for ego gratification and to perpetuate their façades. I've learned not to give away my brilliance so easily and to protect what I've built, *but* I also won't stop sharing ideas that I know can bring positive change to the world, one way or another. We humans are just a fleeting moment in the vast timeline of life on this planet. While I don't get overly attached to my creations or products, I do take great offense when I see influential, powerful people behaving irresponsibly or without integrity. It's not the loss of ownership that bothers me, but the misuse of power and blatant disregard that carries more insulting consequences.

THE YOGI'S LESSONS:

DON'T BLAME YOURSELF

It's easy to fall into a cycle of self-blame after being deceived, but this only prolongs the healing process. Being targeted by a charlatan doesn't mean you're weak or foolish; it means you are trusting and generous with your time, energy, and spirit—qualities that can still serve you well when balanced with wisdom, self confidence, and intelligent boundaries.

FORGIVE YOURSELF

It's really important to forgive yourself for being taken advantage of. Release any shame or regret attached to the experience and take it as an opportunity for growth. There are a lot of abusive, selfish people in our world; you're not alone! The first time a magician performs a card trick, you will likely fall for it—but by the second or third time, you're wiser and you will likely trust your instincts so as not to be tricked again.

THE CHARLATAN'S LESSONS:

THE NEED FOR POWER AND CONTROL

For many, the desire to appear as a charlatan is about gaining control and power over others. When you position yourself as a figure of authority—especially in areas like spirituality, wellness, or self-improvement—people trust you. They follow you, give you their time, money, and often, their vulnerabilities. Charlatans thrive on this control. The more people they can influence, the more powerful they feel. It's not just about admiration; it's about believing that they are controlling other people's lives.

A DESIRE FOR FAME

Some people are addicted to fame and status. They want to be seen as extraordinary, better than others, someone who has all of the answers. By masquerading as a spiritual or wellness leader, they can project an image of esoteric enlightenment. This veneer attracts followers, media attention, and often, celebrity endorsements. The glamour of being a "guru" can be intoxicating for those who crave the spotlight.

GREED AND MATERIAL GAIN

Let's be real—money is a major factor. Charlatans know that spirituality and self-help are lucrative industries. When they present themselves as leaders or experts, they open the doors to book deals, seminars, online courses, retreats, and endorsements—all of which bring in significant profits. Appearing as a spiritual guide or wellness expert is often more of a business strategy than a genuine calling. In fact, Daarun himself has admitted in interviews that becoming a guru wasn't something he set out to do—it was something he figured out along the way. He confessed to starting his journey as an unhealthy doctor. But when fame found him, he saw the financial opportunity and *faked it until he made it.*

VALIDATION TO BE ADORED

Many charlatans are driven by an insatiable need for external validation. They crave the adoration and praise that comes from their followers. Being seen as a "guru" or expert gives them a sense of importance and superiority.

EXPLOITATION OF PEOPLE'S VULNERABILITIES

Charlatans know how to prey on people's hopes, fears, and desires. They understand that many people are searching for meaning, healing, or a sense of belonging. By positioning themselves as spiritual leaders, they can exploit these vulnerabilities for their own gain. They promise quick fixes, enlightenment, and transformation through their extensive programs, knowing that people in need will hand over their trust, time, and money in hopes for a miracle.

Some people are simply manipulative by nature. They enjoy the game of deception, seeing how far they can take their façade and how many people they can fool. Sometimes the thrill comes from knowing they've tricked others into believing something that isn't true.

REFLECTIONS:

Charlatans use the language of spirituality, community, or self-growth to paint themselves as enlightened, but pay attention to what they actually do, not what they say. True spiritual leaders live their teachings; they don't use them as a marketing tool as a means to seduce you.

Never let someone belittle you for wanting fair compensation for your work. Don't buy into the myth that spiritual work should be free, especially if someone is making millions off of others' unpaid labor. Establish your requirements early on. If they push back or attempt to guilt you into giving more, consider it a red flag and move along as quickly as you can.

Lastly, don't let the glamour fool you. The alluring image of a spiritual "guru" can be intoxicating, but remember: it's all part of the marketing. Charlatans are masters at creating an aura of credibility through fame, wealth, and followers, often based on unprovable claims. Don't be dazzled by the flashing fake lights.

Authenticity isn't sold on Instagram or packaged with a wellness retreat. Real wisdom often comes in the quiet, honest spaces of humble reflection.

All personal growth can be summed up with
Gandhi's famous words:
Be the change you want to see in the world.

DON'T BE RULED BY YOUR REPTILIAN PECKER!

PROMPTS & POSITIVE ACTIONS

A charlatan often relies on charm, promises, or vague claims. If you follow a charlatan, what actions or outcomes back up their words?

....

....

....

....

....

Commit to developing greater discernment—being mindful of who you choose to invest your time, energy, and generosity in. Describe those changes below:

....

....

....

....

....

....

How can you live more independently in your spiritual endeavors, without being seduced by charlatans, psychics, or exaggerated promises of false healers?

....

....

....

....

....

....

CHAPTER 5

The Groomer

"The one who loves the least, controls the relationship."
- **Robert Anthony**

THE GROOMER

My friend, Mark, referred me to a man named David, who was looking for a yoga teacher while he was in town for the Grammy Music Awards. As it turned out, David was a big deal in the music industry. A high-level executive, very close with Clive Davis, and a key player behind the success of many of the musical legends we know today. He was delightful—charming, focused, and honestly, a bit mesmerizing because of how attentive and present he was. At first, our yoga sessions included his wife, Kate, but before long, it was just the two of us.

Most of our sessions were held at the iconic Beverly Hills Hotel when he was in town. During one particular session, while I was stretching him out, he suddenly looked up at me and said, "You're a star, you know that?" I remember being flattered and offering a polite thanks, but he wasn't done. "No, seriously," he continued. "You have all the elements of a star. You dazzle. I know how to make stars." His words were smooth, no doubt, and coming from someone like him, they carried weight. It was one of those moments where you're unsure whether to feel empowered or like you're being placed under a microscope.

But who wouldn't like to hear something like that from someone with his kind of experience? It's flattering, no doubt. And after being just a few months out of the abusive relationship with Jack, his words felt like the first sip of an Argentinean Pinot Noir to a socialite after a six-hour private flight without beverage service—unexpectedly rich, soothing, and exactly what I hadn't realized I'd been craving.

To be honest, and not to sound cocky, but I already know that I'm a star—it's just not the first thing on my resume. I'm fully aware of my exceptional talents and potential for greatness in everything I do, so while his attentiveness to my talents was touching, it didn't catch me off guard, it made me feel truly seen. I mean, sure, I could definitely out-dance JLo any day of the week, but launching a music career was not on my radar. I gave up performing a long time ago—I was far more interested in spirituality and mastering the art of becoming the most honest version of myself.

After years of emotional abuse from Jack, David's kindness was irresistible, and I looked forward to every yoga session that he scheduled with me. However, in a world where charisma and compliments can easily blur into something more complicated, I had to be careful. I did my best to keep things strictly professional, making a point to bring up his wife often, always asking about her in a respectful way—subtle reminders to both of us about where the boundaries lay. Yet, there was an undercurrent of tension I couldn't ignore. His compliments slipped beneath my defenses, stirring parts of me still tender from past traumas. I wanted to believe his words were innocent, that he genuinely saw something special in me. But deep down, I knew I had to stay on guard.

He started honing in on me, asking a lot of questions and really trying to get to know me. At one point, he completely caught me off guard by asking, "Where's your accent from?" *My accent?* I thought. I'm as American as they come! So I threw it back at him and said, "If you think I have an accent, why don't you tell me where you think I'm from?" He laughed, enjoying the challenge, and then said, "Keep talking," so I did.

"Keep going, tell me about your day," he said again, listening intently while I recapped my morning, keeping it casual.

After a short pause, he confidently said, "Buffalo… or Toronto." I nearly dropped his leg right there, since I was still stretching him. How could he know that? That was remarkable! I am from Buffalo, but I don't have a mid-western accent. I was floored. What a finely tuned ear and impressive level of attention. I found that incredibly attractive.

At first, it was strictly business—conversations about yoga, my projects, future plans, and the growth of my company. I had recently launched a new collection for my clothing line and even brought some samples for his wife. David seemed genuinely enthusiastic.

"I'm going to invest in your company," he said with such energy that it caught me off guard. "I just left my position at the record label, and activewear is booming."

Wow, I thought, this is really happening! He sounded so committed that when his wife asked how much she should pay for the clothes I had brought, he waved her off with a smile. "Honey, I'm going to invest in this company. Take them," he insisted. In that moment, it felt like the start of something big—like doors were finally beginning to open, with a highly successful, reputable and intelligent man.

At the same time, I was having promising conversations with another private yoga client, Peggy, who was a marketing executive at a major TV network. When I told her about David's excitement and his plans to invest in my company, she was over the moon. Peggy had been itching to leave her hectic position at the network for some time, and she loved what I was building. She, too, saw my potential. This felt like the perfect opportunity for her next chapter.

We sat down together to brainstorm, mapping out a plan that merged her aspirations with her extensive marketing experience. I introduced her to David via text, and we quickly arranged a meeting to discuss a formal investment strategy. It all felt seamless—like every piece was clicking into place. The energy and momentum were exhilarating, and I couldn't help but feel that these were the right partners.

David positioned himself as a business mentor to me, someone who could help me grow my brand and bring my vision to life. His insights and attention felt validating, but he didn't seem to follow through as I expected after meeting Peggy.

During our meeting with Peggy, she took the lead, engaging David in most of the conversation. But David didn't seem as committed in the business discussions with her, although he offered valid analytics and strategic business plans. At the time, I didn't think much of it, but as things unfolded, I began to see that his lack of follow-through wasn't a fluke. He wasn't planning on committing to anything serious—at least not until he got something else that he wanted. His intentions weren't as pure as I had originally thought, despite his confident words, praise and all the excitement he had projected. This was a new breed of shark, one that I really wanted to be a dolphin.

Then one day, David called me while I was out with some friends, excited about an idea. It sounded serious, so I found privacy to take his call. He asked if I would be his guest to an American Music Awards after party. He offered to buy me a dress for the occasion.

I could sense the weight of the invitation—it felt like more than just a casual night out. Still, I reassured myself that he wouldn't invite me to a high-profile industry event if his intentions were anything but honorable. After all, we had become friends, and there was a genuine mentor-mentee dynamic between us. It wasn't unusual for people in our circles to mix business with social events, I reasoned. This felt like an extension of that relationship—an opportunity, not a risk. Or so I wanted to believe.

"That sounds lovely. Thank you for asking," I replied cautiously. "Kate won't be able to join you?"

"No, she'll be on the East Coast," he said, his tone casual, as if that detail didn't change the dynamic.

"OK," I said, keeping my boundaries intact. "But I can buy my own dress." True to form, I wasn't about to let the gesture blur any lines.

The event sounded epic, and I won't lie, I genuinely enjoyed spending time with David. At that point, I was still blissfully blind to his true intentions, but this was not out of the norm; 80% of my private clients invited me to special events, personal celebrations, parties, premieres, weddings, vacations, brisses, record releases—you name it. It wasn't out of the ordinary for me to be included in these things, given the nature of our relationships, and that's really what made my work so special—the relationships. I wasn't just showing up for a yoga session and leaving; I became part of their lives. I watched some of my clients go from dating to getting married, having kids, and all the milestones in between. There was a depth to those connections that made the work feel so much more meaningful.

However, after that night, the clarity set in. The party was delightful. It was fascinating to watch David in his element, effortlessly navigating the room, mingling with some of the most interesting and influential people. He had this charisma, a way of charming everyone with just the right words, and a total rock star when it came to giving his attention to people, which is a quality that I obviously regard highly. It was clear he was deeply connected in this world, and I was grateful to have been invited.

When the evening wrapped up, and David was dropping me off, we pulled up to Judy's house. She was out of town for the weekend, so the house was dark and empty. My guest house was in the back, down a walkway on the right side of the house, and in the backyard. David turned off the car. *Uh-oh,* I thought. My instincts kicked in, but I remained polite, smiling and thanking him for the wonderful evening and ride home. I was still living in Judy's guest house, bless her heart, and it was a cozy, private space, but I really didn't want to complicate things by having David come in.

He insisted on walking me to the guest house, and I insisted back that it wasn't necessary. I told him I was perfectly fine and thanked him again for the fun evening. But he didn't back down. Instead, he shifted his tone slightly, saying that he wanted to see my new dog, Flash. *Hmmmm. OK,* I thought. It was the way he pushed past my polite refusals, the subtle way he was testing my boundaries that was obvious, but historically I am not great at going against the grain.

We walked back together, in the dark, to the guest house. The mini structure was surrounded by windows, so it was easy to see that my little puppy, Flash, was fast asleep on the bed. *Thank goodness,* I thought—this could be my perfect excuse to avoid anything awkward. As we approached the door, I signaled for David to be quiet, whispering that I didn't want to wake Flash. We stood there for a moment, just outside the door, admiring my sleeping pup, using it as a buffer between us.

With my back turned to David, who was standing just behind me, we quietly whispered about how cute Flash was. The peacefulness of the moment didn't last long. Without warning, David slowly pulled my hair to one side, and began kissing my neck. A rush of emotions hit me. It felt good—too good, but I immediately knew this was going down a road I wasn't comfortable with. I had no interest in having an affair with a married man, and this was bound to complicate everything.

The last thing I needed was for things to get messy and awkward between us. My mind was racing—this wasn't just a random guy; this was someone I had to see in a professional capacity, someone who was supposed to be a mentor, not a lover. I gently pulled away, turning to face him, smiling in a way that I hoped would diffuse the moment without making it more uncomfortable. "David," I whispered, "I have an early morning session tomorrow, *hint hint*," referring to David, who had scheduled a yoga session at 8 a.m. at his hotel. He smiled.

He hesitated for a moment, but then nodded, pulling back and holding me by both of my shoulders. "You're right," he said, his voice smooth as ever, though I could see the flicker of disappointment in his eyes. He gave a half smile before turning to walk away. I exhaled slowly, grateful that I'd managed to stop things from going any further. But as I watched him leave, I couldn't shake the feeling that this was going to make everything more complicated moving forward.

Soon, David began flying me to different locations where he had business affairs, still playing the role of *yoga client* and *business mentor* while I continued to focus on his fitness. I would update him on my business objectives and opportunities, but things started to feel off and he never formally stated that he was no longer going to invest in my company. I was hoping to get clarity on that, but clearly David wanted to use it as a bargaining chip for other things.

One night in Las Vegas, I flew in and checked into my hotel, ready for what I thought would be a normal few days of work—yoga sessions with David and a casual dinner, while he was there on business. After dinner, I returned to my room to unwind when something caught my eye. Laid out neatly on my bed was $800 in cash. I froze, staring at the bills. I hadn't left any money there, so how had it gotten there? It didn't take long to realize that David must have had access to my room. Suddenly, the mentor-student relationship was starting to look more like predator-prey. I thought to myself, *does he think I am a hooker?*

Was this a bribe? An expectation? It wasn't just the money—it was the invasive reality of him having a key to my room, entering without my knowledge, as if I had no boundaries at all. The whole thing felt, well, like what I went through with Jack—except the difference here is that David had a soul, and I found him attractive and delightful! But I realized I needed to re-evaluate everything about this "mentorship."

So when he showed up at my room shortly after, I made sure to return the hundred dollar bills he must have "accidentally left on my bed", and we left it at that, without speaking a word of it.

I knew that my strength and integrity only fueled David's desire for me. It was the same magnetic pull that seemed to attract others—people drawn to me because I was a good egg, someone wholesome, someone different, and, to them, worth the challenge. Because, let's be honest, what's more thrilling than the idea of breaking the unbreakable? They're used to people throwing themselves at them, hoping for a shot at fame or opportunity. Don't get me wrong, I was not running from the opportunities or business growth, but I held my ground with selling myself in any deals. I knew with absolute certainty—that would be a one-way street leading in the wrong direction, one I'm never going back down again.

So this went on for years. He became my sounding board for every new business venture, the one whose approval seemed to matter the most to me. We'd do yoga, have dinner, talk through ideas, and inevitably, he'd try to make advances. It was an ongoing dance—me sharing my dreams, him playing the supportive mentor, only to blur the lines yet again. You can't deny that he was persistent! Despite knowing better, there was always a part of me that held onto the belief that his interest in me was genuine, that his mentorship wasn't just a guise for wanting sex. But each time, his actions would remind me of the reality I was avoiding.

He was a groomer, and unfortunately, that's commonplace in the music industry. It's a world where power dynamics are constantly at play, and those with influence often use mentorship or the promise of stardom as a veil for something far more manipulative. They seek out people who are talented, passionate, and perhaps a bit naïve, knowing that their ambition can be weaponized against them. The "grooming": it starts subtly—with flattery and guidance—but eventually, the true intentions emerge, and the line between mentor and predator becomes unmistakably clear. *I can give you fame, if you give yourself to me.* It's not just some wild conspiracy about the Illuminati or deals with the devil; this is the reality of how much of the industry operates. Even now, when I look at most celebrities, I can't help but wonder who they had to sleep with to get where they are. Sure, maybe 40% are genuinely talented and made it on their abilities alone—but I'd bet the other 60% were initiated through means they're far less likely to share.

We were both stubborn, locked in a silent standoff, neither willing to give in first. But here's the thing—I shouldn't have even felt the slightest compulsion to give in to his desires. I resolved to confront him directly and ask whether he ever actually intended to take my business seriously or if I was just a game to him. He was staying at the Beverly Hills Hotel, so after our yoga session, we went to The Polo Lounge for dinner.

David was charming as ever, and as we sat across from each other, the tension was palpable. Just as I was about to bring up the business, he beat me to it. For a brief moment, I felt relief—finally, a conversation about something that needed to be addressed. He smiled and said he was ready to make an offer. He proposed putting $50,000 into my business—an amount that could truly help expand my collections and elevate my brand to new heights. My excitement was short-lived, though, because, of course, there was a catch.

"But," he said, his voice dripping with flirtation, "in exchange for this, whenever I see you, you must teach me how not to want you, because I will always want you." It was an ultimatum wrapped in charm, but it was still manipulation, clear as day. He, too, thought he could buy me, that his money could sway my boundaries. It was a power play—dangling the investment he had been promising while pushing his personal agenda. I could feel the room shrinking as his words lingered in the air. It wasn't just about business anymore; it was about control, about turning what should have been a professional opportunity into a personal conquest.

But I wasn't playing his game. I kept my composure, smiled politely, and responded, "Well, as my long-time business mentor, I'm sure you'd agree that accepting such an offer wouldn't be very wise, now would it?"

His charming smile faltered for just a moment, caught off guard by my refusal to be swayed. He was used to winning, used to people folding under his influence, but I wasn't about to be one of them. I held my ground, knowing that my self-worth wasn't something to be bargained with again, no matter how much money he dangled in front of me. I'll be honest, though, my resolve was definitely bolstered by the fact that he was married—otherwise, I'm sure this story might have had a very different ending, or beginning.

My journey with these types of people has been anything but easy. They have endless time to waste, and the worst part is—they truly don't care if they waste yours in the process. The games they play aren't just a passing habit; they're a way of life. David, in particular, twisted my sense of trust and respect, wasting years where I could have pursued other partnerships or ventures. But here's the thing: while these experiences were painful, the growth that came from them has been invaluable.

David—and others like him—forced me to confront my vulnerabilities, sharpen my instincts, and build boundaries so strong that even the most persuasive charmers can't cross them. It wasn't a lesson learned overnight, but I came out on the other side much stronger. And I've learned that when I rely on myself, I don't need empty promises from people like David.

Yes, it's taken longer. Yes, it's been far more challenging. And sure, I could have built a highly profitable global brand years ago if I had sold out or compromised who I am. But then I wouldn't have my integrity intact—and that's worth more than any business deal or shortcut to success in this make-believe game of Monopoly that humans mistake for real life.

While David is not the only private client to make sexual advances towards me—I won't bother to glorify the major film studio executive who forced me to lay on top of him during savasana, or the top agent who sent me daily dick pics, or the major music producer who brought condoms to every session—but that chapter in my life was filled with confusion, excitement, and deception, still hung over from Jack's abuse.

Sure, these delays cost me, but ultimately each step back towards myself was a lesson in empowerment. I stood my ground—mostly— and walked away with more confidence in myself. And that, in the end, will always be worth more than any check that David could have written.

THE LESSONS:

The Groomer

Groomers are experts at manipulation, often preying on individuals' dreams, insecurities, or ambitions as a way to gain control. Their actions reflect their lack of integrity, not your worth or potential to succeed. Unfortunately, the industry is saturated with people chasing fame and success, which creates an environment where many are willing to comply with the selfish demands of groomers just to get ahead. This toxic dynamic doesn't excuse the groomer's behavior, nor does it make you responsible for their actions.

Groomers manipulate young talents by creating emotional dependency, offering promises of fame, and/or access to influential circles. David dangled the opportunity of partnering with globally recognized female music artists, presenting them as game-changing collaborations. However, he never followed through, making it clear that his offers were contingent on his personal advances.

David's tactics didn't work on me, likely because 1) I wasn't chasing fame in the music industry, and 2) I had already encountered similar manipulations from Jack and was starting to recognize these toxic traits in other people.

YOGI'S LESSONS

My experience with David is another example of how manipulation and exploitation can be disguised as opportunity. It's a situation many face when someone in a position of power uses their influence to blur the lines between business and personal boundaries.

Recognizing Manipulation Disguised as Mentorship: Naturally, at first this relationship seemed legit and innocent—an influential person showing interest in my projects, offering to help, and spending time with me.

Strength and Purity are Attractive: My strength, independence, and integrity likely made me even more appealing to David. These types of people are often drawn to strong people who are also kind, but not because they respect those traits—they see the strength as a challenge and the kindness as their access point. But strength, in my case, also meant not playing his game, and that's why his manipulation failed.

THE GROOMER'S LESSONS:

If you are conscious of your Groomer habits, the first step is to be brutally honest with yourself. Acknowledge that your actions have harmed others, even if they seemed justified or harmless at the time, or if you've justified your actions by simply being how your industry works. Grooming is a form of manipulation and exploitation, and recognizing this is the foundation for meaningful change.

Real change takes time, self-awareness, and consistent effort. This may involve ongoing therapy, regular self-reflection, and actively working to build trust and integrity in your relationships.

Educate yourself on the effects that grooming and manipulation can have on others. Understand the emotional, psychological, and professional damage you may have caused so that you develop greater empathy and awareness.

REFLECTIONS:

Like all forms of injustice, navigating encounters with a groomer, such as my experience with David, involves moving through a series of emotional phases. These phases are complex and often overlap, making it a challenging journey to reclaim personal power. Here's a breakdown of what those stages might look like:

- **Shock and Denial:** At first, it was hard to accept that David could have been playing me. I didn't want to believe that someone I trusted—someone I looked up to as a mentor—was trying to manipulate and control me.
- **Anger and Frustration:** As the initial shock wore off, anger quickly took its place. I felt furious at David for wasting my time and manipulating the situation. However, in my case, the anger wasn't tied to a violation of sexual boundaries. If you've experienced any form of sexual boundary being crossed, I encourage you to seek help from a therapist or counselor and, if necessary, consult a lawyer. You don't have to go through it alone—there are resources available to help you heal and protect your rights..
- **Sadness and Depression:** Once the anger subsided, the sadness hit. I felt betrayed, disillusioned, and taken advantage of. What should have been a professional relationship turned into a twisted power play for sexual favors.
- **Healing and Empowerment:** With acceptance comes healing. Empowerment comes from knowing you survived the situation and grew stronger from it.

Every person's journey through these phases will look different, and healing takes time. What's most important is learning to trust yourself again, rebuilding your sense of worth, and recognizing that the manipulator's behavior is a reflection of them—not you.

PROMPTS & POSITIVE ACTIONS

The first step is recognizing that a relationship is harmful. Be honest with yourself below about the emotional, mental, or even physical damage a similar relationship has caused you.

....
....
....
....
....

Forgive yourself. Then reclaim your values, boundaries, and dreams. How do you want to reclaim these now that you are free?

....
....
....
....
....
....

Even toxic relationships carry emotional weight. Allow yourself time to grieve the end of the relationship and process any unresolved feelings.

....
....
....
....
....
....

DON'T TRIP ON YOUR POWER!

CHAPTER 6

The Posers

"There are more fake gurus and false teachers in this world than the number of stars in the visible universe...

...A genuine spiritual master will not direct your attention to himself or herself and will not expect absolute obedience or utter admiration from you, but instead will help you to appreciate and admire your inner self. True mentors are as transparent as glass. They let the Light of God pass through them." — **Shams Tabrizi**

THE POSERS

I love yoga. I have committed my life to teaching it, practicing it, and understanding the origins of it. However, after owning and running a yoga studio in Los Angeles for eight years, I can honestly say: I hate yogis. Okay, maybe that's a lighthearted understatement, because it barely scratches the surface of how much I deplore the spiritual bypassing, conspiracy theorists with insecurity-driven God complexes worshiping the Goddess of Spandex in a performative spirituality that plagues our modern day communities. The yoga world, too, has become a playground for people who are more interested in looking the part than actually doing the inner work.

In my opinion, we can thank spandex activewear and social media for that. The birth of compression fabric, sleek designs, and perfectly coordinated yoga outfits ousted the frumpy sustainable cottons and flowing linens of the hippie yogis of old. Suddenly, yoga wasn't just a practice—it became a performance, a lifestyle requirement for a well balanced social media feed. I mean, do millennials even know that Koreans have been cold plunging since before Wim Hof took his first breath? I digress.

Now, at first I was all in, +1, for the spandex parties, but I didn't realize we'd be watching authentic yoga slip away as corporations capitalized on the activewear boom, masking themselves as champions of the yoga lifestyle while peddling cheap, toxic nylon fabrics and mindless yoga practices. What began as a spiritual practice was now commercialized into a brand—a more marketable version of yoga that prioritized fashion and marketability over authenticity.

What followed? Women felt hot! Who wouldn't, with compression fabric sculpting every inch of you into a sexy hourglass shape? It was like wearing confidence on the outside. But the problem came when the leggings came off. Suddenly, without that snug fit holding everything in, the sense of empowerment deflated. It didn't take long for the next wave to hit—plastic surgery obsessions swept in as the "solution" to staying hot in those ever so revealing leggings.

I wasn't, nor am I, against feeling hot or flaunting my shapely physique, or even artistically natural plastic surgery—I'll be the first to admit that feeling good in your body is empowering, as well as being a huge aspect of what yoga is about. But I got into yoga for spiritual reasons, not for a delusional vanity contest. As time went on, I started to feel increasingly disconnected from where the practice was heading. What began as a sacred journey inward was now being swallowed by consumerism, competition, and body image obsession.

I had stayed strong on my feet, persevering, after many instances of abuse and manipulation, but this—this was about to be my take-down; I couldn't escape. What I didn't realize until later was that before becoming a yoga studio owner, throughout my entire career as an instructor, I had always been able to self-regulate my environment. I crafted my own schedule, handpicked my clients, came and went to public classes as I pleased, and in the days before social media took over, I had the luxury of quality quiet time for meditation and working on contemplative writing projects. Running a studio, however, was a completely different beast—and it not only opened my eyes to a whole new side of the gossip-ridden, ego-driven, addict-like yoga community, but now other people's behaviors and performances would affect my business and brand.

So, looking back, it's clear that by maintaining strict control over who I allowed into my space, for how long, and on what terms, I was unconsciously keeping my triggers at bay. I never really clicked with the broader yoga community, but that didn't bother me. I was different —my approach was more grounded in reality, science, and psychological alignment. I stayed away from the typical yoga cliques and fellow teachers. I built my own business, organized my own retreats, and produced my own events. I wasn't part of the *scene,* and I preferred it that way.

I remember one of my managers at Equinox once calling me her "stealth bomber." At the time, I figured she was just blowing smoke at me—probably saying the same thing to everyone. But years later, after managing flaky LA yoga teachers myself, I finally understood what she meant. I saw firsthand just how difficult it was to: 1) get teachers to show up on time, 2) ensure they ended classes on schedule, 3) maintain consistency, 4) respect the studio space, and 5) avoid inappropriate behavior with students (more on that later).

She called me a stealth bomber because I showed up on time, delivered a great class with precision, and left without causing any drama or issues. At the time, I hadn't realized how rare—or valuable—those qualities were.

Since I dive into the details of how I fell into yoga in my book *As I Am*, I'll take this opportunity to share the slightly *woo-woo* backstory about how I accidentally became a studio owner here, in this book. Yes, I'm fascinated by spiritual and mystical concepts, but only when they align with reality and science—even if modern teachings on frequency, numerology, and synchronicity aren't exactly mainstream. So, if you're gearing up to judge this next story, I'm not concerned—but try to have an open mind. Owning a studio wasn't part of some grand plan, or hidden desire. It all started with a series of synchronistic events involving the one and only Prince, which led me to lean into my first studio. After that, we'll get into the nitty-gritty of the LA "conscious" communities and the camera ready yoga posers.

PURPLE RAIN

In 2015, I decided it was time to reclaim control of my life and living situation by making the big move back to San Diego. I had only returned to Los Angeles because of Jack's manipulative ultimatum, but the pull toward the tranquil, authentic lifestyle of North County never left me. Encinitas was calling me back, along with its strong sense of community, spirituality, authentic yoga, and surf culture.

I found what felt like the perfect sanctuary: a stunning gem of a house on Neptune Avenue in Leucadia, overlooking the ocean. Situated right across from Beacons Beach, it was everything I had been searching for—a peaceful, beach-side dream far removed from the chaos of LA—although I planned to commute to Los Angeles for work half of the week, just as I had done before. The contrast between the serenity of my Leucadia sanctuary and the hustle of LA felt like the perfect balance. I could immerse myself in the calm, authentic vibe of Encinitas, take my dog for long beach walks, and then shift gears when needed, returning to the city's grind for business.

I poured my heart into that home, carefully furnishing each room, even custom-building several pieces of furniture to create the ultimate beach retreat. The house had a large garage, which I converted into my warehouse and workspace. It was the perfect setup as I was deep into manufacturing large quantities of clothing, toys, dolls, and books for my growing brands.

And then Prince died.

Now, let me be clear—I wasn't a die-hard Prince fan. I loved his music, sure, and I had a few of his songs on my iPod, but I wasn't one to follow his every move, or know every detail of his life. Yet, strangely, on the day he passed something shifted in my life.

I had plans to teach a yoga class to a group of women in my backyard that night, which we followed with some wine on my patio, enjoying the breeze and ocean view. Inspired by his passing, I threw together a Prince playlist for the class that day, dancing around my living room to *Erotic City* in preparation.

That evening, the women arrived for class as usual. The sky was calm, clear, and starry—a perfect Southern California night. We finished the wonderful yoga session with *Purple Rain* playing during savasana. It felt like the perfect tribute to honor such a remarkable musician and deeply spiritual man on the day he passed.

Afterwards, in the exact moment when the last woman had rolled up her yoga mat and stepped underneath my patio awning, out of nowhere, the sky unleashed a torrential downpour. Not a light sprinkle, but a full-on, tropical storm kind of rain. It was so sudden and so intense that we all stood there, laughing at the coincidence. It lasted no more than a few minutes—just long enough for us to joke that Prince had sent us the rain from beyond—before stopping just as abruptly as it had started. We shrugged it off as an amusing, quirky, coincidental moment.

But the next day, everything seemed to change.

Suddenly, my life in San Diego felt off-kilter, like I was completely misaligned with the world around me. Doors that had been opening suddenly slammed shut. It was a noticeable energy shift, as if I no longer fit in here, where I had so carefully crafted a new life for myself. What's the saying, *Man plans and God laughs?* That's what it felt like.

Around the same time, a massive opportunity appeared on my horizon. Things had really taken off with my children's brand, and I had recently secured an in-person meeting with the doll buyers at Target—a huge, beyond epic milestone for my business. Target's headquarters is located in Minneapolis, and the meeting was scheduled for October 14th, and what made this even more significant was that my birthday is on October 13th—a day that has always carried a deep spiritual significance for me. It didn't matter where I was—in India, Portugal, or Peru—something profound would always happen. For a decade, it was like clockwork. But that year, I figured things might be different as I was fully focused on my business endeavors. I had a business meeting in Minneapolis. *What could possibly happen there?* There was so much to prepare before that meeting, and the pressure was on to get everything right. I wasn't focused on or worried about much else.

Meanwhile, back in San Diego, my once peaceful life was continuing to unravel. I had made the well-intentioned but regrettable decision to rent a room downstairs to a man I'd befriended at the beach. What I didn't realize at the time was that he was a complete sex addict. Whenever I was at home, he wouldn't leave me alone— constantly making inappropriate sexual innuendos and coming on to me. The tension in the house grew unbearable, and I found myself feeling distracted in the very space I had lovingly created to be my haven.

Now, I'll admit, I was attracted to him—that wasn't the issue. The problem was, I knew better than to let those feelings lead me. I made it clear that if anything romantic or intimate were to happen between us, we'd need to wait at least six months. I valued the peace in my home too much to risk it. But instead of respecting that boundary, he acted out in defiance.

Suddenly, he began bringing a revolving door of women into my home, practically flaunting them in front of me. It became a weekly occurrence—different women, grand displays of affection, right there in my living room, on my furniture. My space felt tarnished by these disrespectful acts of entitlement.

Despite my requests and efforts, he refused to leave since I had added him to my lease. Due to how important my business endeavors were, I couldn't risk a domestic issue. I was forced to make the difficult decision to let go of my beloved home and, with it, the life I had rebuilt in San Diego. I packed up everything and put my belongings in storage unsure of my next move, but focusing on peace and success. I ended up renting a short term, furnished guest house in Rancho Santa Fe.

In September, I decided to take a road trip to Lake Tahoe for my friend Julie's wedding, and of course, I brought my dog, Flash, along for the adventure. Driving gave me the freedom to take my time, stopping along the way for hikes and to soak in the beauty of nature. But, on every hike a strange phenomenon began, one that I had never encountered: purple rainbows arching over the stream, or foliage in front of me. It wasn't just once or twice—it was five or six. Thankfully I have photos as reminders, but even though I didn't think too much of it at first, by the fifth one, I started to wonder. *Was this a sign?*

On my drive back to San Diego after the wedding, I stopped in Los Angeles to pick up my mail from my PO Box there in Santa Monica. I received something that I needed to ship out immediately, so I headed over to the nearby FedEx store on Wilshire Blvd. While I was standing in line, minding my own business, the female customer ahead of me erupted in frustration, shouting at the clerk. "I said Rodeo Dr.! RODEO DR.!" she yelled repeatedly, her voice filled with annoyance as she gave him her address.

Her outburst immediately jolted me back to a memory from when I had first moved to LA. I had been working as a nanny for a high-profile couple—Warner Brothers producers who I'll call Mr. and Mrs. K. They had two daughters, Nina and Jennifer, and one day, while babysitting them, Mr. K asked me to drop him off in Beverly Hills. It seemed simple enough. But on our way there, he asked me to take Rodeo Drive, believing it to be a faster route. The thing is, I was still fairly new to LA, and in my mind, Rodeo Drive was an area for ridiculously expensive shopping, not a street you actually drove down. So as we approached Rodeo, I didn't slow down, I didn't turn, and Mr. K began to yell at me with the same tone I was now hearing at FedEx, "RODEO DR.! I said Rodeo Dr.!"

The synchronicity of it all hit me like a ton of bricks. Here I was, standing in the middle of Santa Monica, reliving a moment from fifteen years earlier, brought back by the familiar shouts of frustration. Amused by the memory, I pulled out my phone to message Nina, wanting to share the coincidence with her since I was still waiting in line.

But as soon as I opened my Facebook messages to message her, there it was—a message from Nina from several days earlier. My smile faded as I read her words: "Mr. K passed away. His service is Monday at 12pm," which was just two hours away. I froze. The timing was unbelievable. The same family I was just reminiscing about, with a memory so clear and vivid that it felt as though it had happened yesterday. Here I was, standing in a FedEx store, mere hours away from his memorial service.

Without hesitation, I made a quick plan. I had a dress in the car from the wedding I had just attended—it would suffice for the service. I rushed through my errand, changed clothes, and made it to the memorial just in time, still processing how seamlessly all these moments had come together.

After the service, Mr. K's daughters, Nina and Jennifer, came up to me, thanking me over and over again for introducing spirituality into their lives when they were younger. It was such a heartwarming moment, and it made me realize just how much of an impact I had left on them. I hadn't seen them in at least ten years, and yet, they remembered those small but meaningful exchanges from their childhood. As we caught up, Jennifer asked what I was up to and where I was living. I laughed and admitted that I didn't know exactly—I was thinking about moving back to LA but hadn't figured out my living situation yet.

That's when Jennifer casually dropped a bombshell. "You know, my dad owned an apartment complex in Westwood. We have a two-bedroom unit available if you're interested," she said, completely nonchalant, as if she wasn't offering me the perfect solution to my dilemma.

Without missing a beat, I said *yes*. Just like that, the decision to move back to LA was done, and a new chapter was set to begin November 1. But first, Target!

Strangely, around the same time, I found myself being called back to teach at Maha Yoga, the same studio where I had worked from 1998 to 2002. It was another full-circle moment, and I began subbing classes there on the days I was in town. The familiarity of the community was undeniable—many of the same students and members from 15 years ago were still there, and most of them welcomed me back with open arms, as though no time had passed at all.

Also during this time, as I prepared for my trip to Minneapolis, I received an unexpected and fabulous gift. One of my private clients, who worked in the music industry, gave me a ticket to a Prince Tribute Concert in Minneapolis that just so happened to be on my birthday, October 13, the day before my meeting. It felt like a magical alignment —right in Prince's hometown, and on my special day. *Whoohoo*!

Now, I know this might all sound a bit crazy, but there had been a growing series of Prince synchronicities that had been subtly weaving into my life the past few months. In small, seemingly random ways, but it wasn't until hindsight that I began to really connect all the dots. As I mentioned, I wasn't even a huge Prince fan to begin with! So I started paying extra attention.

The night before my flight, I decided to get my nails done at a local salon. While there, I struck up a conversation with a woman across from me named Jessica. She mentioned that her boyfriend's birthday was the following day—the same as mine, so we connected immediately. Naturally, this led to me sharing some of my recent *Let's Go Crazy* Prince moments, and—just as we were talking about it—I kid you not, *Purple Rain* started playing through the salon speakers. We both stopped in awe, wide-eyed, then screamed in delight right there in the salon. We instantly bonded over the magical timing. Then, fifteen minutes after she left the salon, she texted me with all caps, "OMG," including a video to show me what was playing on her car radio after she drove off. Yup, *When Doves Cry*. To this day, she's still saved in my phone as "Jessica Purple Rain."

When I arrived in Minneapolis, things got even stranger. After landing, I went straight to my hotel, quickly showered, and changed for the Prince Tribute Concert that night in St. Paul at the Xcel Energy Center. And here's where it gets wild—I found myself seated not just anywhere, but about forty feet from the stage, with a perfect view. Even more surreal? I was sitting right next to Prince's family—his brother, sister, and close relatives! I believe this was also the birth of my very first selfie, with none other than Tyka, Prince's sister.

The night was already set to be extraordinary, but then Stevie Wonder, Chaka Khan, Sheila E., The Roots, Erykah Badu, Janelle Monae, Maxwell, and other iconic artists took the stage, performing in what turned out to be a six-hour ecstatic experience. It wasn't just a concert; it felt like church—an immersion into Prince's world, filled with private clips of him speaking, intimate stories from his closest friends and bandmates, and performances that left me on a euphoric high.

And then, this is when I had my *"What the F is going on here"* moment. The mayor of St. Paul walked onto the stage at the end of the concert, holding a large scroll-like document. He took to the microphone and declared October 13th—my birthday—"Official Prince Day." As I watched the private clips of Prince and absorbed the energy of the night, I was overwhelmed by the strange synchronicities that had been aligning for months now culminating in this moment, on my birthday? *What was happening?* I thought to myself.

The next day, I had my big meeting with Target, and to my absolute delight, I landed my first order with them. It was a huge milestone, one I'd been working toward for years, and I felt like I was walking on air. With more than a few hours to kill before my flight, I decided to take a chance and visit Paisley Park, Prince's iconic estate, before heading to the airport. However, with the concert and the influx of fans in town, the online ticket site showed the tours were completely sold out. I hadn't planned well enough in advance, but how could I have known all of this before it happened? Still, something inside me just wouldn't let it go. After the surreal experience at the tribute concert the night before, I felt drawn to just go anyways. Even if I couldn't get inside for a tour, I thought, at least I could see the outside and soak in the energy of the place. The alternative was sitting in a cold, chaotic airport for hours, and that just didn't feel like the right way to end such a magical trip. So, I decided to take my chances.

When I arrived at Paisley Park, just as I'd expected, I was turned away at the front entrance. The tours were completely sold out, with a long waiting list of eager fans hoping for a last-minute opening. I stood in the parking lot, feeling a bit disappointed. I had come so close, yet still missed my chance to experience the magic inside this iconic place. Knowing this could happen, I snapped a photo of the exterior, took a moment to soak in the energy of the space, and began to orient myself to head to the airport.

That is until, the universe stepped in again, in fine fashion and impeccable timing. As I turned towards the road, walking straight towards me was Prince's sister, Tyka. Having cheered and danced along together at the concert the night before, she recognized me immediately and greeted me with familiar warmth.

She asked what I was doing and why I was leaving. I explained how the tours were sold out, so I was heading to the airport. Without skipping a beat, she smiled and said, "Come with me." Just like that, I was whisked away on a VIP tour of Paisley Park, courtesy of Tyka Nelson herself.

It was an unbelievable moment that led to an absolutely unbelievable experience, one that truly felt like a divine gift, allowing me to step inside the world Prince had built, filled with music, creativity, spirituality, and impeccable artistry.

Upon entering Paisley Park, I walked straight down the entrance hallway, which was lined with Billboard Awards, gold records, and photographs of Prince accepting his countless accolades. I was in awe of the sheer magnitude of his legacy surrounding me. The hallway opened up into the atrium, a central lounge space underneath large skylights, located at the heart of the first floor.

Behind this central lounge area was a quaint little kitchen. Curious, I walked over and peered inside, marveling at the thought of Prince spending time there, making himself lunch. And then it happened—the most surreal moment of all. Out of nowhere, cutting through the noise of passing tourists, came the silencing sound of two doves singing.

I had only just stepped inside moments earlier, so I had no idea just how unusual this moment was—until six or seven staff members, all dressed in purple Paisley Park t-shirts, came rushing into the atrium. One of them, a woman, clearly in awe, announced breathlessly, "The doves haven't sung since Prince died!" The space fell silent at that moment, leaving only the sound of these sacred birds, which added an almost mystical layer to this already unbelievable experience. It was a scene straight out of a dream.

The weight of her words hit me like a tidal wave. I had chills up and down my body. This wasn't just a routine moment; this was something special, something sacred. The doves, named Divinity and Majesty, were perched upstairs, just above the atrium. They had apparently been silent since Prince's passing, and here they were, breaking their silence in that exact moment, as if they, too, were welcoming me into this surreal space.

I stood there, frozen in awe, realizing that this was more than just a tour. It felt like an ethereal, divine connection. I became hyper-aware, disregarding time in every way, listening to everything, feeling it all. It was a moment that transcended explanation. If you've read my book *Meaningful Coincidence*, you may recall an experience I shared about my time in India in 2004 (also on my birthday), which parallels what I felt in that moment at Paisley Park. Back then, I was overwhelmed by the intensity of synchronistic events—the shock factor of feeling a deep sense of responsibility, fear, confusion, and a desire to run from the perfectly aligned experiences entirely. In India, those emotions had nearly consumed me, but this time, as they resurfaced while standing in the heart of Prince's home, I made a different choice. Instead of retreating or resisting the flood of emotions, I leaned into them. I listened.

Rather than letting the fear take over, or the inner voice speaking "don't think that you're special," I embraced it, recognizing that these profound moments were not meant to be escaped but experienced. Something within me had shifted, and in that moment, I realized how much I had grown since that experience in India. Here, in the place where Prince had lived, created, and died, I chose to stand still and open myself to whatever my spirit was showing me.

As I wandered through the halls of Paisley Park, the weight of everything began to settle in. This wasn't just a museum tour; it was a journey into the heart of an artist who had poured every ounce of his soul into his craft, leaving behind something far greater than mere songs or performances. It was a space infused with the spirit of a man who had stood for something beyond fame or fortune—he stood for truth, enlightenment, and the audacity to defy conventions.

I was granted access to listen to the very last track he had been recording before he passed. The music felt alive, even unfinished. In his private meditation room, the Galaxy Room, I sat in stillness, meditating, feeling the energy he had cultivated in that space. It was peaceful yet electric, and pulsing with funk. I danced under the spinning mandalas in his performance hall, feeling the pulse of the space, as if it were still alive with his presence.

I even had the chance to sit at his desk—his actual desk. It was such a grounding moment, a reminder that this icon, this untouchable figure, was also just a man, with dreams and battles, and paperwork! There were, of course, the tourist areas filled with memorabilia and presentations, but the most profound moments were when I was allowed to simply be in the spaces he had inhabited—spaces that felt sacred, not because of their physical contents, but because of the energy they held.

What struck me the most was the palpable sense of purpose that lingered in the air. Prince wasn't just an artist—he was a warrior for truth, a man who stood up to the injustices of the world, called himself a slave to his recording label, and spoke out in the name of something far greater than fame. He fought for creative freedom, for and he was aligned with I AM consciousness, as am I.

So much of what this book is calling out is exactly what Prince fought against. He didn't just make music; he stood as a fierce advocate for integrity and authenticity in an industry that often chews people up and spits them out if they refuse to submit and conform. He called out the hypocrisy, the exploitation, and the hollow promises that lure people in only to rob them of their essence. I see now that everything I'd been feeling, everything I'd been fighting for, is part of that same battle—to push back against a suppressive system that values profit over soul, image over substance.

In that moment I finally allowed myself to fully align with what had felt like a woo-woo, hippie-dippie exaggerated coincidence. However anyone wants to explain it—whether as synchronicity, divine timing, cosmic resonance, harmonic convergence, or something else entirely— I no longer care. What I do know is this: it was an undeniable force, and my mind has a sharp, almost instinctive way of solving riddles, seeing through people's lies, and piecing together spiritual patterns and synchronicities. It's likely a combination by-product of being both hyper-vigilant from my upbringing, and trained as a yogi committed to peeling away illusions to embrace reality most truthfully. This combination gives me a clarity to see both deceptions and alignments that others might miss, allowing me to navigate life with a sharper lens —one that looks beyond surface-level realities.

As Nietzsche so perfectly put it: Those who were seen dancing were thought to be insane by those who could not hear the music. For those of us who live authentically, and refuse to conform to society's narrow expectations, we may seem "insane" to those brainwashed by the world, but we are the ones fearlessly dancing to the true pulse of life. This is what I've been called to do, and this is what I will always lean into.

The only other person I've ever met with these same refined, hyper-vigilant abilities that I possess is my father, Al. Growing up, I believed his exceptional and fearless ability to read people came from the hyper-vigilance he developed during his time serving in the Army while in the Vietnam War. He was never treated for his PTSD—those were different times. But as I got older and began experiencing similar traits myself, I started to realize that his perceptiveness wasn't solely a byproduct of the war. It was part of who he was, something deeper—energetic and genetic, as well as developmental.

Even as a child, I connected with him on a level I couldn't fully comprehend at the time. I empathized with his pain and frustration, and I was mostly patient with his temper and his moments of isolation when he felt misunderstood. It wasn't that I understood what he was going through intellectually, but I felt it. I must have related to him on a spiritual and emotional level, long before I could consciously grasp the complexities of the situations.

When I returned to California, the synchronicities surprisingly continued to unfold. Just two weeks later, I made the big move from San Diego into the Westwood apartment, exactly as planned. The process was utterly exhausting. And, within a few days of settling in, I was off to lead a three-day Detox Retreat for 42 people in Desert Hot Springs. That experience, while rewarding, left me doubly drained.

By the time Monday rolled around, I was beyond ready to take a few days off—desperate to restore my energy, fully unpack, and mentally regroup. I had a massive task ahead of me: fulfilling my first Target order. The excitement was there, but I knew I needed to regain my strength to rise to the occasion. I literally said out loud, "You're not going anywhere today!"

Then, at 9:20 a.m., just as I was finishing my morning coffee, my phone buzzed with a text from Elise, a fellow yoga instructor. She was in a bind and needed me to sub her class at Equinox in Santa Monica at 10:45 a.m. I hesitated for a moment, then replied, "Sorry, no can do today!" But she asked again, hitting me with a plea that tugged at my heart: her dog was having a health emergency, and she needed to take him to the vet.

Ugh. That got me. As a dog owner myself, I completely understood the panic and helplessness that comes with those situations. So, despite my desperate need for rest, I sighed and texted back, "Okay, I'll cover it." I figured I could push my day off to tomorrow instead. It was just going to be one class, right?

When I arrived at the studio, I decided to play my April Prince playlist. It had been a long time since I played that particular set—since the night Prince passed away, actually. The energy in the yoga room was great and there was a strong group ready for class. But then, something strange and completely unexpected happened.

As Purple Rain began to play over the speakers, a young blonde woman practicing on a purple mat right in front of me caught my attention. She sat down on her heels, towards the back of her mat, gesturing for me to come over to her. I walked towards her, and with an almost concerned look on her face, she pointed to the sweat imprint on her mat. And there it was—a perfect, heart-shaped imprint right in the center of the mat.

Awww, how cute, I thought, but then she looked up at me with wide eyes and asked, "What does it mean?!" as if I had any insight. I crouched down next to her, still teaching the rest of the class. I paused for a moment, not wanting to project anything on her experience, and said, "You know, only the person viewing a sign can truly decipher its meaning. But I have heard that Purple Rain symbolizes new beginnings, so maybe there's something exciting on the horizon for you in love." Her eyes lit up at my answer, smiling, clearly satisfied with the interpretation. She returned to her mat and slipped seamlessly back into the flow of practice, as the song continued to wrap its magic around the room.

I decided to capture the heart-shaped sweat imprint for her, so I made my way to the stereo cabinet to grab my phone. As I turned around, ready to take the photo, something even stranger happened; I honestly thought that I was getting punked! A man in the far back row and far right corner—George, a regular who I knew well—jumped off his mat like he was playing hot potato. His eyes were wide, his hands covering his mouth, and he let out a high-pitched squeal. George was never like this. At first, I was convinced that he was mocking the woman's moment, but something about his expression was too genuine.

He frantically called me over, waving me toward his mat. I couldn't figure out what was going on. *Was everyone playing some kind of joke on me? What the hell was happening?!*

George pointed at his mat with one hand, and the other hand over his mouth, "It's Prince!" he yelled. His sweat imprint sat just above the yoga mat's surface, it hadn't absorbed into the mat. And it was unmistakable—Prince himself, holding his hands in a heart shape. The boots, the pompadour hair, the signature bell sleeves—it was all there. I was stunned, frozen in disbelief, staring at what felt like an impossible image.

George, equally shocked, reached out and rubbed his hand over the sweat mark, but it didn't move or change shape. The mark stayed perfectly intact. I had no choice but to stop the class. This was too surreal not to acknowledge.

"Okay, everyone," I announced, "Let's come into pigeon pose. I'm going to give a lesson on synchronicity today, because I have been experiencing a wild ride with some Prince synchronicity lately, and you are now all witnesses to this today." While they settled into the stretch, I told the class about what had been swirling around my life for months —Purple Rain moments, the concert, sitting next to his family, the unexpected declaration of 'Official Prince Day' on my birthday, the doves at Paisley Park, and now this.

I could see the class leaning in, curious but also reflective. "We live in a world where we're constantly moving, but if we're always in motion, we miss the small things, the details, the moments that are trying to speak to us. Life has its way of nudging us, whether through synchronicities, signs, or just a quiet moment of clarity," I said.

The energy in the room shifted, and I could feel that everyone was beginning to internalize the message. "Pay attention to the little things, the coincidences that don't feel like coincidences." I said, "These moments are guiding us—if only we can slow down enough to hear what they're saying."

For the rest of the class, there was a collective sense of peace and presence, a reminder that magic does indeed exist, and that it is more natural than we're led to believe. This was no accident, and it also felt incredibly refreshing to have solid witnesses to what was happening in my life. No one would have believed me otherwise!

After class, George was still sitting there, staring at his yoga mat in awe. "I don't want to roll it up," he said quietly, his eyes wide with disbelief. He looked up at me, dead serious. "Prince is trying to talk to you."

I laughed nervously, though I knew he wasn't joking. "I know!" I said. "But what? What is he trying to say?"

George was one of the most intuitive, spiritual people I knew—a highly tuned-in, compassionate gay man. If anyone were to deliver a message from Prince, it would be him. He thought for a moment, then finally said, "I think you were lovers in a past life."

I shook my head, unconvinced. That answer didn't resonate with me. It felt too easy, too predictable. People love to default to the idea of past-life romances when faced with the unknown, but this felt deeper—more spiritual, more pure, more present. It wasn't about romance; it was about something bigger, something universal. I just didn't know what it was yet.

"It's more than that," I told him. "I feel like it's about purpose, alignment… something beyond just a personal connection." George nodded, still staring at the mat, and I could tell he understood what I meant.

I glanced down at my hands, and they were trembling. My heart was racing. I could barely process what had just happened. George's words echoed in my mind, "Prince is trying to talk to you." But what could this all mean?

By the time I was heading out the door from Equinox, it was 12:15 p.m., and I was still buzzing from the surreal events of the morning. I glanced down at my phone, as it had started ringing. It was Maha Yoga. I answered the call. "Hi Alanna, it's Ana. We've had an emergency, and Jenny can't teach her 12:45 class today. Is there any chance, please, that you can cover this class in 30 minutes?"

I let out a laugh, shaking my head. It was clear—there was no such thing as a day off for me today. I was only 20 minutes away from Maha, so it wasn't a huge inconvenience, but I was still drunk on what had just happened. My mind was racing, trying to process George's words, the Prince figure in the sweat—everything. But there wasn't time to sit and reflect. It seemed that Prince had more plans for me today.

"Sure," I said, "I'm on my way."

Ana sounded elated and grateful, so with a mix of curiosity and anticipation, I headed over to the studio. As soon as I entered the yoga room, something immediately caught my eye—a striking purple amethyst crystal ball sitting right in the center of the teacher's platform. It shimmered through the studio window light, fully claiming its presence. I had never seen this there before, but what puzzled me most was that nobody seemed to know who it belonged to. Trust me, I asked everyone in the studio, and no one could give me an answer.

Teaching that class, I was admittedly distracted. The events of the morning were still swirling in my mind. Naturally, I played the same Prince playlist I had used earlier; it felt like the most fitting thing to do. Once again, as the familiar notes of Purple Rain filled the space, I guided the class into savasana, the final resting pose.

I took the opportunity to meditate myself. I walked over to the crystal ball, sat down, and gently held it in my hands, feeling its cool surface grounding me. I closed my eyes, heart and mind open, and I silently invited whatever message might be trying to come through.

This room—Maha Yoga—wasn't just any room. It held a deep significance for many people, and for me, personally. It was where I had started teaching yoga, back in 1999. Yes, that's right, 1999. Those early years were so pure, I even called my classes Pure Yoga. A room filled with light, memories, alignments, and beginnings. And then, just as I surrendered to the stillness, I heard it. Clear and unmistakable, as if whispered directly into my soul: "You're home. You're home. You're home."

The words echoed softly, but powerfully, over and over again, leaving me with an overwhelming sense of peace and clarity. It was as if I was being reminded that despite all the twists, turns, and trials—this was exactly where I was meant to be. I was home.

In that moment, everything clicked into place. The house in San Diego, the sudden misalignment I had been feeling, and the myriad synchronicities surrounding Prince's passing—it all seemed to make a little more sense. I had been swept up in a relentless wave of change, but now, with newfound clarity, I understood that I was exactly where I was meant to be. *I was going to make Maha Yoga my home studio, and teach here more frequently*, I thought to myself.

Within two weeks, I was again finishing a class at Maha Yoga when I walked into a conversation in the lobby, one that caught me off guard. One of the owner's advisors was sitting outside, talking about the studio's future. I overheard something that made my heart sink— they were considering closing the studio.

No, this can't happen, I thought. Without hesitation, I stepped into the conversation and asked, "How can I help?"

Bill, an advisor to the owner, explained the financial struggles they were facing. I felt an urgency in my heart—this was the very space where I had begun my yoga journey as a teacher, and I couldn't bear the thought of it closing its doors. "Listen, I have a garage full of activewear inventory," I told Bill, "I'd be happy to donate it to the studio if it would help."

Bill said, "I'm having a call with the studio owner tomorrow, I'll let you know." That single sentence somehow inserted me into deeper conversations about the fate of the studio. Suddenly, I found myself involved in discussions about what it would take to keep the studio open and what that future might look like. I ended up sitting in a formal meeting with the building owner, a lawyer, and several advisors—talk about unexpected turns. I also learned that a fellow teacher at the studio, Jared, was also working on taking over the lease. Great, I thought, at least it seemed that the studio was not going to die.

After the meeting, the owner of the building called me directly. "I like you. I like your energy. You have a great brand. I'm not going to give the lease to Jared. He's trying to shove the terms down my throat. Why don't you take it?" I was taken aback. This was definitely not what I expected. Jared, after all, was very well-known in that community— the most popular teacher there, though not always for the right reasons. He had a bit of a reputation, both as a yoga instructor and, as a former adult entertainer, if you know what I mean, although I wasn't sure about the former part of that. His "conflicting" reputation in the yoga world wasn't always positive.

The building owner explained that Jared's energy and approach didn't align with the changes he wanted to implement at the Town Center where the studio was located. He wanted something fresh, something positive. In his eyes, I was that change. He saw my energy, my brand, as exactly what the space needed.

And just like that, the lease was mine for the taking. However, my brain immediately shouted, Hell no! My first instinct was to reject the idea entirely. I wasn't ready to run an entire studio, nor had I ever wanted my own studio, but it was exciting nonetheless. Knowing that the option with Jared was not going to happen, I reached out to the studio owner to see if there was room for me to partner with him in some capacity.

Here's the catch, though—the studio owner was one of the most unresponsive people I'd ever dealt with. He'd start a conversation and just vanish, leaving you in limbo without finishing any of the plans or giving any real answers. I found myself in this strange situation, thinking I was stepping in to help save the studio, but instead, the owner slowly ghosted me, leaving me holding the idea of owning the yoga studio entirely on my own.

The long and short of it? I was left with a question: *could I, should I, really take on the responsibility of owning a yoga studio?* There was no clear direction, no guidance from the owner—just me, a space and community I cared about, and a purple crystal ball telling me that I was home. As terrifying as it was, it was equally intriguing.

That week another sign came in that was a stop-in-place moment pushing me towards the decision I was terrified to agree to. I received a notification from Spotify announcing the release of a posthumous track from Prince, get this: titled *As I Am*. I signed up for the release, however, before the public could hear it, the release was pulled by Prince's estate several weeks later.

Well, I think you've already figured out what happened next. Yes, my ego got the best of me and I chose to *Party Like It's 1999*—and let me tell you, the shit show was about to begin! I decided to make Prince the studio muse. Purple became the official brand color, of course, a nod to his iconic legacy, and the synchronicities that led me there. I incorporated spinning mandalas into the décor, blending them with the music-driven classes that had already been a staple of Maha Yoga. The vibe was set: sound, soul, and spirituality.

As another nod, I added something special above the entrance to the studio—a decal that read, *Dearly Beloved, We are gathered here today to get through this thing called Life*. It was more than just a lyric; it was an invitation. Prince's words felt like the perfect mantra for everyone who would walk through those doors.

LET'S GO CRAZY, LITERALLY

The last conversations I had with Jared before I officially took over the studio were positive—we had known each other for over a decade.

Jared had attended my yoga classes regularly over the years, and had even worked as a massage therapist during several of my yoga retreats. There was a sense of camaraderie between us, and I genuinely believed we were friends. I was led to believe that we shared mutual respect, which is why I assumed stepping into this new chapter together would be smooth and supportive. We were yogis, after all, right?

We had both agreed that regardless of who ended up taking over the space, we would support each other, continue teaching, and create a positive environment for the community. At the time, it seemed like we were on the same page—ready to create a positive solution to this potential closure, and keep the community thriving. At least, that's what I thought. I had been teaching mostly privately over the last ten years, traveling a lot, and living mostly in San Diego. While I was confident as to being an outstanding teacher with a nationally bestselling yoga DVD, I wasn't looking to be the star of the studio. I wanted to be respectful to everyone. I gave Jared the space to arrange his class schedule however he chose. My intention was to fully support him, and the other teachers, and make this a positive experience for everyone involved.

But shortly after this transition began, it became clear that Jared had no intention of honoring this. He wasn't keen on reciprocating the respect and support as I had hoped. Instead, it became evident that Jared was very fickle when it came to supporting me. If he could take credit for the positive aspects of the studio, he was all smiles and optimism. But if some random rich woman didn't like the color of the new floors, Jared was quick to pile on other reasons to belittle me. He was easy to bend with the wind when it came to the wealthy and influential clients in this upscale community.

This began to create a toxic environment that was invisible to others. You see, when students and members were around, Jared played the role of a jolly, kind, and loving teacher. He was always charming in public, projecting an image of unity and support, while behind the scenes, he was undermining my efforts, generating false gossip, including telling people that I "stole the studio from under him." I had already been through an emotionally abusive relationship with an insecure man (Jack); I wasn't stoked about this one, even if the relationship with Jared wasn't intimate.

Yoga teachers often carry an interesting and complex sense of narcissism. I firmly believe every teacher should be required to manage a studio before stepping into the role of instructor. It's a humbling and eye-opening experience to witness how teachers behave when they're not on the mat and to see the reality behind the metaphorical white robes. We lead groups of people through their bodies and emotions, and in the end they feel relaxed, euphoric, and better than when they had walked into class. Students have a habit of praising the teacher for these highs, instead of realizing that it was all their own doing; we simply guide the process. It is very easy for yoga teachers to develop an inflated ego as a result of this, especially men, who have a harder time than women when it comes to turning away praise and adoration.

Whenever I lead teacher training courses, the first thing I tell future teachers is that, as yoga teachers, we must be very mindful not to let ourselves be placed on a pedestal. Being on a pedestal only leads to a few outcomes: isolation, fear of falling, believing a false sense of grandeur, or eventually falling. None of these paths lead to anything positive. We're just yoga teachers, not gods.

The discrepancy between how Jared acted in front of others and how he behaved privately towards me was disorienting. It wasn't obvious at first, but soon enough, the cracks in his façade started showing. For him, it wasn't about fostering a thriving studio or maintaining a partnership—it was about his classes, ego and control, no matter what it cost me. This carefully hidden side of his was far more damaging because it made it nearly impossible for others to see what was really happening. The well known saying, Manipulation is when they blame you for your reaction to their toxic behavior, hits the nail on the head here. And I made it easy for him, because I became reactive; making it even easier for people to believe his lies. It is no different than how cancer spreads through someone's body, one metastasized gossipy cell infecting the next, until it is out of control.

The truth is, Jared was afraid that I would become a popular teacher at the studio, which would threaten his class numbers, his income, and his status as the "king." I could understand and empathize with that, but I had made it clear to him that I wasn't like that. He was resentful that my brand was the face of the business. Slowly, I started to see his irritation surface—whenever I appeared happy, or if I looked attractive, or when students liked me. He couldn't hide his scowl and squinted eyes, and the shift was palpable. It started with passive-aggressive remarks, but those soon escalated into derogatory texts filled with insults about anything he could project onto me. He demanded that I consult with him before making any schedule changes. Worst of all, he began spreading hurtful gossip, slowly poisoning the atmosphere in the studio, which really started to affect me emotionally and professionally, in and out of the studio.

The situation became even more toxic when I learned Jared was sleeping with many of the women who attended his classes; oh and there was their monthly group orgy. Whatever, that didn't bother me; do you, has always been my motto, as long as no one is getting hurt. But that energy came into the studio. The majority of women who came to Jared's classes came for his massages, his "adjustments," and his flirtatiously inviting side glances.

Some of these women began to treat me like another woman in his life, simply for being the studio owner who happened to be a woman;

to them it was a form of relationship that they wanted so badly to have with him, so they took their pent up frustrations out on me. Some of these women were outright emotionally unstable sex addicts, hurling insults at me, and breaking down in childish tantrums when Jared was out of town, or if he had requested a last minute sub for his class.

I remember one time I had to sub for Jared's class. He had decided to extend his vacation at the last minute, only informing me that same morning. I had started class flustered due to the aggression I experienced during check in, dealing with Jared's angry groupies, who had not received word in time that he would not be there. Regardless, I made it through the class successfully. Until, during savasana, one of these unstable "students" got up from her mat, and came after me. She was triggered when I gently complimented the group for being open to staying for my class. "You're talking about me!" she screamed, jarring everyone out of their rest.

If it weren't for Constance Marie, a well known actress, who stood up and stopped this woman in her tracks I might've gotten punched in the face right there in class! Constance scolded her, "What is wrong with you?! She just gave us a beautiful class and you're berating her?!" Constance will always hold a special place in my heart for her fearlessness, and standing up for me when no one else did. So, if you ever see her in a film of TV show, send her some love—she's one of the rare, real ones.

Jared's groupies brought attitude and baggage into the studio every single day, and it started to wear me down. Their energy was toxic, and it became increasingly difficult for me to maintain a positive environment. The negativity wasn't just directed at me either; I witnessed other teachers suffer too. Once I saw a male instructor who subbed for Jared's class walk out of the yoga room in tears. Jared found the whole situation amusing—he encouraged their antics because it reinforced his inflated ego. He laughed whenever I was forced to deal with the chaos. It was cruel, and over time, I resented him for perpetuating it.

But one of the worst moments came when the parents of a 14-year-old girl walked into my studio, furious. They told me Jared had massaged their daughter's ass inappropriately during a class, while she was in pigeon pose, specifically touching her in a way that was highly inappropriate for a minor. I was horrified, not only by what had happened but by the gravity of the situation. I begged them not to call the police, promising to deal with it internally, convincing them (and trying to convince myself) that it was just a yoga adjustment misunderstanding. This was no longer just about a toxic work environment—he was putting my business at risk.

I spoke to Jared about this and made myself very clear: "If this happens again, it's over." In that moment—and in the surprisingly productive changes that followed—I realized that no one had ever set boundaries for him before. He was used to doing whatever the fuck he wanted, whenever he wanted and to whomever he wanted. But something shifted after that conversation.

I saw him change, little by little. He'll probably never thank me for helping him move beyond his turbulent past and bad reputation, but I know I did, and I was happy to see him grow. He found a way to balance just the right amount of bad boy edge to live a good life.

But it was still a total shit show! And I am only grazing the surface as to what went down, to give you a general idea of this time in my life. You see, I wasn't expecting my contemporaries and community to become so consumed with envy. One of the most shocking instances came from a former yoga manager at Equinox. When I shared the exciting news that my dolls had been picked up by Target, she didn't offer congratulations—instead, she replied to the news by telling me:

"go to hell and never contact me again." I was floored by the extreme venom of her response.

This wasn't just an isolated incident; it was a harsh reality that any entrepreneur eventually has to learn, worsened with my particular industry. Yoga teachers often hold a quiet belief that they're the best at what they do. For one, there's no one else in the yoga room to compare themselves to, and the process naturally makes students feel great— often independently of the teacher's skill, although they take the credit. If someone, like me, all of a sudden has real worldly success, well *hold onto your mats*, because their twisted egos will not be happy!

When people sense success, greatness, or authority in someone else, they can often feel threatened or insecure, triggering an instinctive urge to tear that person down. It's a mix of intimidation and a sense of inadequacy within themselves. Now, imagine if that internal sense of lack clashes with their own inflated ego, which is based on people's responses to their yoga class? The result can be a toxic blend of imposter syndrome and denial-driven defensiveness.

Instead of reflecting on their own feelings, it becomes easier to generate untrue, hurtful gossip as a way to smear the very thing or person making them feel bad about themselves. It's a defense mechanism rooted in envy, and unfortunately, celebrities and world leaders experience this abuse exponentially. I have compassion for what they go through and the debilitating mental illness it can induce.

I learned quickly that my friends were not my audience, and they were certainly not my customers. The people you expect to cheer for you often find it hardest to see you grow or succeed. It's really important to not take these reactions personally, but I did—big time. Remember, I was a functional people-pleaser, so it hit me harder than most. It can feel isolating and disappointing, but it's part of the journey —learning that success often comes with a price, and not everyone in your life is going to celebrate with you.

I wasn't fully aware of how much the toxic negativity at the studio was affecting me. As a hyper-vigilant person, I sensed people's aggression and envy more acutely than most. I felt every side glance, every backhanded comment, whisper of untrue gossip, and every unduly rejection. The stress of it all was killing me, because remember, I couldn't escape! I was experiencing a deep, visceral reaction to the negative energy I was constantly absorbing.

In an attempt to deflect this kind of attention, I started changing how I looked. Appearance was the easiest thing to control. I began to dress down, to hide myself under hats and loose clothing, anything to avoid drawing more attention and triggering further resentment. I was shrinking into myself just to navigate the shit show of retaliation and judgment from people I had thought were my peers, my community, and practicing yogis! But this strategy came at a cost. I was dimming my own light, sacrificing my authenticity, just to make others feel more comfortable around me.

Looking back, it's heartbreaking to realize that I felt the need to alter my appearance, and even my energy, simply to survive in that environment. It was a defense mechanism, a way to shield myself from the storm. But in doing so, I was losing even more of myself, and I started to feel depressed. It's a lesson many of us learn—how easy it is to compromise who we are to make others feel more at ease.

I found myself in a constant uphill battle to defend my efforts, reputation, and the very vision I had for the studio. It was disheartening and exhausting. People knew Jared longer than they knew me, so they believed his lies. They didn't see him insult me, or push me, so they believed him. It soon became apparent that what I thought would be a mutual support system was instead turning into a one-sided, draining endeavor. Jared was out for himself, no matter the cost.

One member told me, "Harness his ego and you'll make a lot of money!" Sure, if I were running a sales agency, I understand that strategy. This was a yoga studio, and harnessing an ego for profit just didn't ring very true for me. I am simply not motivated by that kind of approach.

After a while, Jared's playbook ran dry with the same old predictable tricks. I finally accepted him for who he was. I knew I couldn't change him, so I did the next best thing—I avoided him. I hired staff to cover his classes and adjusted my schedule so I wouldn't be at the studio when he was. It was a simple strategy: if he didn't see me, he couldn't sabotage my happiness or disrupt my peace.

I also had to be realistic. I depended on his classes to keep the studio profitable. As much as I wanted to stand up for myself more aggressively, I couldn't afford to rock the boat. I figured I just had to get through my lease, and then reevaluate my options.

It wasn't ideal, but at least it kept things from escalating further. I compartmentalized things—Jared was a situation I had to manage, not a battle I needed to fight. In the meantime, I made the studio my own in every other way I could, building a community and focusing on the people who truly wanted to be there. I actually understood where Jared was coming from, and who knows, I may have acted similarly selfishly if I were in his shoes. It just wasn't easy being in mine at that time.

Also, let me paint a wider picture for you—it wasn't just Jared. About 80% of the teachers I "inherited" from Maha Yoga were alpha dog wannabes: tall, strong, cocky womanizers, some of whom had personal lawyers on retainer due to their rotating misconduct issues. And here I was, a feminist female boss in a world that revolved around their fragile egos. Imagine that—these were the men I had to manage! It was a nightmare on both sides.

And I am not even going to get started on Rocco! The chemically imbalanced, stimulant-addicted yoga teacher with severe anger issues. The one who stole the keys to my studio, kicked down a door, and for an entire year, made it his mission to sabotage me because I fired him. Like clockwork, he'd show up and break my business signs, at least once a month—until I finally captured it on camera and threatened to have him arrested— haven't seen or spoken to him since! Managing personalities like his is a whole other chapter in the madness of running a yoga studio in LA! I'll save the rest for another bedtime story!

I hadn't realized it yet, but there was a contrasting parallel at play. The more I became aware of my people-pleasing tendencies, the more I realized how they had pigeonholed me into a role I was beginning to resent. It had been much more enjoyable when I only had to manage myself, finding genuine satisfaction in bringing positivity to my private clients—I could please them without issue, and my dysfunction felt rewarded. But now, dealing with toxic teachers and the riff-raff of desperate housewives parading through my studio looking for a hot trainer to flirt with—it just didn't satisfy me, or check my boxes.

So, I did what anyone else in my shoes might do in Los Angeles—I pitched a reality show! I mean, why not? This was drama gold. You had the classic battle of the sexes, the clash of personalities, the Brent-itled customers, the sex appeal, the addicted groupies throwing themselves at Jared, and me, trying to hold it all together. And let's be real, the story practically wrote itself. I didn't even need to exaggerate the drama—it was all there, raw and real, just waiting for the cameras to roll.

But, be very careful what you ask for.

I received interest from a nearby production company that had close ties to a major network, one infamous for its reality shows. The network was intrigued and eager to move forward, but they wanted to run some casting auditions first. I immediately knew I didn't want to include Jared or any of the biggest offenders in the main cast. The last thing I needed was their toxic energy taking center stage. But, as luck would have it, the studio dynamics alone—along with all the eccentric personalities—could easily become storylines without Jared or his crew becoming key players. Again, the tension, drama, and day-to-day absurdities at the studio practically wrote themselves.

So, I went through three rounds of casting, picking up some valuable lessons along the way. It became clear that we all needed to have real relationships, dynamic and interesting lives, and—importantly, to the network—we had to be open to dating as a storyline. Ultimately, the network passed on my pitch because the cast wasn't exciting enough—after all, I was choosing cast members who I genuinely liked. Of course, they wanted more tension. Anyways, I chalked it up as a fun experience with some great lessons learned.

But get this, seven months later the same exact network put out a casting call for the same, exact premise as what I had just pitched. Oh, what a sneaky way to usurp control? And they even informed me of the auditions for it! Honestly, I didn't care which way it came, I jumped back in to try casting again.

At one point in the new casting process, I remember a producer looking at me and saying, "So basically, you threw your career away to babysit LA yoga teachers who think they're God?" I just sat there, speechless. I mean, I didn't say it—he did—but wow, did that hit hard. It was like the culmination of all my frustrations rolled into one brutal truth. I had spent years managing the egos, drama, and chaos, all while trying to stay true to my own path. Hearing it put that bluntly? Let's just say, it really made me rethink everything.

The casting process was moving at a snail's pace, and all the while, the aggravation from the studio was wearing me down. When my lease was nearing its end, I knew it wasn't worth renewing. I had invested so much time, energy, and effort, but my peace of mind was more important. I wanted out.

With no clear commitment from the network, I decided to call it quits. It wasn't an easy decision—after all, I had poured my heart and soul into the studio, hoping for a breakthrough that would make all the struggles worth it. But in the end, the uncertainty, combined with the toxic environment, made it clear that walking away was the best choice.

And then, as fate would have it, and as you can probably only predict, three months after closing the studio, I got *the* call. The network was ready to issue a contract for the reality show. Oh, the timing—just as I thought I was ready to close that chapter and move on. Now, here I was, faced with a decision: dive back into the madness or walk away from an opportunity that had taken so much energy and sanity to bring to life.

I chose the opportunity, which meant that I would have to re-open a studio, because, deep down, I knew there was more at stake than just a reality show. I truly believed that exposing the behind-the-scenes antics of the yoga world would not only be hilariously entertaining but also incredibly enlightening. It was no different than the premise of this book—a chance to pull back the curtain on the superficiality, the hypocrisy, and the absurdities that plague industries we hold up as sacred, or designed to serve humanity. I've always been driven to lift the lid on anything fake, and what better way to do it than with a quirky, fun TV show that highlights an authentic brand sharing real life lessons? I signed the contract!

POSERS TV

Things were moving along beautifully. Finally, it felt like all the pieces had come together. *It won't be soon, before long* was my motto, inspired by the Maroon 5 song that felt fitting to my life's ever twists, turns, and near touchdowns. What could possibly derail this train this time? Mmmmm. Guess again...oh, a global pandemic?! Yes, a global pandemic. Just as everything was falling into place, the world flipped upside down. COVID hit, and suddenly the entire landscape of business, entertainment, and fitness studios, particularly in California, were upended as we knew them.

As someone who believes deeply in the power of recurring patterns, I've always made a point to pay attention when similar situations show up in my life again and again. Whenever I seemed inches away from the goal line, something would inevitably come along to deter my bigger success. Naturally, I started questioning myself: *Was I self-destructive? Was I afraid of success? Was there something unhealed or unaddressed lurking in my subconscious mind, like an anchor preventing me from progressing?* Probably, yes, to all of those, in some form or another.

In order to make the reality show around my business a reality, I needed to reopen my yoga studio. Timing, as always, was everything. A good friend of mine, Barry, owned a prime building in Santa Monica—a place he had been trying to get me into for years, even while it was occupied. The space was beautiful, a former church, former movie theater, and right in the heart of downtown Santa Monica. It had incredible energy, a mixture of history and light that made it the perfect space for what I envisioned.

Barry had plans to tear down the building, but not in the near future. I didn't want a long lease, as I wanted to see what would happen with this reality show contract before committing to a longer term. It seemed a perfect fit, and I *mostly* trusted Barry. The opportunity felt too aligned to ignore, so I jumped, heart first, once again pouring my soul into creating this space. Anyone who has been there knows how special it was. I have a knack for decorating spaces, while making them feel welcoming and sacred. It was an absolute dream studio, and I was proud! A new chapter for my business. A show that would expose the realities behind the yoga world while uplifting authenticity. This was it. *What could possibly go wrong this time?* You'll have to jump to the next chapter to find out the full answer to that. :)

All in all, though, it was a dream start. The space was perfect, I trained and hired teachers who I admired, and who I chose! Hallelujah! And, the clientele were amazing—finally! Real yogis who were kind, who came for the practice, not for the gossip, and who appreciated what we did, and what we offered. They showed up for themselves, and respected the community we were building. Dream come true!

I was meticulous in curating my staff, making sure not to hire anyone with an ego grande, or attitude problems. *Hell, no!* After all my prior experiences, I had zero tolerance for that energy. My boundaries were strong—stronger than ever—and it was making a huge difference. I even had minimal patience for entitled or difficult clients, when those inevitably rolled in. The result? A peaceful, thriving studio with a sense of authenticity and respect that was palpable. This was how you make positive change, I thought. This was my Auroville! I was watching it in action.

For the first time in a long time, I felt in control of my environment, in control of my business, and aligned with the people around me. Everything was finally flowing, again, like I had finally found the sweet spot of balance between business and boundaries.

We had cast the reality show with an eclectic crew of fun yoga posers, each more eccentric than the last. There was another porn star, who had to be excused once we discovered her side gig. An absolute egomaniac who thought he was a real life superhero. A delusional and bipolar shaman wannabe. A glam yogi former escort. A model queen. A snarky sound healer, and a co-dependent, two-faced future therapist who offered unsolicited advice between her personal breakdowns.

I have to admit, I was kind of obsessed with them, and we would have, hands down, won an Emmy for this show had it aired. However, things changed with them once they each signed their network contracts. Suddenly, they didn't care about actually working. Teaching classes? *Eh, too much effort.* Showing up on time? *Why bother?* The allure of potential fame had taken over, and the reality of running a studio seemed burdensome if cameras weren't rolling.

The egomaniac, Greg, was really starting to get under my skin, as I'm sure you can imagine, with the little I've shared with you about my personality. He had crossed the line in the most unforgivable way— soliciting one of my receptionists to extract my student email list for him —which included 11,000 names and email addresses. That was years of trust and hard work boiled down to a sneaky, underhanded data grab. I was livid.

This wasn't the first time he had crossed boundaries, either. I had already fired him four times before, each time hoping things would improve for the sake of the show. I had tried to be patient, tried to keep my cool, but this? This was an unforgivable level of betrayal. I couldn't look past it any longer. It wasn't just about the show anymore; it was about integrity and protecting what I had built. How could we carry a show with someone I planned to fire on the first episode?!

I made it crystal clear to the producers: if he was in, I was out. There was no way I was going to continue working with someone who had so blatantly violated my trust, and certainly not while cameras were rolling. This was beyond drama for TV; it was my real life, and I wasn't willing to compromise my values for the sake of keeping a character on the show.

Suddenly, I missed Jared. Well, not really—but I found myself appreciating that, despite all his antics and insecurities, at least Jared was communicative with his schedule, took responsibility for his classes, gave his all when teaching, and had a certain level of maturity that I did appreciate. I never thought I'd say this, but in comparison, Jared almost felt...likable and manageable.

And that's when it hit me—what I was committing to. The reality show, the studio, the drama, the egos, and the lack of respect—it was all starting to feel overwhelming, and not worth it all; it scared me. I had spent so much time building my brand, pouring my heart into it, and here I was, about to dive headfirst into a whole new world that felt completely out of my control. I was nervous as to where this endeavor was heading, and how it would affect my business.

Was this really what I wanted? Could I handle this level of intensity? Would I want to work with these kids day in and out, season after season? Suddenly, the glamorous idea of exposing the yoga world's dark underbelly wasn't feeling as exciting.

I had expanded from a 2,500 sq ft studio with one room and a store to a 6,500 sq ft space that included two studios, a store, a lounge, a kitchen, multiple offices, and four wellness treatment rooms. Managing it all demanded nonstop effort—simply too much for one person to handle alone. As the initial endorphin rush began to fade, I found myself weighing my responsibilities against my original objectives.

It forced me to confront a tough question: If the show were no longer a factor, would I still want to keep the studio? Was this truly the life I wanted, or had I been chasing a means to justify the reality that I had landed into a big pile of shit show yoga four years earlier?

CHOCOLATE COVERED KARMA

The past few years, I've started to recognize that sometimes synchronicities can masquerade as "chocolate-covered karma," as I like to call it—at least for me! They're sweet, exciting, seductive, irresistible moments, tempting me to take a bite, when I otherwise wouldn't have —like the time I opened a yoga studio based on one—only for me to realize that I had to confront unresolved aspects of myself. They act as invitations, wrapped in something promising, only for me to realize that underneath the sweetness hides the karmic, internal work I still need to do.

They're not just random coincidences; they're reminders that healing is an ongoing journey, not a final destination. Each synchronicity carried with it an understanding, a lesson, a challenge, a blessing, or an opportunity to face the parts of me needing my attention. And while these synchronicities may have initially felt like signs pointing me toward something magical or transformative, the magical portions couldn't be fully actualized until I did the necessary healing.

The opportunities were there, but they stayed just out of reach until I became more whole. The potentiality is always within each of us, waiting for the right conditions in our mind and body to broadcast the right frequency. The more that we resist and fight our natural process, or the more distracted and disconnected we become, the less light we're able to project into our experiences. The mundane vs. magical aspect of living is up to us.

My impeccable practices had unknowingly created extraordinary alignments, which opened portals into the workings of synchronicity and quantum physics. However, when I had to then step into an imperfect, cruel and greedy world, the lights quickly blew out, like candles in the wind. I bet you know the feeling.

But here's the thing I've learned: wherever we go, there we are. No matter how tantalizing the synchronicity, or how aligned things might seem on the surface, we can't outrun the lessons we're meant to learn, or expect to be perfect without practice. As long as we're engaged in our lives, the same themes and lessons will keep showing up, waiting for us to realize them, whether we're managing a yoga studio, selling new cars, or just starting law school. How we view the world is shaped by an internal lens, and that lens can only be corrected from the inside.

I also view synchronicities like viable pregnancies—full of potential and opportunity, ripe with promise. But not all pregnancies take hold. In some of my experiences, my unhealed traumas have often acted like hidden landmines, or scars, preventing these "spiritual pregnancies" from going full term. It's like there's a dance we're engaged in: the dance of free will, the dance of karma, the dance of desire and opportunity. If we're dancing while carrying the heavy baggage of past wounds and unaddressed pain, it inevitably changes every step, and it alters the outcome to every opportunity that comes our way.

Had I not carried wounds from narcissistic men, I probably wouldn't have had issues with Jared or the likes of him. But if I hadn't been affected by those experiences, I might have settled into a deeply dysfunctional situation without realizing it. So, one isn't necessarily better than the other; both are part of the learning process, and I believe that we have to trust our intentions and timing. The changes we seek, the healing we crave, they all source from inside. Everything else— every person, every challenge—is just an opportunity, an exercise, to grow and learn from our experiences.

I learned the hard way—I had to stop everything. I had to turn inward, stop chasing the next distraction, believing that when *that happens*, then I can heal. Instead, I had to trace where the cracks from past abuse and disappointments had formed, not to keep sealing them back up, but to let the light in and the darkness out. That's when real healing began for me—not by avoiding the pain or trying to override it with distractions, but by sitting with it, listening to it, letting it unravel, and ultimately allowing it to naturally step out of it's constraints and into a new, liberated life.

We are energetic beings, constantly emitting energy coded with our heart's purpose and our mind's intentions. We have the power to create harmonious energy that is aligned with our truth—or, conversely, we can emit discord, confusion, and chaos. The beauty of it all is that it's entirely up to us. We are the conductors of our own energy, and how we choose to resonate shapes the experiences that we create.

THE LESSONS:

The Posers

"You can't be friends with someone who wants your life."
- Oprah Winfrey

REFLECTIONS

Listen, yoga is going to attract people who are trying to 1) improve their lives, 2) get fit, 3) avoid their problems. Running a yoga studio is not as easy as say, managing a car dealership. You're selling wellness and everyone is going to have a different history, different triggers, and different solutions. It's not easy!

After thirty years of teaching and eight years of running yoga studios, I've encountered many absolutely amazing and compassionate yogis, as well my fair share of inauthentic yoga posers. Real transformation takes time and hard work, and I am sure that I've fallen into my own version of a yoga poser at different points in my journey as well. Remember, everyone is doing their best with the tools and understanding they have in each moment.

THE YOGI'S LESSONS

As a yogi turned yoga studio owner, I've learned some hard but invaluable lessons about the intersection of passion and practicality. I let my love for teaching yoga and my awe of synchronicity lead the way, at the expense of grounding my decisions more pragmatically. Running a studio required more than just sharing my passion—it demanded navigating leases, staff management, building upkeep, marketing, and finances, none of which aligned with the initial passion.

One of the most profound lessons I learned was the importance of maintaining a healthy buffer between myself and the sheer volume of people I interacted with daily. As a yoga teacher, I thrived on personal connections and uplifting others, but as a studio owner, the demands of hundreds of students, teachers, and community members overwhelmed me, as I am very sensitive to, and highly aware of energy. Be mindful of the energy you surround yourself with, because if you are not the strongest force, you will adapt to your environment. The amount of time and energy it took to keep the studio running rocked me out of balance, leaving me with less capacity to extend grace and patience to the very people I wanted to serve. This imbalance was compounded by the toxic elements I encountered—a hurtful, gossipy, and at times jealous community that felt hypocritical to the very principles of yoga.

Despite the challenges, I've cultivated compassion for myself and for those I've encountered along the way—it's all growth. It's not easy to deal with the undercurrents of human behavior in a space that is supposed to be a sanctuary, and I've learned to forgive myself for the missteps I made while trying to manage it all. At the same time, I've come to understand that while I deeply love yoga and teaching, the performative aspects and surface-level spirituality I've encountered in the modern yoga world feel disconnected from the deeper truths I aim to cultivate and share. This has allowed me to refocus on what I am more passionate about—living and teaching authenticity.

As for *The Posers*, if they're even subconsciously drawn to yoga and healing practices, I'd wager they're on their own journey toward greater awareness and healing. I genuinely wish everyone healing, love, and truth. For a little amusement, however, enjoy these common poser archetypes for how they are meant to be—*fun and funny*, with a dash of consideration that you may relate to:

⟩ *The Festival Fiend* ⟨

- Spiritual community festivals have become less about mindfulness and more about how many fringe kimonos and glitter pasties they can fit into one weekend.

○ From single-use glitter to plastic water bottles, they leave a trail of waste behind—because nothing says "eco-conscious yogi" like trinkets and disposables littered across the sacred festival grounds.

⟫ *The Plant Medicine Junkie* ⟪

○ **The Ceremony Hopper:** This person treats ayahuasca like a nightclub lineup, hopping from one ceremony to the next, bragging about how many shamans they've sat in ceremony with—because more trips = more spiritual relevance, right? They claim they've obliterated their ego, and just can't stop reminding you just how ego-free they are.

People who develop a dependency on plant medicine often do so as a way of substituting their former addictions, whether to hard drugs, party drugs, even sex or food. While plant medicines like ayahuasca, psilocybin, and ketamine can offer profound healing when used mindfully, and with a certified guide, they can also become a crutch. In some cases, individuals trade one form of escapism for another, using these substances to avoid addressing the deeper issues at the root of their addictions.

• Example: Below may have been part of a real conversation I had with someone wanting to offer Kambo ceremonies at my studio:

Egoless Someone: "These marks on my shoulder are from my Kambo ceremonies—my ego's basically dead at this point and I am free of all addictions."

Me: "Where does the Kambo come from?"

Egoless Someone: "It is harvested from frogs. We spread their legs on a stick and tickle them to get the kambo."

Me: "Sorry, I can't take on that legal responsibility at the studio."

Egoless Someone: "Fuck you. You're such a bitch!"

Sorry, but, in my opinion, if you have to jerk off a frog to get high, that's probably not yoga. But, you know, it's **not** about the high... it's about the healing...

❧ *The Spiritual Bypasser* ❧

- **Unreasonable Reason:** The "everything happens for a reason" response has never been my favorite. The universe is formulaic and mathematical. Yes, everything does happen for a reason, and sometimes that reason is our own missed opportunities, lack of awareness, and poor judgment. Using this phrase to dismiss someone's grief, hardship, or trauma shifts the focus away from real emotions and encourages avoidance of uncomfortable realities. Huge faux pas!

- Example: When spiritual bypassers dismiss other peoples' struggles with phrases like, "It's all meant to be," or "Just be grateful."

Before "spiritual bypassing" became a widely recognized term, I identified a similar personality type in my book *As I Am*, which I called the **Airy Fairy**. This type embodies much of the same behavior—floating above real issues, often using spirituality as a means to avoid confronting deeper emotional wounds. While I want to tread lightly here, since dissociation from early-life trauma may be at play for some of these individuals, let's be honest—we've all encountered a few Airy Fairies in our yoga classes! They're the ones who lean heavily into cosmic jargon and positivity, while subtly dodging things of this world.

❧ *The Phony Ambassador* ❧

- These personalities claim they only support brands that match their "energy" but conveniently forget their values when a toxic company cuts them a check. Who knew fast fashion and mindfulness went hand in hand?

- Example: I may have seen the below captioned on a social media post:

✦ Welcome to Grati-Tuesday! I only align with brands that resonate with my highest vibration ✦—that's why I'm so honored to be working with [insert toxic fast fashion company]! Remember, I created my own wealth by following my dreams, and I can show you how to do the same for only $4,444! True abundance flows when you believe you deserve it. Use my code 'ENLIGHTENED11' for 11% off your soul-aligned purchase that will manifest your best life!

⚝ *The Hedonist* ⚝

- **The Savasana Subpoena** – When your savasana is disturbed by a process server issuing sexual misconduct papers to your yoga instructor. Namaste, indeed, because I have seen this happen!
- **The Tantra Femme Fatale** – We all know the "tantric goddess" yogini persona. But let's be real—it's just a lucrative way to perpetuate objectification while packaging it as empowerment. Her "sacred sensuality" feels more like an Instagram thirst trap, after all even yogis know that "sex sells."
- **The Creepy Perv** – Every tantra event is guaranteed to have at least one creep on the prowl, hunting for a "sacred hookup" or a willing partner for some awkward eye gazing.

I enjoy learning about Tantra, which was originally one of the earliest forms of spiritual worship centered around a female deity. However, over time, simple minded humans reduced its depth to focus on sexual enlightenment, as if women's significance could only be tied to a one dimensional value: sexuality.

⚝ *The Toxic Positive* ⚝

- **Just Love Me, Please:** This person is completely allergic to any negativity, they'll shut down any real talk with a cheery "Just stay positive!" The Toxic Positive desperately needs to be adored by everyone in the room.

- Example: There was a workshop leader at my studio who seemed more interested in being seen as a guru than actually doing the work required to become one. He demanded free spots for guests at his events, and yet complained about not making enough profit for himself. At first, I tried to help him understand the value of my time and space, but when I broached the subject, he dodged any conversation by sending me voice memos, saying, "Just tell me you love me—that's it! No need for a conversation about this."

⸱ *The Miserly Healer* ⸱

- **Preaches Abundance, Practices Scarcity:** Loves to talk about abundance consciousness—right after trying to haggle down a studio rental rate. Because yoga and spiritual work should be free, unless it's for their services! #DoubleStandardVibes

- Example: Besides offering their energy healing services without any legitimate background in therapy or counseling, these self-proclaimed "master energy healers" frequently inquired about booking my studio for their services. During negotiations, they insist they're raising the vibration of my space, and therefore deserve a discount or free use. This kind of behavior is a perfect example of a performative abundance mindset: they expect generosity and free services from others while fiercely defending the value of their own time and work.

⸱ *The Gossip Guru* ⸱

- **Living in the Past Pose** – Every new teacher gets compared to some long-lost yogi from 20 years ago. People often struggle with change, especially when emotions are involved, because emotional attachments create a personal sense of identity, but it just may be time to let this go.
- **Masters of passive-aggressive gossip**, these yogis live for drama under the guise of "community connection."

⋛ *The Pseudoscience Biohacker* ⋚

- ○ **Dependency Peddler:** Their daily routine includes 72 pills, powders, daily cold plunge that Vikings and Koreans have been doing for thousands of years, and—oh, don't forget the tech gadgets—even though red light therapy may be causing retinal disease, but they'll have a new, alternate "life-changing" product to sell you next month after today's formula gets debunked. *Spoiler:* Aging is still undefeated and death is inevitable.

I included the longevity guru with an extra bit of humor, but the truth is, I do believe in many longevity techniques, except that I prefer techniques that assist my body to find balance, not to be excessively dependent on supplements or gadgets to maintain my health. I believe in moderation. I believe wellness should complement a balanced life. No one can escape death and if we become excessively fixated on anti-aging, the natural and inevitable process of aging will feel devastating.

In today's world of excessive food consumption, the results of fasting feels like a miracle to many—but really, it's simply more natural. We've normalized eating far more than we need, often indulging in foods packed with unhealthy chemicals and preservatives that offer minimal nutritional value. Fasting helps reset our systems, giving the body space to heal and function more optimally. It's a reminder that less is more when it comes to food, and that sticking to natural, whole sources is always best.

PROMPTS & POSITIVE ACTIONS

Give examples of when you have believed gossip told to you,
then re-told the gossip that you had heard to someone else.

....

....

....

....

....

How can you immerse your current wellness routines more deeply
into authentic practices of mindfulness and truth?

....

....

....

....

....

....

Write and repeat with intentionality:
*I am committed to speaking only from my own experience and
honoring the truth of my experiences.*

....

....

....

....

....

NAMASTAY OUT OF MY STUDIO!

CHAPTER 7

The 22

"Teach me how to trust my heart, my mind, my intuition, my inner knowing, the senses of my body, the blessings of my spirit. Teach me to trust these things so that I may enter my Sacred Space and love beyond my fear, and thus Walk in Balance with the passing of each glorious Sun". **- Lakota prayer to Wakan Tanka**

THE OMEGA Ω 22

I was incredibly proud of what we built at the Santa Monica studio. It validated my disappointments about the Brentwood location and proved that I didn't need to operate under Jared's influence or endure such hurtful abuse from a community. Stepping out of his shadow allowed me to reclaim my peace of mind and teach without judgment. For the first time in a long while, I felt free from toxic relationships.

However, LA is a city where gossip spreads like wildfire, and I wasn't immune to it. Despite moving on, I still heard echoes of false rumors—embers Jared had lit years ago that continued to linger. It was frustrating to know that even after leaving behind that toxic environment, the residue of his influence persisted, but I was content in knowing my truth, compassionate with myself for how I reacted to such a challenging situation, and resolve in trusting that the right people will make their own decisions, not based on gossip.

The experience also deepened my compassion for others, especially women in the public eye. Whether it's a young pop star, a politician, or an Olympic athlete, any strong woman stepping into a leadership role often faces relentless cruelty. The harsh public judgment directed toward women reflects not only societal biases but also the discomfort that insecure men feel when they see a woman succeed independently.

Unfortunately, I wasn't immune to this toxic dynamic. What saddens me more is seeing some women knowingly align themselves with these men—choosing to protect and enable these bullies as a way to feel secure themselves, hoping to maintain their own favor and fearful of losing their status or connection.

This pattern, where women endure more scrutiny simply for asserting authority, speaks to a much larger cultural problem. It's a reminder that solidarity among women is critical, especially in environments where success is punished by untrue gossip and smear campaigns. The emotional toll these experiences take is real, which makes every small act of support—from a kind word to standing against false narratives—all the more essential.

However, just two months after opening my Santa Monica studio, I was hit with two bogus lawsuits tied to an incident that had occurred one year earlier. It all began when a woman named Ivanka reached out to me through Airbnb. Her message was desperate, almost pleading, asking for a short term stay in my home. She explained that she was struggling financially because of the pandemic and begged me to let her pay directly, bypassing Airbnb's platform fees to save a little money. I empathized with her situation and, regrettably, agreed. You know that saying: *no good deed goes unpunished.*

I expected her to be grateful for my generosity, yet to the contrary, she immediately became quite demanding, in many ways. From wanting me to replace the office chair in her room to overusing (and eventually losing) my guest parking passes, it was becoming clear that she had a strong sense of entitlement. She argued about every basic cost for utilities. Still, I tried to be accommodating, assuming that maybe it was just the stress of the pandemic taking a toll on her. Plus it was only a two month stay.

Then one day, a new children's book I had written during the pandemic, *Bounce Back!*, arrived in the mail. I was excited to finally hold a copy in my hands and eagerly showed her the cover, happy to share the moment with someone. Her reaction, however, was anything but supportive. With inquisitive, squinted eyes, she asked, "You write children's books? What else do you do?"

Her newfound interest in my business didn't seem sincere at all—it felt opportunistic, as if she was sizing me up, measuring my worth against her own ambitions. It wasn't admiration or curiosity; it was as though she was calculating how she could take advantage.

In 2022, I found myself confronting one of the most challenging and disruptive personal situations of my life—just when everything seemed to be falling into place. I had finally built the dream studio I'd envisioned for years, and I was on the verge of a major breakthrough with a promising network TV show development deal centered around my business. The timing couldn't have been more ironic or difficult; just when I thought I had finally pulled myself back up from the depths of past struggles, and that success was just around the corner. Yet, despite everything I had worked so hard to rebuild, I was about to face a new wave of chaos I didn't see coming.

After Ivanka's perked interest in my business successes, she ran a Google search on me. Once she discovered the breadth of my work— my business, clothing brand, toys, books—*and* after witnessing camera crews filming casting presentations for the TV show at my house, her opportunistic mindset went into overdrive. Instead of showing support or even asking genuine questions about my endeavors, she saw a golden opportunity to exploit what she perceived as my success.

Oh, and get this—remember the whole *Hamptons Magazine* fiasco?! When they called me to fact-check an article about Jill Monroe, the wife of a well-known billionaire, who had claimed to be the founder of my company? After hearing the truth from me that Jill was not the founder of AZ I AM, the magazine swiftly updated their online version of the story, but the damage had already been done with their print versions. They couldn't alter the hard copies in time, and other outlets had picked up the story based on the hard copies, perpetuating Jill's lie and creating a seed trace of that false story online, which Ivanka found with her extensive sleuthing.

Ivanka's eyes gleamed with a smug grin as she asked, "Sam Monroe is your business partner?" as if she thought she'd hit the jackpot. When I told her no, that wasn't true, she didn't believe me. The look in her eyes, paired with that sly, entitled smile, told me everything. She was convinced I was lying, certain I was hiding wealth or connections. In her mind, this was her moment to latch on and manipulate some claims.

Her calculating mind went into overdrive as she began fabricating a claim, trying to frame me as being in violation of the pandemic's eviction protections. It was clear she had assumed that, with the visibility of my work, the TV crews, and everything else she'd observed around me, I had to be sitting on a fortune. Months later, I uncovered a text that her attorney had sent, bluntly stating: "Sam Monroe is her business partner. There's a lot of money to go around."

It was now painfully obvious that her intentions had never been genuine. From the moment she messaged me, then stepped into my home, she had been sizing me up, carefully plotting how she could benefit from the recent pandemic ordinances in Santa Monica.

Ivanka seized the opportunity, driven by her irrational beliefs and assuming that I would simply settle her claims. Instead, what followed was a two year legal battle—draining, relentless, traumatizing, intrusive, and deeply destructive. You see, I'm less motivated by the prospect of financial gain through legal action as I am motivated to rectify an injustice. I will not settle to something that I am not guilty of. Period. This was war.

Though I ultimately emerged victorious, the toll it took on me was undeniable. It wasn't just a fight over false claims; it became a battle of capacity and endurance that tested every aspect of my resilience— mentally, emotionally, and spiritually. During this time, I began to develop a deep distrust and dislike for people—it wasn't just Ivanka's behavior that wore me down. The so-called 'conscious community' in Los Angeles had morphed into a conspiracy-driven mob, and suddenly I found myself in their crosshairs. They came at me like vigilantes, arguing and fighting with me at the front desk of my studio, as if I were personally responsible for enforcing Governor Newsom's strict COVID protocols, mask requirements and business closures. It was as if they saw me as the stand-in receptionist for the state government, taking out their frustrations on me instead of understanding that I had to comply with the state's restrictions.

LA hipsters weren't having it, and their entitled aggression grew unbearable. On top of the legal battles I was already fighting each day, and the extreme homelessness issue in Santa Monica, I had to deal with their hostility, too. The constant pushback from people who were supposedly all about peace and love was exhausting—and it left me disillusioned with the very community I was serving.

As awful as this experience was, it marked a pivotal moment in my life—the first time I chose to fight for justice. I had endured countless betrayals before: plagiarism, domestic violence, defamation—you name it. Yet, in all those moments, I never fought back. I had always let things slide, I could never get past an internal resistance to fighting back; it always felt too overwhelming. But this time was different. It felt like the breaking point—the moment when I could no longer remain passive in the face of injustice. Something inside me had shifted, and I put everything aside to focus on these matters.

There came a point when a sign convinced me to lean in to the situation instead of questioning how it had happened. The dark side of synchronicity, I call it, whispering for me to trust even this process. 22 —appearing again and again, and again. But what did it mean? Was it a reminder, a calling, or a nudge? I didn't fully understand it yet, but I knew it held meaning, something waiting to be revealed. So, I continued to listen for an answer.

Fittingly in February of 2022 (yes that's 02/2022), while preparing for court, I came across a copy of Ivanka's passport and nearly fell over. Her birthday? 2-22-88. The shock hit me like a freight train. Let me explain. February 22, 1988, was a date forever etched in my memory—a day filled with immense tragedy and heartbreak. On that day, the children I used to babysit for as a young teenager, were murdered by their stepfather in a fire. I was supposed to be at their house that night, watching over them, but I had canceled last minute because of a high school party that I ultimately never attended. This story is one of the pivotal moments of my life, and one of the other times in my life where I acted beyond my control—much like what happened in Costa Rica, as I described in *Chapter 1*—I share this experience with the children in greater detail in my book, *Meaningful Coincidence, Volume 1*.

This was the first instance where 22 became not just a number, but a confirmation, albeit painful, and it is when I surrendered to the negative situation. It all felt like a cruel joke, frankly. Here I was, bogged down by a legal battle that was draining and distracting me from what I thought was my true path forward. But we can't break free until every bind is untied.

As the year went on, the number 22 and its variations began interjecting themselves into every corner of my world. I was dragged into the national spotlight during a former client's cheating scandal. His production company? 222 Productions. I had stopped working for him years earlier due to Jack breaking my wrist in a jealous rage—and Jack's birthday was, fittingly, 4-22. Daarun Sharma's birthday? 10-22. I was seeing a clear pattern, and very eager to understand a meaning.

Shockingly again, later that year, I found myself in the public eye, giving national news interviews, this time speaking in support of a survivor of a quadruple homicide in Idaho. The address of the house? 1122 King Road. My life seemed inextricably linked to this number, yet not in a pleasant way! The signs were heavy, dark, and morbid.

STRIKE A GONG

I couldn't ignore it anymore. The synchronicities were too clear, too powerful, and happening too frequently to dismiss as mere coincidence. I was being forced to relive and release old wounds at what felt like breakneck speed.

Then it hit me—*was it the gong?* It seemed like these shadow synchronicities began shortly after I started to play the gong, which is a powerful instrument of vibrational resonance that can initiate a vibrational detox, clearing out stagnant energy from the body and mind.

Could playing the gong have set off this massive release of long-held traumas within me, like champagne bottle corks popping with such force after being held down so tightly, for so long? It certainly felt that way. I wasn't just remembering these traumas—I was reliving them, and each one was surfacing with a purpose, and let's not forget—front page news coverage!

I'm not sure I'll ever fully understand why I instinctively shied away from fighting when I had been wronged in the past—why it felt easier to just move on. But for these cases, I dug deep, deeper than I thought I could, and I fought. The turning point came when I was finally able to present a pivotal piece of evidence: a video that showed Ivanka calling the police, claiming she was locked out of my home, while she was, in fact, inside the house the entire time. When the judge saw that, his demeanor shifted completely. He stated, "Ms. Zabel will prevail in court, and she could sue the City for malicious prosecution," which was a game-changer. The truth was finally laid bare (two years later!), and my legal case *against* Ivanka was allowed to proceed. That's when the lawyers called, asking to settle.

If I wasn't so utterly drained, and frankly depressed, from two years of this insanity—the endless legal wrangling, the web of lies spun by lawyers, the invasions of my privacy, and the emotional toll—I probably would've kept fighting, just to see justice carried out to its fullest. But I was done. I hadn't taken good care of myself over the past year, with the massive stress and inhuman amount of workload to keep everything afloat. I felt like I aged 10 years overnight, I had put on weight, both which added to the emotional heaviness. It was finally over and I could move on, victorious, but frankly, I felt like crap.

On the last day, as I walked out of the courtroom, the clerk handed me a bar of chocolate and said, "You should have been a lawyer." Maybe he was right, because I seemed to be the only one besides the judge focused on truth and justice, but for now, I simply wanted to step back into my own life—one that didn't involve courtrooms, unethical lawyers, or legal battles, at least for a while.

RING OF FIRE

Now that the stressful legal battles were behind me, I was finally able to refocus on my studio and invest more time into offering events and classes, if there was still time to salvage my business. It felt like a breath of fresh air after so much emotional strain.

As a yogi, it is common practice to follow astrological shifts and occurrences, like full and new moons, as well as solar and lunar eclipses. I had been following a particular pattern of eclipses which had aligned with powerful moments in my life since around 2005. When I learned that a powerful *Ring of Fire* solar eclipse was set to align right after my birthday on October 14, 2023, I decided to get away that weekend, to heal. There was a new hot springs spa that had just reopened in Durango, Colorado, so I decided to head there for the weekend. I reserved a house on AirBnB and invited my family to join me, if they'd like.

When my family declined my offer, I decided to organize a small fasting retreat at that house, and, as fate would have it, I learned that the direct path of the solar eclipse was set to pass right through Durango.

As I began researching Durango, I realized it was very close to Mesa Verde National Park—a place that would offer an absolutely breathtaking view of the eclipse. Mesa Verde is home to ancient sites built by the Ancestral Puebloans, often referred to as the Anasazi, with roots connected to Hopi and Navajo traditions.

Being from Buffalo, NY, which has rich Native American history, and having been given the name *White Buffalo* during a Native American sweat lodge ceremony in Mt. Shasta in 2002, I've long felt a deep connection to Native American history, culture, and spiritual practices. The thought of exploring Mesa Verde during such a powerful celestial event filled me with great excitement that I had not felt in awhile. This felt like more than just an opportunity—it was a remembrance and reminder that life can be magical and meaningful. And it was pretty cool that the pattern of magical birthday experiences seemed to be returning, too!

Early on, I made the decision to dedicate this trip and retreat to two key intentions: first, to heal the traumas woven into my family lineage, and second, to send waves of hope and inspiration to future generations. The theme of the journey felt crystal clear—a chance to honor the past while paving the way for the future.

Just days after setting this intention, my mother emailed me a newspaper clipping detailing her father's (my grandfather's) death. He had died in a very tragic work accident in Niagara Falls at the age of 29, *in a fire*. And as if the universe wasn't finished nudging me, the article listed his birthday: 11-1-21. It seemed that the 222 code was starting to shift.

When the weekend of the retreat finally arrived, I walked into the car rental company to pick up my rental car. I was expecting an economy vehicle, which I had booked. I had mentally prepared for a run-down Hyundai or Toyota—something practical and unremarkable. What I got instead completely blew my mind. The Midway rental agent handed me the keys to an Alfa Romeo sports car. At first, I thought there had been some kind of mistake. I even tried to argue, reminding them of the small, budget-friendly car I had reserved. But they assured me, with a smile, that the Alfa Romeo was available at no extra charge, if I wanted it as my car rental for the weekend. For a moment, I stood there stunned, holding the keys—what an unexpected luxury for a journey that already felt destined to be extraordinary. That would not be my last synchronistic experience with Midway, by the way, and because of this they're always my personal *go-to* for a car rental journey in California.

Now, I may not have mentioned this earlier, but my mother's side of the family is 100% Italian. My grandfather, Thomas Emanuele, who tragically lost his life in the work-related fire, had become a powerful figure in my intentions for this particular retreat. His tragic and unjust death impacted my mother's life in profound and devastating ways, forever altering her personality, outlook on life, and, ultimately, her fate. The weight of that loss rippled through generations, shaping not only her path but mine as well.

I personally believe that healing isn't limited to the present or the future—we have the power to heal the past, too. When we heal ourselves, we begin to unravel the trauma and burdens carried by those connected to us, both living and departed. In this way, healing becomes a sacred, cyclical process—we are all connected. At the end of this book, I include an entire section on *Healing Ancestral Trauma*.

My grandfather's energy became a powerful presence in my intentions. I also thought of the children who I used to babysit, who had also perished in a devastating fire back in 1988, and the *Ring of Fire* eclipse took on many meanings than simply a catchy Johnny Cash song.

Family, children, fire—and now, the *Ring of Fire* eclipse. It all felt like a symbolic convergence, as if these elements were weaving together with meaning far beyond coincidence. There I was, winding through the mountains in an Alfa Romeo, with the Italian flag emblem beneath the gear shift—its red cross logo strikingly similar to the emblem of the Knights Templar.

As I drove, I listened to Paulo Coelho's *The Pilgrimage*, a book recommended to me by a guest who had visited my studio just one week before. I was unaware until that very moment that the book's premise was about the protagonist tracing the same path once walked by the Templars. *Hmmmm*. The symbols, the journey, and the story were aligning, and I began to drop into attentive awareness to the spiritual signs unfolding. The connection between past and present, my heritage, future generations, and this unexpected pilgrimage, felt undeniable. And, I was re-learning how to get back into the moment, after the deeply chaotic, aggressive, and disruptive past two years.

As I listened to the audio book, October 13 was a central theme to the Knights Templar. *Interesting that we can also experience synchronicities through the stories being told in an audio book, at the right time,* I thought. You're probably tired of me bringing up my birthday, but it really has been the most illuminating day of my life in such profound ways—just as the card given to me at Sri Aurobindo's ashram in Pondicherry, India, confirmed: *Your birthday is the most auspicious day of your year. There is no coincidence that you are here.* I share the full story of that journey in my book, *Meaningful Coincidence* as well. Our birthdays are the origin point for connections, insights, and journeys, the focus point of our lens, so to speak. It's not just a personal milestone; it feels like the axis around which so much of my life's synchronicities, and very likely your story revolves around yours, too.

October 13 holds significant historical weight, particularly with the Knights Templar, because it was on this day in 1307 when the infamous massacre and unjust arrest of the Templars by King Philip IV of France took place, marking the end of their powerful order. This date became a symbol of betrayal and injustice for centuries. Even more intriguing is that in 1938, Adolf Hitler deliberately waited until this date, October 13, to take possession of the Spear of Destiny—the relic believed to be the spear that pierced the side of Jesus Christ during his crucifixion. This object held great mythical and religious significance, especially for those who believed it granted invincibility to whoever possessed it, as Hitler believed.

As I drove, I encountered a thick fog just beyond Palm Springs. It was later than I had planned—around 8 p.m.—as I had been delayed by traffic leaving LA. A wave of fear swept over me. I considered turning back to stay the night in Palm Springs, but the thought felt discouraging since it would set me back half a day. The fog was so thick I could barely see a few feet ahead, making it impossible to judge what lay in front of me. I was afraid to continue at freeway speeds, worried that traffic might have slowed suddenly, or that another driver might not see my car in time, risking a rear-end collision.

The awareness of my fear felt unsettlingly familiar. I realized that fear had been my constant companion for the past two years, with no real reprieve, and here it was again, like a cloud of daunting anxiety. As much as I was hoping for a solely miraculous and positive journey, I also knew there was an equal chance of tragedy—the perfect yin and yang of light and dark, balancing each other as it often does.

In between my audio book chapters, I stayed updated on the recent tragedy that had unfolded just days earlier in Israel—the horrific Nova Festival massacre and ensuing acts of terror on October 7. Shortly before I left for this trip, I saw in the news that the jihadist terrorists had declared October 13 as their "Day of Jihad." Once again, I was struck by the duality of this day—which was just a couple days away—where profound darkness and profound light seemed to coexist. This added to the looming fear and uncertainty I was feeling.

I decided to pull over and assess the fog, trying to gauge how far it stretched and how much it would limit my visibility. As I exited the freeway, I had zoned out to what was happening in the the audiobook I was listening to, but suddenly Petrus, the main character, mentioned that he was encountering a thick patch of fog on his journey. *"What?!"* I yelled, alone in my Alfa Romeo, stunned by the eerie synchronicity. I rewound the audio to re-listen. Like me, Petrus was gripped by fear as the dense fog disoriented him. Suddenly, I felt a little less alone, curious about how his story would unfold for both of us.

So now, a simple book recommendation unexpectedly became a key to setting the theme for my journey to Colorado. With my nerves slightly calmed, I changed course, following the slower pace of local traffic streets in the same direction, but continuing on towards my destination. Though I knew I was losing time, the slower route felt safer, and I felt more grounded in my decision.

People have often asked me, "Why do these mystical synchronistic experiences happen to you?" The answer has always been clear to me: I allow life to unfold more than most people do. Most people try to control their lives so fiercely that they constrict the magic, they're often afraid of the unknown, but once you've tasted the extraordinary, infinitely layered, divine coincidences and in-the-moment synchronicities, nothing else compares. The ordinary world, shopping for gimmicky gadgets online simply feels mundane and manufactured —and I find that dreadfully boring.

About 40 minutes into my detour along local streets, the fog finally lifted, revealing clearer skies ahead. With a sense of relief, I merged back onto the freeway, feeling a small but reassuring boost of confidence from having navigated through the dense fog unharmed, having faced just a handful of my fear and knowing I had trusted my instincts to come out on the other side safely.

SEDONA

I stopped in Sedona for a night, where I visited my friend Larry Geller, the former spiritual advisor of Elvis Presley, the next day. With all his wisdom and spiritual insight, I asked Larry about the number 22, hoping to hear his thoughts as to its meaning, as well as its continued presence in my life.

Larry suggested it might be linked to a soulmate or twin flame. Initially, that didn't sit right with me—it just didn't feel true to my situation. Much like the synchronicities I experienced with Prince, I've noticed that people often default to romantic connections when trying to make sense of meaningful alignments, as if romance is always the answer. It struck me as the simplest, most convenient explanation, but not necessarily the most thoughtful one.

That is, until later that night. As I was crossing a street, something clicked. In a moment of pure ecstatic revelation, I threw my hands up in the air and laughed out loud, Oh my God! (much to the amusement of the passing drivers). I mirrored the two 2's in my mind, imagining them facing each other like twins. And then, boom—it hit me! They formed the Omega symbol, Ω, the ancient symbol of endings and beginnings. It was a powerful a-ha and shift in my understanding. This wasn't just about revisiting trauma; it was about transformation, healing, and rebirth. I realized then that the number 22 was guiding me through cycles of closure, release and renewal.

Anyone who knows me knows how much I love the letter Z. My initials are A and Z, and twenty years ago, I trademarked *Gen Z Girlz*, long before I knew exactly when Gen Z would emerge. There's just something about Z's that has always drawn me in, and now, the omega symbol felt like it fit right into the same family of meaning—both representing closure, completion, and transformation.

Before continuing on to my journey to Colorado, I made a stop at St. John Vianney Church in Sedona to visit one of my favorite priests, Father Ignatius Mazanowski. He was hearing confessions at the magnificent Chapel of the Holy Cross, which overlooks the stunning red rocks of Sedona. Father Mazanowski is one of those rare Catholic priests with whom I have never felt a need to hold back about my spiritual beliefs—he's intuitive, non-judgmental, and highly knowledgeable.

I shared with him some of what was happening, my spiritual experiences and synchronicities. As we spoke, I noticed a statue of St. Philomena in the church. St. Philomena has always held a special place along my journeys and seeing her statue instantly reminded me of a profound moment I had while traveling in Mysore, India in 2004. I had stumbled upon a twin-tower cathedral dedicated to St. Philomena, which held catacombs with her relics inside. Her presence felt powerful to me, particularly in my personal mission to guide and protect children.

As I told Father Mazanowski about this, he leaned back in his chair with a reflective look on his face. "Alanna," he said, "We literally just received a relic from the Vatican last week. It's a relic of St. Philomena, and it's still on my desk." Yet another recurring synchronicity to add to this journey.

I shared with him the intentions I had set for this journey to Colorado, and the upcoming eclipse. He listened carefully, nodding in understanding before asking permission to offer me a blessing, which I consented to, happily. He placed one hand over my heart and the other on my head, offering a prayer for the cleansing of my family lineage. The healing energy flowing from his hands was palpable. It was one of those rare moments where I felt truly supported in the spiritual work I was doing.

MESA VERDE

On the first night of the retreat in Colorado, our group gathered around a family-style table to reflect on the journey we were about to begin. We spoke about the fast, the alignments, and the significance of the upcoming eclipse. The atmosphere was both calm and charged with anticipation, as we stood on the threshold of a group journey. It was a shared acknowledgment that this experience would be about more than the physical journey, opening our minds to whatever insights and transformations the retreat had in store for each of us.

In many Native American traditions, eclipses are seen as deeply spiritual events. Some tribes, such as the Navajo and Lakota, traditionally engage in fasting, prayer, and reflection practices during eclipses. The act of fasting aligns with detaching from the physical world to connect more deeply with unseen, energetic forces, while also recognizing that such moments are not for action but for inner spiritual alignments.

Experiencing the energy of Mesa Verde during our fast, particularly under the alignment of the full solar eclipse, was pretty profound. NASA was on site with telescopes as well, creating a close up view of the eclipse as it was happening. Mesa Verde as a landscape holds a palpable sense of history and immersion with nature, making it an absolutely incredible setting for self-reflection, healing, and renewal, and our fasting amplified our sensitivities to the experience.

You've likely heard the Lakota phrase "All My Relations," which holds deep significance in many Native American traditions. It reflects the belief that all beings are interconnected. It's an acknowledgment that everything in existence is part of a sacred web of life, and it is a reminder that all of our actions ripple outward to everything we are connected to—past, present, and future. This all perfectly aligned with my intentions and exactly where my mind was focused. It felt powerful.

As we were relaxing that first night, someone in my group pointed out that the final eclipse in this particular family of eclipses that we were experiencing would fall on April 8th, 2024—4/8/24. *Hmmmm.* And get this: the direct path of the eclipse will pass right through Buffalo / Niagara Falls, my hometown. At that moment, I knew, without question, that I had to be there on April 8th, 2024, at 3:22 p.m. To fast, cleanse, and align under the twin celestial event as to the current one, in the very place where indigenous tribes renounced war in the early 1800's. It felt significant and connected, and the next bread crumb in this unfolding journey. It was also a reminder that the ripples of resonance never end. Life continues on and on and on, for eternity.

Niagara Falls is also where Nikola Tesla harnessed the natural forces of the Falls to generate power for the benefit of all humankind. Nikola Tesla, one of the most brilliant minds in history, was treated horribly throughout his life by the government and fellow engineers. Despite his groundbreaking contributions to electrical engineering and physics, he and his work were marginalized, exploited, and overshadowed by others. Even though his visionary ideas were ahead of their time, and we all use his innovations today, the combination of his eccentric personality, lack of business acumen, and personal conflicts with powerful people led to many injustices and intellectual property thefts.

There is an immense burden that comes with someone who is a visionary genius, like Tesla—the isolation, the misunderstandings, and the constant struggle against the status quo. True innovation requires more than just intelligence; it demands the courage to defy conventional thinking, to envision something not yet manifest, the ability to present these concepts and ideas, and the strength to endure skepticism, rejection, and exploitation. And if you're a woman, enduring the inevitable: being called "the c word": *crazy*.

So now, my hometown would be in the path of this *final* eclipse— creating a vortex of light and dark that I couldn't ignore.

NIAGARA FALLS

So, immediately after the Colorado retreat, I began planning the retreat to Niagara Falls for the April eclipse, knowing that the Canadian side, with its stunning views, would be the ideal spot to host the weekend event, Friday through Sunday. Then, we'd view the eclipse on Monday from the Canadian side, which is called Horseshoe Falls. *Hmmmm*. Horseshoe—that's another omega symbol, Ω, the mirrored twin 2's, marking endings and new beginnings. I started to listen more attentively.

A couple weeks later, stirring a daunting concern around my upcoming journey, I was struck by some shocking and devastatingly sad headline news in November 2023. A Bentley Flying Spur car crashed into the Rainbow Bridge at Niagara Falls, bursting into a ball of flames at 11:22 AM on 11/22. The symbolism was impossible to ignore —11/22, fire, Niagara Falls, all wrapped up in a violent and tragic death of a hard-working Italian couple from Grand Island. I started to feel a sense of looming doom, nervous about what this "ending" would bring. For this reason, I didn't actively promote the retreat, aside from friends from my hometown; preferring to see who would find it organically, instead.

When April came around, and I flew into Buffalo, I arrived early to shop, prepare and set up the house before retreat attendees arrived. Niagara-on-the-Lake was absolutely incredible. The scenery was breathtaking—our house sat on a peaceful orchard, complete with a barrel sauna and just a short walk to the beach on Lake Ontario.

Having more time than I expected, and knowing very little about Canadian history, I decided to visit Fort George, where I explored the site of General Brock's legacy. The first historical plaque that I read gave me pause right away—General Brock had died on October 13th. *Great,* I thought, sarcastically, *another sign of death and my birthday.* Ugh. Naturally, that detail caught my attention, given how I've been tracking this date as a significant marker throughout my journey. It felt both daunting and oddly fitting.

But I didn't linger too long on that thought—there was no time to dwell. I had things to do—groceries to buy, preparations to make, and a lot of produce to juice. There was something grounding about slipping back into the rhythm of practical tasks, even while the deeper meaning of it all hummed quietly in the background.

I had a small group for this retreat, but it was as if they were hand selected perfectly to embark on this journey and mission together. They were experienced at yoga and retreating, as well as being very independent and easy going, so I didn't have to cater to a lot of individual needs. We began our retreat by juicing, focusing our energies, sweating, and clearing—a detoxifying process that felt both spiritual and physical. Plus, they were a lot of fun! There's far more to say on this experience than can fit into this space, but it was transformative from the start.

One afternoon we took a walk to the beach of Lake Ontario. Immediately as we were arriving at the shore, a young blonde Canadian girl came running toward us, clearly excited. "Are you American?" she asked eagerly. We nodded, and she squealed with delight, pulling out her phone to show us a photograph of something that had washed up on the shore near her home that morning.

I took a quick glance and felt overwhelmed. The image she showed us triggered that unshakable fear that had been building within me, leading up to this weekend for months now. I immediately walked away while the rest of the group looked at the photo and spoke with the girl. Strangely, the photo was of an election plaque for the New York State Coroner. *Coroner*! There was that symbol of death again, surfacing in the most bizarre and unexpected way, almost as if it was confronting me head-on. *Who takes a photo of something like that, and then runs up to share it with strangers?* It made me feel uncomfortable! As I walked away I tried to shake off the sense of doom, but the thought of death lingered. I didn't want to bring that up to a yoga retreat group —because it's not very inspiring!

That's when, moments later, I had the most glorious and refreshing realization. *I AM dying!* I thought. "No one else is dying—the old ME is dying!" In that moment, I understood the symbolic nature of all these death signs that had been haunting me. They weren't warnings of physical death, or death of someone else, but rather signals of an internal transformation. This death I had been seeing signs of, and resisting with dread, was a symbolic death of my former self—making room for a rebirth. Now, I could exhale.

I was filled with a deep sense of relief. This daunting fear that I didn't want to speak of to anyone had been about someone else dying, or my actions inadvertently causing harm to someone else. I started to open my mind to the idea of a rebirth being on the horizon, and this retreat, this journey, was leading me directly into its path.

On Sunday, I set out to scout the area near the Falls, wanting to get a feel for how crowded it might be for the eclipse the next day. The news was stirring up some panic, warning about massive crowds, traffic jams, and general chaos surrounding the area as tourists flew and drove in for the experience. On my route, I unexpectedly came across a small town called Queenston Heights. There was a towering monument that caught my attention, so I pulled over to check it out.

The monument was dedicated to the death birthday guy from Fort George, General Brock. The monument stood tall and solemn, radiating a sense of history and purpose.

As I explored the grounds, I read every single historical plaque that I encountered along the route, and they all referenced October 13. As I learned, it was the exact date when the Americans launched an attack on Canada, right there at Queenston, attempting to seize control of the bluffs overlooking the Niagara River, just south of Lake Ontario.

The story carried significance. Native American allies had joined forces with the Canadians to repel the American forces, securing a hard-fought victory. But that victory came at a cost—General Brock himself was killed there, in battle, on October 13. There it was again, as if I was getting closer to the source: the end of one thing and the beginning of something new, marked by struggle, sacrifice, and victorious new beginnings.

I stood there, absorbing the weight of it all, feeling the undeniable power of the moment. Here was a fragment of history that mirrored the pattern I found myself in—a cycle of victory born from loss. At that moment, I realized that transformation is rarely gentle. It's born from upheaval, pain, and the willingness to surrender to forces beyond our control.

After an hour or so walking the grounds and taking it in, I continued driving, again making my way towards Horseshoe Falls. Since I was still juicing as part of the retreat, I needed a restroom break to offload some liquids, and I pulled into a parking lot near the Falls. I walked to the nearest building, where I noticed a relatively new attraction called *The Tunnel*, which apparently had opened just 18 months earlier.

I asked the staff at the check-in desk if I could quickly use their restroom, but they politely declined, explaining that access was only allowed with a ticket. Understandable given how many tourists would want to use their restrooms for free. At first, I felt a little frustrated—but something nudged me, almost intuitively, to just go ahead and buy the ticket, even if it was merely to use their restroom. It was only $20, after all, and that celery juice had done its job.

Well, *WOW*—was that ever the right decision! What I thought would be a simple pit stop turned into an unexpected experience that took my breath away. After using the restroom, I thought, *well I may as well look around while I'm here!*

As I descended 180 feet below ground in an elevator, I could feel something powerful was about to unfold with a heightened sense of presence. This experience, The Tunnel, was built around a part of an old hydroelectric power plant that used to harness the energy of the Falls. The journey in the tunnel, which was an old drain pipe, takes you along the same path traveled by water, leading you to a viewing platform at the base of the Horseshoe Falls, where the tunnel emptied into the Niagara River. The tunnel itself runs 2,200 feet through this old discharge pathway.

For the past two days, one of the women on the retreat, Alison, had been drawing the Yemanya card from our Goddess deck—a symbol of the Goddess of Water. When I stepped off the elevator, it finally hit me: the symbol of water was everywhere in this experience, in full force. And now, I felt as though I was moving through this massive birthing canal in a manner far greater than I could possibly have imagined, planned or expected.

The walls were a massive 50 feet high and wide in the tunnel, moving toward the powerful, rushing water, I literally felt as though I was being physically, emotionally, and spiritually reborn. Emerging from the dark passage and stepping out onto the platform where the full force of Horseshoe Falls surged around me, and a thick mist cleansed my body and spirit was an utterly out-of-body experience. I was at the base of the Falls, and it felt like the water was washing away layers of the past, cleansing every part of me.

The symbolism of birth, cleansing and transformation—of being carried through the tunnel into the rushing, life-giving force of water— was overwhelming. I stood there, speechless, for at least 45 minutes, unable to fully comprehend the magnitude of what I was experiencing. It was as if the tunnel, the water, the energy, and my entire journey were merging into this incredible moment. It was a moment of pure, profound realization that words can barely describe. Just...*wow*.

The next day was the big Eclipse. The energy in town and with my group was feeling frenetic but I was trying to keep the metaphoric horse calm, centered, and in the moment (without success). Alison and Suzy had booked a room at the Marriott Falls View Hotel, literally right there at the Falls, with a gorgeous Falls view! The street that the hotel was on was scheduled to be blocked off, but since they had the room booked, we were able to park at the hotel, and gain access to the area without any issues or delays.

However, Alison and Suzy decided to break their fast that morning, and they went off in search of breakfast at the hotel, leaving me with a bit of time to myself. I waited in the hotel lobby, settling into a large, cozy chair by the window with a perfect view of the Falls. As I sat there, watching the water cascade over the cliffs, I felt a peaceful stillness settle over me. The relentless power of the Falls—this unstoppable force of nature, constantly in motion, yet somehow calming in its rhythm.

It was one of those moments when everything feels suspended, as if time itself slows down. I sat there, simply observing, simply being. I wasn't thinking about schedules or the next task on my list. I also didn't want to rush through this hyped up experience, either. The retreat was officially finished, but I had planned to view the eclipse with Alison and Suzy there at the Falls, even though I grew up nearby and have been to the Falls countless times in my life. I was just letting the experience unfold.

Well over an hour had passed, and a new feeling was setting in; an overwhelming, almost nagging sense that I was wasting precious time by just waiting for them to eat their pancakes. I couldn't shake it. I glanced around, wondering where they had gone, and how much longer that they would be, when a woman sat down next to me.

We struck up a conversation. She told me she was from San Francisco and had traveled with her husband to witness the eclipse. There was something serene and inviting about her presence—a warmth in her voice and a sense of calm in the way she carried herself. It felt natural slipping into conversation.

She asked what had brought me to the hotel that morning, and I explained that I had just finished leading a weekend yoga retreat. Then she asked where I was from, so I shared that while I currently live in Los Angeles, but that I was born and raised in Buffalo.

We talked easily, and for a moment, the rush of people and the

Falls faded into the background. Then she paused, her demeanor shifting entirely. She made a distinct turn in her position to face me in my chair, looked me directly in the eyes, as if what she was about to say carried weight beyond casual conversation. "Are your parents still in Buffalo?" she asked.

"Yes," I replied, caught off guard by her shift in demeanor. Her gaze didn't waver as she spoke, each word deliberate and full of meaning: "If I were you, I would go spend this eclipse with your parents," she said.

Her words landed heavily, reverberating in a way I couldn't fully explain. It felt like advice, but more than that—like a strong nudge or hint, disguised in the form of a stranger's suggestion. At that moment, I knew that she was right. I wondered if I had time, or if I would be able to cross the Peace Bridge without traffic delays or border issues. The weight of it settled in, though. I realized then that the eclipse wasn't just about celestial events or symbolic transformations. It was about something more personal, something tied to my roots, to family, to the very essence of who I am. At that moment, I knew what I had to do.

At that precise moment of realization, Alison and Suzy walked up to me, their timing almost uncanny. They seemed relaxed, already discussing their plans to explore the Falls. The weight of my conversation with the woman from San Francisco still hung heavy in the air. I turned to Alison and Suzy, hesitating for a moment before speaking. "Would you mind if I headed out?" I asked, unsure how they'd feel about me leaving.

They smiled, completely unbothered. "Not at all," Alison said warmly. "We were planning to go check out the Falls anyway."

With their easy going response, a sense of relief washed over me. I knew, without doubt, that the next step in my journey wasn't here—it was with my parents, my personal sun and moon. That was exactly where I needed to be for the eclipse.

As it turned out, the eclipse wasn't just passing through Niagara Falls—it was set to align perfectly over the vicinity of Buffalo and Niagara. But here's the real kicker: the absolute direct path of the eclipse, where the alignment would be 0 degrees exact, ran straight through my hometown of Hamburg, just southwest of Buffalo. Something was guiding me back home—quite literally—calling me to witness this rare and powerful event, with such precise alignment, from the very place where my journey as Alanna began.

The eclipse would be a mirror as I stood at the intersection of where everything started and where everything seemed to be shifting. It was a new birth, in my birthplace.

As I approached the Peace Bridge, I had to decide if I would make a pit stop at the Fatima Shrine in Lewiston, which was only 15 minutes away, but on the US side, or continue directly to Hamburg. The Shrine has special meaning to me, and I thought I may not be in this area again for a long time, and I still had plenty of time before the actual eclipse.

So, I went for it. I drove to the Shrine, dedicated to the miracle and feast day of Our Lady of Fatima on, you probably guessed it, October 13th. The Shrine is filled with impressive relics, including those of St. Philomena (the lovely patron saint of the youth), and a replica of the Shroud of Turin. I wandered through the grounds of the Shrine, detached from time, and just allowing myself to take everything in.

I had arrived just in time for Confession and Mass. Still in the midst of my fast, I felt light—almost too light, as if my body had become pixelated from reality. Fasting can make you feel that way, balancing on the edge of clarity and lightheadedness, as if the barriers between the physical and spiritual worlds start to dissolve. That's how I felt; like I was walking through a lucid dream, each step purposeful yet surreal.

During Mass, the priest mentioned the eclipse. Obviously because it was a big deal in the area, but I was surprised to hear a Catholic priest reference it symbolically, as they tend to be more strict in keeping their language and focus on the Bible readings. As a spiritual person with Christian synchronicities and reverence, I appreciated the acknowledgment—after all, I've never believed that scientific and natural alignments, like eclipses, should conflict with religious faith and teachings. They are of nature, interconnected parts of the same divine order. In my opinion.

Even though I was struggling to stand due to being lightheaded, my attention peaked when the priest shared something even more striking: today was, "ironically, but not ironically, the Feast of the Annunciation of Christ," he said. This took me by surprise. The Annunciation—the celebration of the angel Gabriel announcing to the Virgin Mary that she would bear the Son of God—is traditionally held on March 25. But due to an unexpected scheduling change from the Vatican this year, it had been moved to April 4. *How very interesting!* I thought. This event is considered one of the most significant moments in Christian theology, as it marks the incarnation of Jesus.

Here was a celestial event marking new beginnings, paired with the Catholic feast celebrating the divine message of a divine birth— both coinciding on this day, with an ironically altered religious calendar, seemingly by chance. Yet nothing about it felt random.

The priest reminded us that even Christ didn't know the exact hour of what was expected of him until the moment was upon him. I had never really considered that, and it was a powerful thought that sank into my heart. There it was again, everything about our existence comes down to living fully in each moment, embracing the unknown, and trusting life's unfolding exactly as it comes—the good, the challenging, and even the seemingly bad. The key to living a divine life is surrender and trust—learning to flow with what life presents, even in the moments when they don't match our expectations.

This reflection continued to reverberate powerfully within me as I sat there, absorbing the atypical source of such a message, in a church instead of a yoga studio. I recommitted myself to be fully open to life's unexpected turns, and in that moment, I knew, with deep certainty, that I was exactly where I needed to be—at the right time, in this very place, on this very day, in these very moments. The timing of this realization felt deliberate and impossible to manufacture, with the realizations making themselves known for me to understand right now.

The lesson was unmistakable: we only know when we know, and that is enough. Life doesn't require us to have all the answers ahead of time, and there are far too many variables in life to predict our moments with exact precision. Jesus Christ didn't even know all of the details of his journey, but he trusted God. Embracing the uncertainty and trusting the natural unfolding of events is how we align ourselves with grace and the divine rhythm of our co-existence.

Knowing that each moment, whether joyful or challenging, arrives exactly when it's meant to, as long as we don't fight or force—allows us to live in harmony with the interconnectedness of everything. Imagine if the world lived with this same reverence and conscious connection to nature. The sense of urgency, greed, and separation that dominates modern life just might dissolve. Instead, we'd learn to trust the wisdom of the world around us, understanding that, like nature, we are part of a greater whole.

I arrived back in Hamburg, NY, just in time for the eclipse, and I cannot fully express how powerful it was to stand in perfect, zero-degree alignment of the sun and moon, with my parents by my side. It was chilling, surreal—extra-ordinarily simple, yet impossible to explain. In that moment, it felt like the most profound rebirth I could have ever imagined, arriving quietly, without warning, away from the bells and whistles.

There was something deeply moving about my father, who rarely entertains such things, wandering outside to join me and my mother, standing next to her as I lay on the driveway at my childhood home, fully absorbing the experience. It was *simply* powerful. Nothing grand or elaborate—just the three of us, together under the cosmic shadow, sitting through the sudden darkness and cold, as if all the chaos, history, and pain we had carried for so long was eclipsed, too, without elaborate words or ceremony. And then, just like that, the sun came back out.

For 24 hours after the eclipse, I felt completely renewed—light, protected, and genuinely feeling on the other side of my bridge of troubles. The suffering I had endured throughout my life no longer felt pointless; it now carried meaning. Everything had come full circle, and I knew, deep down, that none of it had been in vain.

And then, uh-oh!...I checked the history on my Ring camera back home in Santa Monica. On April 8, 2024, at 11:22 am PST and 2:22 pm EST, someone broke into my yard and tried to access my car and house. My heart sank into my gut as I watched the footage unfold, fearful of what could have occurred. The intruder knocked over plants and furnishings, searching for a key, removing every screen on the first level of the home, even bending back my sliding screen door, trying to gain access. But ultimately, and thankfully, he failed. At 11:44 am PST, 2:44 pm EST, he left the property, unable to gain entry, and never returning.

At first I felt a wave of panic, dread, that my 24 hours of peace was gone, but I quickly realized how incredibly lucky I was not to be home, instead. Because, when I am, I always keep the sliding glass door open, which includes Flash's doggie door. Standing there, just after this cosmic rebirth, it hit me that the number 22, which had haunted me for so long, had now shifted. It was a symbol of protection and alignment. We're not only lucky to be in the "right place at the right time," but we're also lucky *NOT* to be somewhere.

A long time ago, I remember hearing a story about a woman who was warned by an astrologer that she would get into a car accident on a certain day. Terrified, she decided not to leave her house when that day inevitably came, thinking she could outmaneuver fate. But the force of the planets couldn't be denied, apparently. That same day, a pile-up on her street ended with a car crashing through the wall of her living room.

The story stayed with me, and in the aftermath of the eclipse, it resurfaced in my mind like a subtle warning. I felt like the Ring camera footage was a subtle reminder that if we succumb to fear—paralyzed by the signs we perceive as looming dread—what we're avoiding will still find us, because it's an inside job.

PURPLE RAIN FINALE

Nine months later, after this eclipse experience in Buffalo, on January 22nd, 2024, I was faced with the incredibly difficult and very sudden decision to close my beloved Santa Monica yoga studio. It wasn't something I had anticipated, and it was particularly painful because my friend, Barry, the original owner of the building, had passed away two years earlier. In his absence, a new figure emerged—a disbarred attorney with a questionable reputation and an aggressive bedside manner. For nearly two years, I tried to renegotiate new lease terms with this new owner, as mine had expired. I was deeply committed to the Santa Monica space and the beautiful community that had grown there. But despite my best efforts, the owner refused to fix severe roof leaks, which had been wreaking havoc on my business for over three years. Every time it rained I would have to sleep at the studio in order to empty buckets every few hours. And I can't begin to tell you how many rugs I had to throw out after each flooding.

January brought some serious rain storms—we had a wet winter alright— relentless, torrential downpours courtesy of the infamous Pineapple Express. Maybe Prince was closing this chapter with me. After all, I had only opened this location as part of my network contract for my reality show, and with that prospect no longer proceeding, it seemed that maybe it was time to move on, even though the unexpected end result had manifested as a wonderful business, community and space. Maybe, too, it was simply time for me to stop serving everyone else before myself.

Massive leaks flooded the studio, making it undeniably clear that the space was no longer sustainable without proper terms. Though the decision felt sudden, almost overnight, it also felt right—it was time to move on. Within just four days, I made the bold choice to let everything go—literally everything, turning in the keys on 1/22/24. When the moment came, I didn't hesitate, fight or try any further. I gave it all away—no regrets, no hesitation—about $30,000 worth of furniture, one by one, giving it all away to people in Santa Monica who could use each item. It was a silent understanding that this chapter had run its course. It was time to move forward, unburdened and ready for whatever came next. It was all a dream.

It was an ending, yes—but more importantly, it was the beginning of something new. And you know what I just realized? I've been feverishly writing this book over the past fifty days—with a flood of urgency pushing me to pour these thoughts, stories, and explanations into these pages, as if they were waiting all along for the right moment to emerge.

And now, as I reach the final chapter, I see another layer of significance: it has been exactly nine months since I closed the studio. This book isn't just the end of that chapter—it is also a birth. A new creation, born from all the experiences, transformations, and lessons that led me here. What began as an ending has transformed into a beginning, and this book is both the culmination and the start of something more organized and more thoughtfully presented and processed. It fills me with immense peace to finally share these experiences.

11/4/2024 UPDATE: I had finally finished editing this book on the morning of 11/4/2024, and I had the eager thought of sending a copy to Tyka in Minneapolis, as well as other people who have blessed my journey.

I was leading a *5-day Goddess Detox Retreat* starting on 11/4/2024 in the afternoon. At 3pm, a delightful and colorful woman named Edith arrived. She was treating herself to a birthday retreat, and today, 11/4, was her birthday. She was a regal African American woman, originally from Kenya, who now lives in San Jose, CA.

As Edith sat in my living room, she opened a coffee table book I hadn't touched in at least seven years. She called me over, pointing out the inscription in one of the books, DIGNITY, dated exactly seven years ago, 11/4/2017, by its author and photographer, Dana Gluckstein. This book, filled with stunning photographs of indigenous people, was created as a powerful call to action against racism.

A bit preoccupied with finalizing the retreat details, I didn't give much thought to the coincidence of Edith's birthday and the book. However, we continued talking. She asked me about my purple velvet couch and a painting of Prince. I explained that I felt a special spiritual connection with Prince, and she shared her own love for the color purple. Half-jokingly, I said, "Maybe Prince is going to send a message through you." She seemed positively open to the idea.

The next day was the U.S. presidential election. I was leading a meditation class at 8 p.m., right in the middle of the election tally. A woman named Edith signed up, and at first, I thought it was the same Edith, since I'd never had an Edith sign up for my classes before—it's not exactly a common name. But it turned out to be a different Edith.

When Edith #2 arrived, she shared a bit about herself—an Armenian woman feeling anxious about the election results and preparing to leave for San Jose, CA, the next morning. Edith #1 and I found the coincidence intriguing, though we weren't quite sure what to make of it.

The next day, Edith and I were sitting in the sauna when she mentioned that her niece's name is Tica. I excitedly replied, "Prince's sister's name is Tyka!" Edith then responded that Prince's sister had passed away. Shocked, I thought, *What does she mean?* I jumped out of the sauna to check the news on my phone. Sure enough, Tyka had passed away that week—on the morning of 11/4/2024, Edith's birthday.

Often, we don't fully understand what synchronicities mean, and sometimes they hold no meaning beyond the symbols they represent. Double Edith's, intersecting paths in San Jose, an infant niece named Tica, and Prince's now late sister named Tyka. Another twin crossing and symbol of rebirth. Blessings to you, Tyka. Thank you for the epic experience at Paisley Park!

22 FREQUENCY

With 22 on my mind for several years, I began to notice outside patterns involving the number 22 as well, connections that initially seemed coincidental because they were not my personal experiences that I could feel and understand—if coincidence is even the best choice of wording.

One striking example is Alexei Navalny, a figure embodying undeniable truth and righteousness, whose life appeared to be threaded with the same number. He married his wife when they were both 22, and they remained married for 22 years. Dates of his arrests, times of persecution, and pivotal moments in his life echoed with the resonance of 22. It was as if Navalny's Christ-like perseverance in the face of persecution was symbolically connected to this number, reflecting a similar, but far greater, battle of light versus dark, a fight against injustice that transcended his personal experiences.

Then, after watching the award winning film, *Oppenheimer*. There, too, the parallels were undeniable. Oppenheimer's birthday? April 22nd. His wife Kitty's? August 8th. And eerily, he passed away 22 years after the first successful test of the atomic bomb. The number appeared again, subtly for sure, but as if it marked pivotal shifts in human history —the creation of a destructive force that forever altered the world, a moment when humanity stood at the crossroads of light and dark, creation and destruction. Again, far out, but maybe, just maybe.

Could these instances really be dismissed as mere coincidence, or are they clues pointing to something deeper—a universal pattern or frequency marking the intersection of light and dark? The Omega. I believe that time and space are conceptual illusions, intricately coded with mathematical frequencies, and our belief in them makes them more real. Of course, much of this is subjective. But I tend to trust my intuition—those "spidey senses" that nudge me to pay attention—and this is one of those times.

I also believe that the world as we know it is like a radio station, a collection of frequency signals broadcasting alongside many other stations or realities that we cannot see or hear. What we experience as time and space may actually be dimensions interwoven with non-physical realities, each broadcasting at distinct, unrecognizable frequencies. These dimensions, bound by vibrational energies beyond our current perception, could explain the layers of unseen reality that we can feel, or sense, but cannot yet fully comprehend.

I share similar theories of mine in my book, *Meaningful Coincidence*, in particular when I share my experiences with Virgin Mary apparitions, and the helix lights that I witnessed during the Virgin's apparitions in Medjugorie, Croatia. To me, that explained how the visionary children could see her apparition, but the rest of those present could not. It's a frequency that they could tune into.

So, I encourage you, if it arises in your life, to *Find your 22* and surrender to it. We all have these signs, these numbers, these patterns that seem to call to us repeatedly, that resonate with our personal experiences, leading us toward a greater understanding of who we are and our innate purpose. Follow the trail. You never know what it might reveal until you begin the process of letting go of what you think you want in this worldly life, allowing more divine, spiritual messages to be heard and felt.

WHITE BUFFALO

I have also shared stories around my connection to the White Buffalo in my book *Meaningful Coincidence*, but 2024 brought another miracle. On June 4, 2024, a beautiful white buffalo calf was born at Yellowstone National Park. After the news of the calf's birth appeared in the news, I received more texts and messages from people than I typically get on my birthday and Christmas combined. For nearly 25 years, my life has been filled with white buffalo synchronicities, and the timing of this birth—just two months after the eclipse in Buffalo—still resonates with the additional, glorious symbol of renewal and transformation.

In case you are not aware of the White Buffalo Lakota prophecy, I am happy to share a small portion of it with you here, but I encourage you to do a deeper dive into this beautiful legend. It holds profound spiritual significance, particularly within Native American traditions. It is a symbol of hope. The birth of a white buffalo is considered an extremely rare and sacred event, symbolizing a time of great change, transformation, and the return of peace and balance to the Earth.

One of the most important stories linked to the White Buffalo is the legend of White Buffalo Calf Woman. According to Lakota Sioux tradition, White Buffalo Calf Woman appeared to the people during a time of famine and turmoil. She brought with her a sacred pipe and specific teachings that emphasized living in harmony with nature, respect for the Earth, and the interconnectedness of all life. After imparting her wisdom, she transformed into a white buffalo calf, promising to return again during times of great need, indicating a period of spiritual awakening.

THE LESSONS:

The 22

*"Synchronicity is an ever-present reality for those who have eyes to see." - **Carl Jung***

REFLECTIONS:

Leaning into discomfort is a powerful process for ultimate healing, as it not only allows us to confront and transform the root causes of our pain but also serves as an access point to spirituality and the power of being present. Most of my spiritual growth has come from moments of enduring suffering. The most well known example of this is the story of Jesus Christ, who endured torture and crucifixion without objection or reaction. I've often wondered if we, too, can tap into this higher state of being and transformation by choosing not to react to life's inconveniences and injustices.

Perhaps it's the same "vortex" that extreme sports enthusiasts touch when they are propelled into the present moment, balancing on the edge of life or death. In both cases, there is an undeniable connection to something greater and more real—fully embracing and surrendering to the moment, no matter how intense or challenging it may be.

We all have different capacities for pain—just watch the reactions of men trying a menstrual cramp simulator! It's a hilarious yet eye-opening reminder that pain, like most experiences, is deeply subjective and that one person's inconvenience is another person's devastation.

THE YOGI'S LESSONS

Since hindsight is 20/20 there are definitely some things I would change if I could. I have come to realize more fully that unaddressed traumatic responses to my safety were knee-jerk triggers from my past. Ivanka's acts caused me to feel unsafe in my home, triggering the time I found my housemate brutally raped and beaten in our college home. To onlookers, it's a nuisance, but to someone reacting from a safety trigger, it was excruciating. I wish that I could have worked harder to de-escalate the issue before the mole hill became a mountain.

At the same time that these issues were occurring, I was negotiating a TV show contract with a major network, casting the show, opening a brick and mortar studio to accommodate the show, and all of the personal pressures and insecurities that creep up when the idea of exposure and fame become realities. I can only imagine the stifling challenges of being a celebrity after the little that I have experienced, and it is very common for celebrities to isolate from the public in order to feel more safe. During this time, my cup of capacity was full and overflowing, and, again, I wish that I could have worked through those intense feelings more thoughtfully and less reactively.

When trauma triggers arise, the key is to pause and ground yourself before reacting, which can feel like the most challenging extreme sport of all when you're in it. Take slow, deep breaths to calm your nervous system, creating space between the trigger and your response. Acknowledge what you're feeling—naming the emotion or sensation can help you take control of it rather than letting it control you. Remind yourself that triggers are echoes of the past and not necessarily reflective of the present moment. Grounding techniques, like feeling your feet on the floor or focusing on your surroundings, can bring you back to reality. Practice self-compassion by recognizing that it's okay to feel the way you are feeling. Remember, responding to triggers instead of reacting takes practice and patience, so be kind to yourself as you navigate this journey—and maybe, just maybe, it's the doorway to enlightenment. *To whom much is given, much is required.*

PROMPTS & POSITIVE ACTIONS

What practices or habits can you introduce into your life where you are connecting with nature's rhythms in a present state of mind?

What kinds of meaningful patterns have you experienced in your life?

What brings you a sense of peace or connection beyond yourself, and beyond the things of this world?

CHAPTER 8

The Predators

"We must end this predatory attitude, which makes us feel that we are masters of the planet and its resources, and authorizes us to make irresponsible use of the goods God has given us." **- Pope Francis**

CORPORATE GREED

A corporate predator is a business entity or individual within a corporation that engages in exploitative practices for profit and power at the expense of others. These corporations turn a blind eye, operating with little regard for ethics, sustainability, or the well-being of their employees and/or customers. Instead, their primary focus is on dominance, expansion, and maximizing profit, often employing manipulative tactics in order to gain these advantages.

Corporate greed has grown increasingly subtle and pervasive in recent years. It's no secret that profit drives the corporate world, but today's corporations have mastered the art of *appearing* customer-centric, yet beneath their polished exterior, they are dismantling small businesses, eroding trust, neglecting customer support, and using manipulative tactics to turn their consumers into mere data points. Every interaction—from your browsing history, to your purchase preferences, and even your personal interests—is collected, analyzed, and sold to the highest bidder. Your choices are no longer private or personal—they're assets that corporations trade, profit from, and use to sway your future buying decisions.

They've, essentially, become digital *pimps*, exploiting your behaviors and desires to serve their own bottom line. And the worst part? We're being coerced into their services, often without realizing it. Whether it's through targeted ads or manipulating your social media feeds, these companies embed themselves into your life in ways that make it almost impossible to opt out.

Customer-centric? Guess again. Most major U.S. companies offshore their customer service, use misleading advertising, and swallow up small businesses under the guise of "partnerships." It's a subtle but calculated takeover, one that undermines the personal connections and trust that used to define commerce. If I cannot trust a company's business practices, I am certainly not going to trust the quality of their product's ingredients, resources, and manufacturing processes, let alone their safety practices.

Business used to be fair—a simple transaction where one person offered something of value in exchange for another's of equal value. It was a relationship built on mutual benefit, transparency, trust, and equity. But today, corporations have shifted their focus toward winning at all costs, ensuring that their value not only exceeds, but usurps yours.

IMPACT ON AGRICULTURE, ANIMALS, AND OCEANS

Corporate greed has also infiltrated nearly every sector of agriculture, overtaking natural means to grow food, how animals are raised, and oceans are harvested—all in pursuit of profit, regardless of the environmental or ethical consequences. The industrialization of agriculture, fishing, and farming are depleting our resources, driven by bottom lines rather than the well-being of the planet, animals, or humanity. We're consuming far faster than nature can replenish.

Factory farming, one of the largest contributors to corporate agriculture, treats animals as mere commodities rather than sentient beings. In these industrialized systems, animals are crammed into confined spaces where they barely have room to move. Chickens, pigs, and cows are bred for rapid growth, usually with the help of hormones and antibiotics, straining their already fragile bodies, which often results in chronic diseases in the very meats which humans then ingest. Most of these animals live in filth, standing in their own waste, developing sores and infections that go untreated. The sole focus is efficiency and profit—producing the highest yield of meat, eggs, or dairy at the lowest possible cost.

The same greed is depleting our oceans, where industrial fishing operations strip ecosystems bare. Trawlers and commercial fleets use massive nets that capture everything in their path, including endangered species and other marine life, like dolphins and turtles. These by-catch animals, caught unintentionally, are often thrown back dead or dying, an unspeakable suffering and waste that only illustrates the greed and disregard for anything other than profit.

As a result of over-fishing, key species—like tuna, cod, and salmon —are now critically endangered, and entire food chains are unraveling. With fish populations depleted, marine animals are forced to migrate toward new waters or even into urban areas in search of food. It's not uncommon to see whales stranded near shorelines, sharks swimming closer to coastal waters, and marine mammals scavenging in human habitats because their food sources have been wiped out by these relentless corporate fishing practices.

On land, industrial agriculture prioritizes growing single crops like corn, soy, or wheat for maximum profitability. These crops are preferred for their resilience, thriving even with the extensive use of chemical fertilizers, pesticides, and herbicides, which not only pollute the soil but also strip it of essential minerals. Although resistant to these chemicals, traces of these poisons still wind up right in your Unlucky Charms cereal bowl. Year after year of over-farming leaves the ground with little to no nutrients left to support future crops.

This depletion of minerals affects not only the health of the soil but also the quality of the food we consume. Fruits and vegetables grown in overworked soil contain far fewer nutrients than they did decades ago, meaning that even when we try to eat healthy, we aren't getting the same nourishment.

Corporate farming also encroaches on wildlife habitats, driving animals out of their natural environments. With forests cleared for grazing land and oceans emptied of fish, animals are left with no choice but to migrate toward human settlements in search of food. In recent years, it's not uncommon to see wild animals—bears, deer, coyotes, and even mountain lions—venturing into urban and suburban areas because their traditional sources of food have been exhausted. We've all likely witnessed the ignorant, fear-driven reactions people post on neighborhood apps when they encounter these "intruders" on their lawns. But the truth is, we are the real intruders, having encroached on the animals' natural habitats. If only more of us recognized that these creatures are not invading our space—we've taken over theirs.

It's not too late to change course, but doing so requires that we adopt sustainable farming practices that restore the soil and nourish the planet. In the oceans, stricter regulations on fishing practices are needed to prevent overfishing, to protect marine life, and to keep our oceans clean of toxic waste.

Most importantly, we must change how we view the natural world —not as something to be exploited for a quick buck, but as a system we are deeply connected to. Every action we take has a ripple effect, and we must begin to treat animals, oceans, and soil with the respect and care they deserve. The future of life on this planet depends on our ability to shift away from greed and toward practices that promote regeneration, harmony, and balance with nature.

EXCESSIVE CONSUMERISM

Corporate greed also has fueled a culture of excessive consumerism, where profit margins are prioritized over sustainability and quality. Through relentless advertising and deceptive marketing tactics, corporations encourage a never-ending cycle of buying, discarding, and replacing. Isn't it *interesting* how our phones don't work as well when a new phone model just launched? This hyper-consumption model is not truly about meeting consumer needs—it's about keeping people perpetually dissatisfied and always craving the next product, or trend.

When I was in the process of researching manufacturing for my yoga doll productions, it took me an extra three years of research before going to market, so that I was certain to secure a factory in China that used phthalate-free, recycled plastics, which is not an easy task! Unfortunately, that particular factory went out of business during the COVID-19 pandemic. Since then, I haven't resumed production because it feels too hypocritical to manufacture a doll that promotes healthy practices while using toxic plastics.

Phthalates and other toxic chemicals commonly found in plastic toys and dolls pose serious risks to children's health. These substances are used to make plastics more flexible and durable, but at a significant cost—exposing children to harmful chemicals during critical stages of development. Convenience and corporate greed directly affects the health of our children. Obviously the best non-toxic alternatives use natural materials like wood, cotton, or rubber, or plastics that are BPA- and phthalate-free, certified by safety standards.

If customers become more educated and begin demanding higher-quality, non-toxic products, it will create a shift in the marketplace. Ethical manufacturing companies, which prioritize health, sustainability, and fair labor practices, would not only survive but thrive. But we have to consciously support these businesses, sending a powerful message to the industry: that long-term value, safety, and integrity matter more than convenience or low prices.

However, the price tag on a product isn't always a reliable indicator of quality or ethical manufacturing practices. Having manufactured activewear for over ten years, I understand the costs of quality fabrics and sustainable production processes. Unfortunately, many large brands cut essential corners—choosing cheap fabrics and toxic manufacturing—then inflating their prices to maintain a "premium" brand image.

One well-known activewear company based in Los Angeles exemplifies this. They produce their garments overseas at minimal cost, using cheap nylons, only to mark them up by 1000-1400% when they hit the shelves. What consumers are really paying for isn't superior quality—it's the glossy marketing campaigns, the perfectly curated brand image, the cost of gifting celebrities and influencers free clothing, and the cost for those same celebrities to post on social media, creating the illusion that wearing their products is a symbol of status and exclusivity. In reality, you're paying for that company to market cheap clothing as a luxury brand. I'll say it again: you're paying for it.

Nylon contains a variety of chemicals that pose risks to both human health and the environment. While nylon itself is a synthetic polymer derived from petroleum, the manufacturing process requires several additional chemicals for dyeing, finishing, and enhancing the fabric's performance. These chemicals have been proven to leach out during wear, particularly when in contact with sweat or heat, raising concerns for consumers who wear them regularly, especially during heated yoga classes. Additionally, nylon fibers release microplastics into the environment with every wash. These microplastics enter waterways, accumulating in marine life and food chains, posing long-term risks to ecosystems and human health.

Let me be more clear—nylon is nothing more than thread made from plastic. These brands disguise unsustainable practices behind glossy ads, an illusion of wellness, while paying huge marketing dollars for influencer endorsements, banking on the fact that consumers will choose convenience and cost over ethics and environmental responsibility. Why leggings? Because they are very cheap to make! Consumers are complicit in their own sham by supporting these predators.

And I can't even begin to tell you how many "wellness influencers" and yoga teachers I know personally who have bought into and consent to the marketing hype of this particular company, and many like them. Every time I see one of them posting about the brand, two things immediately come to my mind: 1) I know they're getting paid, and 2) it's obvious that money is more important to them than the well-being of their followers. #Posers

What's worse, this company isn't just guilty of deceptive marketing —it's one of the biggest knockoff operations I've personally encountered. On two separate occasions, I caught their employees in my store in Santa Monica, where they openly admitted to me that their bosses had sent them to scout for designs and ideas they could copy. I followed up by sending a cease-and-desist email to their corporate office, complete with security footage of the incidents. Of course, no apology or explanation ever came. #Predators

This experience didn't come as a complete surprise, and is incredibly common in the fashion industry. I once worked for the founder and designer of a major fashion label. On several occasions, I accompanied her on shopping trips where she would purchase 10 to 15 pieces of clothing. Once back at her office, she would casually toss the shopping bags onto her assistant's desk and say, "Knock these off." That was it—no discussion, no acknowledgment of the original designers' work, just a straightforward directive to copy.

Naturally, my production costs are 30% higher than most brands due to the fact that I source sustainable fabrics and use less toxic manufacturing processes. Over time, I realized that, for most consumers, price point mattered more than ethical and sustainable practices, unfortunately. There will always be an activewear company pouring billions of dollars into marketing their clothing as premium, all while selling you cheap, toxic garments. Question is, will you buy it?

So, as you can imagine, in addition to scaling back doll and toy manufacturing, I also scaled back the production of yoga leggings and activewear—for all these reasons. Sure, I absolutely could have been a gazillionaire by now if I had compromised my values and chased profits like many others in these industries. But, at the end of the day, is it really worth selling cheap, toxic products just to be rich? For me, the answer is no. I wasn't born to play this human Monopoly game, I was born with a spiritual purpose.

There are plenty of ways to build wealth, but if that wealth comes at the cost of integrity, the health of others, or the planet's well-being, then what's the point? I'd rather stay true to my purpose, keep my karma clear, and leave a legacy I can be proud of than chase after short-term riches built on the backs of exploitation and toxic practices.

I mentioned above that corporations thrive by cultivating a false sense of urgency in consumers, manipulating emotions to make people feel like they need to act quickly or miss out. In the next section, I outline some of the most common deceptive tactics these corporations use to psychologically influence you—tricks designed to keep you buying more junk and clutter you don't even need. By understanding these strategies, you can recognize when you're being manipulated and break free from the cycle of excessive, unnecessary consumption.

I've also outlined how the environmental impact of excessive consumerism is devastating. Factories producing fast fashion and electronics rely on exploitative labor practices, with workers in developing countries forced to work for minimum pay in unsafe conditions that negatively impact their physical and psychological well-being. Toxic landfills continue to fill with discarded clothing, older model gadgets, and packaging because the next collection or model has launched.

Realize your power as a consumer by focusing on intentional purchases—choose quality over quantity, support ethical brands, and maybe even consider embracing second-hand and upcycled products. Along with focusing on sustainable resources and manufacturing, I include a disclaimer on my businesses' ecommerce sites to inform our customers that we reuse packaging. This way, they know to expect their orders in previously used boxes. We repurpose packaging from incoming shipments for outgoing orders, minimizing waste whenever possible. Meaningful change begins with small, everyday actions that support the environment.

By truly embodying the understanding that self-worth emanates from within—rooted in your spirit, not in your material possessions—you begin taking crucial steps toward breaking free from the psychological manipulation that corporations rely on. They thrive by instilling feelings of inadequacy, creating a false sense of dependency on their products for you to feel worthy or complete. Knowing your true inner worth disrupts their abusive tactics, creating a resistance to these false pressures.

Corporations must be held accountable. Governments and consumers alike must push for transparency, ethical labor practices, and sustainable production models. Since governments are often influenced by hefty donations from corporations, we can't entirely trust them to protect us. Consumers have the power because they decide where to spend their money. Ultimately, shifting away from excessive consumerism requires redefining success and fulfillment. Real happiness doesn't come from accumulating things. As I shared with you in the first few chapters of this book, wealthy people are not always happier. They actually tend to be more dangerous in their desperate means to cling to status based relevancy founded on these illusions of success. No amount of "stuff" can hide a lie forever.

The bottom line is this: corporations driven by greed will never prioritize the well-being of others over their profits, just as a power-hungry politician will never be able to empower the people. Those who benefit from power are rarely motivated to share it. Once they've attained power, they cling to it fiercely, unwilling to let go. Think of a big wave surfer. If someone didn't do the work to paddle into a big wave, they won't be able to handle the power if they were lucky enough to land on top of one. In the frenzy, they'll focus solely on surviving, clinging desperately just to stay on the wave. Power is simply too powerful.

The paradox is that the people most suited for power are often the ones least interested in pursuing it. Only someone with the integrity to resist the seduction of wealth, status, and influence is truly fit to wield power. Genuine leadership requires humility, selflessness, and a deep commitment to serving others—not personal gain. The challenge lies in creating governance and platforms that elevate such individuals, and allows them to be heard, rather than rewarding those who are the most ruthless, ambitious, willing to sacrifice others for their own advancement, and/or blindly submit to a corrupt system.

Earlier, I mentioned the fact that street gangs secure loyalty from new members by requiring them to participate in a crime as part of their initiation. This tactic implies mutual liability, making recruits less likely to betray the gang or expose its activities, since they too are implicated and risk facing consequences. As I mentioned in the Preface, the rich and powerful operate in much the same way—and predatory business leaders are no exception.

Again, I've refused to compromise my integrity throughout my journey. Yet, that hasn't stopped me from sharing powerful, inspiring ideas to some of the biggest sharks in the industry. It wasn't all out of naivety or foolishness—it was because my drive to create meaningful, positive change has always outweighed my ego's need for recognition.

About twenty years ago, I wrote a children's book about a girl on an overcrowded ship, where merchants were too busy selling their goods, and passengers were fixated on buying, all of them oblivious to their surroundings and the ship's direction. Even the captain of the ship was caught up in the distractions, leaving only the girl aware that the ship was headed for disaster. Desperate, she tried warning everyone, running from person to person and microphone to microphone, but no one would listen. So, she planted the idea in the mind of the loudest merchant—knowing that if he believed it was his own, he could sell the idea to the crowd and convince them to change course to avoid a catastrophe.

This story reflects the difficulty of communicating vital truths that go against society's norm, in a world dominated by distractions and consumerism. It highlights how those in control (corporations and government), driven by their own greed, often disregard warnings that could benefit the collective, until it becomes profitable for them. The story serves as a powerful metaphor, illustrating the need for society to shift its focus toward what truly matters—before it's too late. By planting the positive solution in the mind of the loudest merchant, the girl demonstrates that sometimes the only way to create change is through indirect influence, leveraging the systems already in place to enlighten the deluded masses as quickly as possible.

YOGA DOLL INVENTION

You think Barbie was a feminist icon before Margot Robbie's 2023 blockbuster? Think again! I spent 13 hardworking years creating the first moveable fashion doll, driven by research showing how damaging traditional plastic dolls were to young girls' developing minds, self esteem, and body image. A 2006 study led by Dittmar, Halliwell, and Ive found that girls aged 5 to 8 who were exposed to Barbie dolls experienced a stronger desire to be thinner compared to those who interacted with more realistically proportioned dolls, like the Emme doll, or no dolls at all.

This research suggested that Barbie's unrealistic body ideals could influence young girls to internalize thinness as a standard of beauty, potentially increasing the risk of dissatisfaction with their own image, and related issues such as disordered eating. Understanding these valid concerns about how toys can shape young children's perceptions of beauty and self-worth at critical developmental stages, I began working with my yoga teacher's salary to bring my idea and innovative invention to life, The World's First Yoga Doll®.

When I finally had a prototype, I pitched it to several toy companies, hoping to license it to one of them. I never wanted to manufacture myself. I flew to NY, Minneapolis, drove to San Francisco, and had several meetings in Los Angeles, pitching my new patent-pending moveable plastic doll design. I wanted to give young girls a doll that celebrated who they are, as they are, not merely focused on looking glamorous. And let them move, for goodness' sake!

Then I got a call from one of the designers at the major toy company I had just pitched. She warned me that the company was planning to knock off my concept of a moveable fashion doll. This is always a risk when pitching ideas to large corporations—part of the unspoken reality of the industry. Still, a part of me had hoped, perhaps naively, that they would act with integrity and respect my work rather than copy it outright.

Well, I am not going to let that happen, I thought! Knowing I was ahead of them with my design—and with finalized molds already complete—I made the bold decision to put my life savings on the line to produce *The World's First Yoga Doll®*. My brand, AZ I AM, became the first to market, with a moveable, plastic fashion doll designed specifically to move with a full range of motion, *just like you*!

Because of this, other companies that released similar dolls after mine were limited to market them under different names since they legally couldn't use the term "Yoga Doll." But still—what a low move, right? Unfortunately, that's just how the world works, and these risks are expected when dealing with cut throat businesses trying to stay at the top of their industries, which increases the chances that they are led from corporate greed.

Undeterred, however, I presented at ToyFair in 2015, which was absolutely epic! There I met one of the buyers from Target, who took a chance on my innovative collections, opening a line of conversation to officially present my dolls and toys to sell at Target.

I remember watching the film, Joy, based on the life and business of Joy Mangano. I remember crying with relief during the scenes where the main character flies to China and crawls through an air vent to find her molds after unethical business partners tried to shut her out of her own business. In that moment, watching another fiercely innovative woman who truly understood the exhausting struggle of manufacturing, safeguarding molds, and protecting patents and intellectual property, I felt an overwhelming alignment with her story.

THE TARGET

Although I am not currently manufacturing or selling my products at Target, they remain the most integral company I've ever worked with. I'm not saying this just because they were the first retailer to take a chance on a small business like mine. Their commitment to integrity, clear communication, thoughtful product selection, sustainability, and dedication to diversity are unmatched by any other major retailer I've partnered with, ever.

Due to several factors, I had to temporarily stop selling to Target. The Trump administration's tariffs during the 2018 trade war significantly impacted small businesses importing from China, increasing costs and massively disrupting supply chains. My reps and brokers in Asia were frustrated with U.S. businesses, increasing all of their costs, making it impossible for a small business like mine to produce at a reasonable price.

Additionally, the COVID-19 pandemic forced the closure of one of my manufacturing facilities, which I relied on to ensure recycled plastics and sustainable resources. On top of that, managing a brick-and-mortar yoga studio left me overwhelmed, making it impossible to meet demand. As a result, I had to reject orders and pause operations.

THIRD PARTY INTRUDER APPS

During the time I had paused manufacturing, I was focused on running a brick-and-mortar yoga studio and wellness center. Now, just before opening my first studio in 2016, a third-party app entered the fitness industry, devaluing the services that fitness and yoga studios offered by siphoning our customers with discounted access to their app. The studio I had originally tried to help in Brentwood was struggling financially because of this shift, and many other fitness studios were hit just as hard during that period. This uninvited disruptor altered the landscape of the industry, forcing small businesses to compete with their own services being resold at lower prices.

In the next section, I'll share my thoughts on this now-popular fitness app based on my experience as a yoga studio owner. Over the past 15 years, I've seen firsthand how this app has significantly contributed to the closure of small fitness studios. While it offers users the convenience of variety and affordability, its success has come at a steep cost to independent businesses. For the businesses that partner with this app, it's a financial nightmare. They take 50-70% of profits from individual businesses—small, local studios that are already fighting to stay afloat in a world dominated by corporate gyms and fitness chains.

What's even worse? The app takes credit for the hard work these businesses do, creating the illusion that the app itself is responsible for customers' positive experiences. The app markets a "first-class free" offer to attract new users—but it's the businesses footing the bill for these freebies, not the app. The app's executive team mandates this practice, forcing small studios to absorb the cost. The truth is, however, this creates a cannibalistic system that thrives on exploiting small businesses while gaslighting them into thinking they need the app to survive.

These deceptive practices are a prime example of how corporations prey on smaller, independent businesses by exploiting their need for exposure and then profiting off of their hard work. These local businesses put in the effort—creating programs, maintaining brick and mortar businesses, staffing, training, building relationships with their clients, offering high-quality service—yet the app swoops in, devalues the businesses services, takes the credit, and slashes the businesses' profits more than half—which means that the businesses now have to work twice as hard! This isn't a partnership; it's extortion and hijacking.

And what do these predatory corporations have in common? A total disregard for the people who support them—whether it's their customers or the small businesses they claim to help. This app is draining the very businesses that make the convenience possible. That's not good wellness.

So, what's the takeaway? It's about recognizing the growing disconnect between corporations and the people they claim to serve. It's about understanding how far corporate greed has reached into our lives, manipulated our choices, and convinced us that we need them when, in reality, they need us. Without consumers, without small businesses, these corporations have nothing. But as long as we continue to support them—whether by using their services, buying their products, or accepting their version of reality—they will continue to exploit us. It's time to tell them to **_Knock It Off!_**

CUSTOMER SUPPORT RAGE

I have tried to illustrate the slow and subtle means of corporate greed, sneaking into our lives. These larger corporations scale down their costs to maximize profits, sacrificing the unthinkable: customer service. I bet that you can relate to this frustration—customer service rage. Remember when you could call a company, speak to a representative based in your country, and have an actual conversation where your issue was understood, and you received support? Those days are almost extinct. Today, most large U.S. companies no longer have U.S.-based customer support. Instead, they offload this critical service to offshore call centers where English is not their first language, and language comprehension is challenged. It's not just about returning a pair of socks that don't fit; it's about personal and important matters related to finance and home safety, where more than basic language comprehension is necessary to feeling heard.

You call with a simple issue, and you're funneled through and looped around AI bots that can't understand nuance, or worse, you're connected to a human who also can't grasp your problem because they don't comprehend the local language fluently. Then, if they didn't hang up on you, you're routed around to someone else, where you have to retell the same issue again, feeling trapped in the hellish loop of an automated and dysfunctional service system. You know the kind of rage this stirs.

Again, this frustration escalates to an entirely different level when the issue at hand is something far more serious than returning an ill-fitting item of clothing. Home and driving sharing apps, for instance. While they market themselves as a friendly and personal alternative to hotels and cabs, the truth is that their customer service is mostly outsourced, and near impossible to get a hold of in the event of an emergency. These are companies that 1) use your home and/or vehicle to market and harness their profits, and 2) deal with safety protocols for domestic services within people's homes and on ride shares. Customers, however, cannot reach support agents who speak the language of their home country. And if they ask for this, they risk being labeled discriminatory.

Think about that for a moment. You're staying in a stranger's house, something goes wrong—maybe there's a safety issue—and your lifeline to solving this issue is a customer service agent thousands of miles away, who is only available at 1:00 a.m. your time, and who struggles to understand or prioritize your concerns. They're often reading from a rigid protocol manual, without fully grasping the complexities of your specific situation. This is where the gap between corporate greed and customer safety becomes not just frustrating, but dangerously serious.

Perhaps this neglect is intentional. Maybe these companies bank on the hope that frustrated customers will be less likely to call back, ultimately reducing service costs for the corporation—regardless of whether the customer's needs are met.

In recent years, customer rage has become an increasing issue, fueled by frustration with poor service, deceptive terms, negligent practices, and the feeling of being powerless. This rage is more than just impatience—it's a response to feeling unheard and taken advantage of.

In the end, these businesses may lose customer loyalty and have scathing reviews online, but they are still profiting financially, therefore they're not motivated to make changes. They would rather damage their reputation and face legal payouts than risk losing profitability.

Oh, that brings up another catch: many companies have found ways to shield themselves from accountability. By requiring customers to agree to binding terms and conditions—often filled with dense legal jargon—they force consumers to forfeit their rights to take legal action.

Arbitration clauses and waivers are now standard practice, ensuring that even when harm occurs, the corporation escapes liability.

Ultimately, corporate predators thrive when unchecked and when they have dominated an industry. Remember, their strategies are designed to maximize efficiency and minimize costs, not to protect or serve customers. Their intentional shift toward impersonal, outsourced service isn't just inconvenient—it is abusive.

The psychological impact of customer support rage is reflected in The American Customer Satisfaction Index (ACSI) report that 80% of consumers who experienced poor service felt increased stress and frustration. Likewise, a study published in the Journal of Service Research found that 74% of customers reported feeling angry and 42% feeling trapped when unable to resolve their issues efficiently.

Personally, I believe that there should be a governmental requirement for all U.S. based companies to provide U.S. based customer support, even if that is only for escalated matters.

INFLUENCERS

I find social media exciting, I really do, so please don't get me wrong in this next section. It is connecting the globe in ways we never imagined possible, and I do feel that it will someday heal more than it currently harms. However, most influencers and celebrities are being used by corporations as modern-day snake oil salesmen on their social media feeds. We've all seen those glossy Instagram posts where a famous face endorses a product with a glowing caption. But how many of those influencers actually use the products they're peddling? Spoiler alert: not many. The influencer economy is built on deception. Brands pay influencers enormous sums to market their products, and in return, influencers pretend they use and love said products, regardless of whether they actually do. It's a transactional relationship, with little regard for the truth or authenticity.

How many celebrities can you name with their own makeup, skincare, or perfume collections? The list is endless. And do you know why they all jump on this bandwagon? Because they don't lift a finger while getting paid big bucks for it! The ingredients in these products are often strangely similar across the board—just repackaged with different labels and a famous face slapped on the front. This kind of marketing manipulates millions of followers into buying things they don't need, and often, products that those celebrities didn't create. Yet, despite knowing this, people keep falling for it—buying into the hype, quite literally.

This being said, there are great influencers! There are those who do share quality items, review products authentically, and we can consider them the small business owners of influencers. They are the original "word of mouth" advertising sharing quality products and services that have enhanced their lives. They use their platforms to promote products they genuinely believe in and have personally tested. These influencers focus on building trust with their audience by being transparent about their recommendations. Rather than pushing items for a quick payout or commission, they carefully curate what they endorse, aligning their content with their values and the interests of their followers. Many influencers take pride in supporting local, sustainable brands, and ethical companies, using their influence to highlight products that align with important causes.

PHOTOSHOP & CGI

With social media, influencer marketing and digital advertising comes the overuse of Photoshop, CGI, and special effects, enticing you with altered imagery. Celebrities, influencers, and brands embrace these tools to craft flawless images that set impossible beauty standards. Once used to touch up slight imperfections, they are now used to create a deceptive world where everything appears unnaturally perfect —smooth skin, sculpted bodies, and enhanced features—all of which are far removed from reality.

The overuse of these tools sets a standard of beauty that is simply unattainable, creating an endless cycle of insecurity. When celebrities and influencers present themselves as effortlessly perfect, consumers, particularly young people, begin to compare themselves to these false images, leading to body image issues, depression, anxiety, low self-esteem, and in extreme cases, suicide.

A good friend of mine worked as a high-level creative director at a major network. He quit his job there because he was fed up with spending countless "creative" hours digitally shaving off 20 pounds of back fat from a famous actress-singer personality during her publicity campaigns. Here is a woman promoting wellness while selling low quality make up, bogus supplements through massively photoshopped and filtered images on social media. I cannot be the only person who thinks that this is madness!

It's exhausting to watch these celebrities create completely fake personas and profit off the insecurities they help cultivate. The public eagerly consumes these carefully crafted images, unaware of the smoke and mirrors behind their creation. Having had the opportunity to meet many famous personalities, I can tell you this with certainty—they look just like you and me. The perfection we see on screens and in photos is an illusion, the result of filters, retouching, and curated lighting, as well as facial fillers, Botox, and facial restructuring. Strip away the digital enhancements, fillers, and plastic surgeries, and what remains are ordinary people, complete with imperfections, just like everyone else.

Another friend of mine, a high-level FX producer, gave me even more insight into the insanity. She shared with me that around 90% of actors spend millions—sometimes their own money—on CGI services to look younger, thinner, and more attractive on screen; CGI is basically photoshop for film. Yes, the faces and bodies you admire in the movies?

Most of them are digitally enhanced to meet impossible standards. It's yet another illusion. Ironically, these same actors complain about and picket against AI rights and the dangers of technology taking away their creative integrity—while they're basically outsourcing their own humanity, creating AI-like versions of themselves that they claim to be real.

The hypocrisy is staggering. If you're going to argue for artistic authenticity and human creativity, maybe start by being real about what you look like and stop relying on digital trickery to manipulate your audience.

THE BIRTH OF DETOX RETREATS

Let's face another reality while we're at it: we're all going to die—even those longevity wellness gurus. I'm all for enhancing well-being and guiding our bodies and minds toward staying healthy, but some of these wellness influencers, or so-called "biohackers," take it too far, frequently promoting a "one-size-fits-all" approach to wellness, based on pseudoscience.

While some longevity gurus have legitimate expertise and offer scientifically backed advice, many regurgitate over-hyped claims, and unproven methods to sell products, services, or programs aimed at achieving a longer, healthier life. They often ignore the complex, individual factors that influence aging—such as genetics, environment, mental health, socioeconomic status, and unique body chemistry. What works for a twenty year old woman is certainly different than what will work for a fifty year old woman, let alone the other myriad of variables influencing someone's health.

Their solutions are often packaged with expensive subscriptions, supplements, or personalized coaching, once again preying on people's insecurities and fears. And, their extreme programs often backfire—leading to burnout, malnutrition, and weight gain instead of weight loss.

Human beings are diverse, and what works for one person could even harm another.

I learned this the hard way. When I was younger, I was a little guilty of thinking everyone would benefit from celery juice, meditation, and yoga. But, I still believe that—except now I focus on a more minimalist, customized, and mental approach vs. dependency on supplementation and over-hyped technology.

Twenty-eight years ago, I was a young yoga teacher making waves in the blossoming Los Angeles yoga community. My approach was unconventional—strong, fluid, and blended with dance and fitness movements that hadn't yet made their way into traditional yoga classes. At the time, the LA yoga scene was just beginning to take root. I didn't think much of my unique style at the time—it was simply how I liked to move, drawing from my background as a dancer and experience teaching fitness. But it didn't take long for word to spread that my classes offered something different.

One day, after class, a woman approached me with excitement in her voice. "Oh, Alanna," she said, "if you were to lead a yoga retreat, I would definitely sign up!" Her enthusiasm caught me off guard, and without missing a beat, I responded with playful sarcasm, "If I were to lead a retreat, it would be all women, and we'd fast the entire weekend!" What I expected to be a quick laugh turned into something much more profound. Neither of us smiled. Instead, we locked eyes, and in unison, we said, "That's a great idea!" And just like that, the seeds of *Goddess Detox Retreats* were planted.

Those early retreats were nothing short of intense. We dove in headfirst, stripping away physical, emotional, and mental layers through fasting, movement, hot springs, meditation, and intentional silence. The weekends were raw in every sense of the word. I vividly remember the smell of garlic clinging to my hands, a sensory reminder to the intense detox process we had embarked on. I worked closely with Native American tribes, incorporating sweat lodges, silent nature hikes, and rituals that connected us to the land and our deeper selves.

There was no playbook, no template, no social media to show me what a retreat "should" look like. It was never done before, so I was following my instincts and a willingness to explore. It was exhilarating —liberating, even—because I wasn't limited by expectations or preconceptions, I was in the moment! Instagram wasn't around back then, and in retrospect, I'm grateful for that, even though countless extraordinary moments have to live in our hearts and not in our social feeds. There was no pressure to make things look wanderlust-perfect or photo-ready. It was messy, uncomfortable, beautifully real, and always in divine time.

We peeled back layers, sometimes too fast, and sometimes too deep. That's the thing about transformation—it isn't always gentle. Early on, I noticed how profoundly people responded to fasting, and we began to see the almost miraculously drastic changes in our lives post-retreat. We were manifesting before manifestation became a hashtag. Some experienced breakthroughs they weren't ready for, while others seemed to thrive in the freedoms that fasting created. It became clear to me that this work required balance, a delicate dance between pushing limits and knowing when to pull back.

LESS IS MORE

Over time, I developed a more thoughtful approach, refining the structure and intensity of the retreats. I've come to believe that true transformation only happens when we enter a state of surrender—when we meet ourselves at the edge of our personal boundaries, whether physical, emotional, or mental. Lasting change arises not through force but through gentle acceptance, allowing the body to tap into its innate ability to heal. When we give our extraordinary spirits the space to restore balance to both mind and body, profound and sustainable shifts naturally unfold. I discovered that, more often than not, less truly is more—especially when it comes to the human body and personal transformation.

Extremes and force only hinder growth and restrict our ability to expand. Just as children struggle to learn under pressure or coercion, adults need space and gentleness to thrive. The most powerful gift I could offer my retreat participants was a safe space—a place where they could breathe, pause, and allow themselves to unfold naturally, in their own time.

Today, there's an overwhelming abundance of supplements, which can easily become another avenue for corporate greed. While many supplements are marketed as essential for health and well-being, the wellness industry also preys on people's fears and desires for quick fixes. Some companies push unnecessary or ineffective products, again prioritizing profits over consumer well-being.

After completing a cleanse, you'll likely notice a heightened sense of awareness around what your body truly needs. When the blockages of processed foods and toxins are cleared away, your body's signals become easier to interpret—whether it's a craving for certain nutrients or a newfound sensitivity to foods that don't serve you. This intuitive connection allows you to make more informed decisions about your health and helps you identify when something feels out of balance.

While intuition plays an important role, it's still valuable to consult with your doctor. A basic panel of blood work can identify deficiencies, such as low levels of vitamin D, iron, or B12, which can subtly impact overall well-being. Especially as we age, mild supplementation can be very beneficial to maintain optimal health. However, it's important to approach supplementation with caution, rotation, and intelligence, not with dependency.

Our bodies are inherently designed to seek balance, a state known as homeostasis. This biological process ensures that various systems—like body temperature, blood sugar levels, and fluid balance—stay within optimal ranges to maintain health and function. When something shifts too far in one direction, whether through stress, overexertion, lifestyle imbalances, or excessive supplementation, the body compensates by pushing back in the opposite direction to restore equilibrium.

For example, if we overwork ourselves physically or mentally, the body responds with fatigue, signaling the need for rest and recovery. Similarly, consuming too much sugar can cause a spike in insulin, followed by a drop, resulting in a craving for more glucose to reestablish balance. This "push-pull" dynamic is the body's way of recalibrating, which we have to be aware of and honor.

If we consistently push ourselves too far—whether through chronic stress, over-training, over-supplementation, or poor diet—the body's attempts to correct itself can lead to burnout, illness, or imbalances such as adrenal fatigue, metabolic and/or mood disorders. This is why paying attention to our limits and practicing self-care is crucial: it allows the body to maintain homeostasis naturally, preventing the need for extreme corrections or supplementation.

Many people fall into the trap of over-supplementing, not realizing that most excess vitamins and minerals are excreted through urine—literally flushing money down the drain. In some cases, overuse of supplements can even backfire. For example, when your body receives high levels of certain nutrients from supplements, it may stop producing them naturally, assuming they are already in excess. This can disrupt your body's natural balance and leave you reliant on the supplement.

The key here is finding the right balance: understanding your body's needs through medically drawn bloodwork, supplementing intelligently, and listening to your body's cues. Quality matters too—

opting for high-quality, bio-available supplements ensures that you get the most benefit without inadvertently introducing toxins into your system. Ultimately, the goal is to support your body, not replace its natural processes.

SUPPORT SMALL BUSINESSES

So, the solution to lessening the grip of corporate greed lies in supporting small businesses. These are companies rooted in communities and built on trust, authenticity, and genuine customer care. And you've likely heard the following slogan: *When you support a small business, you're not just buying a product or service—you're investing in a person, a dream, and a community.* Unlike faceless corporations driven by profit, small businesses are built on passion and a commitment to quality over quantity.

Additionally, supporting small businesses contributes to healthier market competition, which helps keep larger corporations in check. It shifts the power balance away from monopolies that dominate industries and ultimately limit opportunities for entrepreneurs.

Make buying choices that align with your values, and vote with your wallet by supporting businesses that prioritize authenticity, fairness, and human connection. Say "no" to impersonal, profit-driven models that disregard consumer well-being or put health at risk. Through small, intentional actions, we can revive the original spirit of business, and every mindful purchase that you make contributes to a shift away from exploitative practices and corporate greed.

You hold the power to make these changes.

DECEPTIVE TACTICS OF

The Predators

*"Earth provides enough to satisfy every man's needs,
but not every man's greed." - **Mahatma Gandhi***

DECEPTIVE TACTICS

In today's world, the deceptive tactics used by companies and influencers to harness followings and maximize profits have become increasingly sophisticated, creating a marketplace driven by illusions rather than authenticity. Below are some of the common deceptive strategies employed to build and exploit followings, along with the methods used to push products with questionable integrity:

☽ CREATING A CULT PERSONALITY ☾

By using personal stories, behind-the-scenes glimpses, or emotional narratives, influencers and companies foster a sense of intimacy with their audience. In reality, this curated content is often designed by teams of marketers and brand managers whose main goal is to increase sales and keep followers emotionally invested; that's not very authentic.

Deceptive tactic: This "cult of personality" creates an illusion that followers are part of an influencer's inner circle, when in fact they're being positioned as nothing more than potential buyers and data points.

☽ FAKE AUTHENTICITY ☾

One of the most common tactics is fake authenticity. Influencers frequently claim to "keep it real," showing their supposedly unfiltered and unedited moments. However, even these moments are often staged to appear relatable.

Deceptive tactic: By presenting themselves as "just like you," influencers gain trust and credibility, which they leverage to push products or services. The more followers trust their authenticity, the more they are willing to buy into their recommendations, despite these being paid promotions.

☽ FOMO (FEAR OF MISSING OUT) ☾

Influencers and companies often exploit followers' fear of missing out by using scarcity tactics or limited-time offers. By promoting exclusive deals, limited-edition products, or once-in-a-lifetime experiences, they create a sense of urgency. Followers feel pressured to act quickly, believing they might miss out on something important or rare if they don't buy now.

You've probably seen the "Only 3 left in stock" alert when

shopping online suggesting a sale ends in a few hours. However, the scarcity is typically fake, and there is no real limit on the products available.

Deceptive tactic: This pressure-driven marketing manipulates consumers into making impulsive decisions.

☽ FAKE TESTIMONIALS (ASTROTURFING) ☾

Companies, politicians, and influencers frequently use astroturfing to create the illusion of grassroots support. This can involve using fake testimonials, reviews, or even hiring bots to generate engagement on social media posts. By inflating the popularity of a product or service with fake endorsements, they manipulate followers into believing that many other people are already benefiting from the product or service, or that it is of high value and popularity.

Deceptive tactic: Inflated reviews and testimonials create a false consensus that tricks consumers into believing a product or service is more popular, effective, or in-demand than it actually is.

☽ INAUTHENTIC SPONSORSHIPS ☾

Many influencers will endorse products that they don't personally use or believe in because they're paid to do so. This is often masked by pretending the product is a genuine recommendation. Influencers use phrases like "I've been loving this product lately," or "I can't live without this," even though the product was sent to them for free and may never have been used before, or will ever be used in the future.

Deceptive tactic: Followers are misled into believing these are genuine endorsements when in reality, they are paid advertisements. The lack of transparency about sponsorships or affiliate commissions can make followers feel manipulated.

☽ FALSE OR MISLEADING CLAIMS ☾

Many companies and influencers use exaggerated or outright false claims to sell their products. Whether it's a beauty influencer promising that a particular skincare product will "change your life" or a fitness influencer claiming that their workout program will "get you shredded in 30 days," these tactics tap into people's vulnerabilities and desires. Some companies are notorious for using "before and after" photos that are manipulated, showing unrealistic results that can't be achieved by using their products. Diet and fitness supplements, in particular, are known for making bold claims that are rarely backed by solid evidence.

Deceptive tactic: These claims capitalize on consumers' insecurities by over-promising and under-delivering.

☽ FAKE BOTS & MANIPULATIVE ALGORITHMS ☾

Many companies and influencers use social media algorithms to artificially boost their visibility. This includes buying followers, likes, and/or engagement to make their accounts appear more popular than they are. Bots are often used to increase comments and likes, giving the illusion that the influencer has a more significant following and higher engagement than is real.

Remember, celebrities and influencers often buy their own fake popularity and expect you to pay for their costs after you've been tricked into believing their hyped up hype. ***Don't believe the hype!***

Deceptive tactic: Fake engagement metrics trick platforms into giving posts more visibility, and trick followers into believing that the influencer or company is more influential than they are, thus making their endorsements seem more credible.

☽ FAKE TITLES, 'BEST OF's' AND VANITY AWARDS ☾

Many corporations and influencers use fake titles, awards, and rankings to build credibility and manipulate consumer trust—strategies that are far more common than most people realize. Book and music publishers often buy their own books and albums in order to hit the minimum requirement for the titles to become "bestsellers."

One of the most well-known examples of this deception is how some authors and publishers game the system to achieve coveted spots on bestseller lists, like *The New York Times*. Instead of relying on organic sales, publishing houses (and sometimes the authors themselves) purchase large quantities of their own books through various channels, carefully distributing the purchases to avoid detection by the algorithm. These bulk buys artificially inflate the book's ranking, landing it on the bestseller list and giving the public the false impression that the book is a runaway success.

Deceptive tactic: These tactics work because people naturally trust authority and recognition. Seeing "bestseller," "award-winning," or "voted #1" gives consumers the impression that they're making a smart purchase. But in reality, many of these accolades are just illusions designed to manipulate behavior and drive sales. The result? Consumers waste money on products, books, or services that don't live up to the hype, all while truly deserving creators and businesses get overlooked.

The digital world is full of predatory behaviors aimed at manipulating consumers, harnessing followers, and turning authenticity into a commodity. By understanding these tactics, you can arm yourself against being exploited and making informed decisions about where to spend your money and place your trust. Influencers and corporations may look like they're giving something valuable, but far too often, it's just another form of exploitation disguised as friendship or guidance.

Be vigilant, think critically, and above all, remember that authenticity is a rare commodity in today's media-saturated landscape. Don't let carefully crafted illusions fool you into paying for your own foolery. Anyone can look glamorous. *Anyone.* But not everyone can be real.

PROMPTS & POSITIVE ACTIONS

List the influencers and retailers that you are most influenced by. Do you trust the validity of their advertisements? Do you trust the quality of the products that they are selling to you?

....

....

....

....

....

Have you experienced customer support neglect or rage from being denied proper customer support? Maybe it is time to find other providers of these services. What options do you have?

....

....

....

....

....

....

Which ethical and sustainable small businesses can you support, while minimizing purchases to companies ruled by corporate greed?

....

....

....

....

....

....

**DO NOT FOOL ME TO PAY
FOR MY OWN FOOLERY!**

Conclusion
The Healing

*"The wound is where the light gets in." ~ **Rumi***

HEALING

Writing this book was anything but easy, and sharing it felt excruciating at first. I wrote it in its entirety in 58 days, including writing, editing, formatting, designing, and self-publishing. I received interest from a major publishing company, but the timing for release didn't match the motivation behind writing it. I felt a tsunami like urgency to finally share these experiences, even though it's never easy to share personal traumas—especially not in the public eye. What helped me through this discomfort was knowing that the lessons and themes woven throughout can help readers lead more empowered, spiritual, and consciously authentic lives.

I've tried to illustrate that since the dawn of humanity, humans have struggled between living morally, or perpetuating lies for profit. You can also likely see the arc of my growth as I finally found the strength and voice to stand up to abusers and fakes. Hindsight is always 20/20, and looking back, it's clear that I was both sought after and mistreated for my bright light and unique connection to spirituality. It's not every day you encounter someone more interested in the truth of their spirit than the glitter of the world. I simply didn't realize how unique I was.

Now, here I am in 2024, nine months after closing my yoga

studio, giving birth to this book. I've felt a strong pull back toward the work that has always defined me: wellness, writing, and helping others navigate their own paths to deeper healing. I began leading smaller group detox retreats in my home, allowing me to also heal in a safe space where I could simply be in alignment with who I am, free from unnecessary judgment or jealousy based ridicule.

FLASH

When people ask me, "How did you get through all of these experiences?" One word comes to my mind and heart: *Flash*. There is a short animation film by Eleonora Stella Hariyono Oei, titled *Side Effects: Helping Others*, that follows a simple yet powerful premise: a man who loves helping others slowly learns the importance of caring for himself. As the stick-figure protagonist leaves his home, he encounters several people struggling with difficult moments. Each time he offers assistance, he unknowingly absorbs a bit of their dark energy, visually depicted as a growing shadow that engulfs him more and more with each encounter helping others.

By the end of the film, he stumbles back into his house, exhausted and overwhelmed by the darkness he has accumulated. But just as he feels consumed by the weight of everything he has taken on, his dog runs up to him with unconditional love and joy. In that moment, the darkness begins to drain out of him, showing how unconditional love can replenish us in ways nothing else can.

The film illustrates a profound message about the balance between helping others and taking care of oneself. It suggests that while compassion is vital, we can't truly give our best to others if we neglect our own well-being. So when people ask how I got through so much disappointment and trauma, that is my answer: my dog, Flash.

I wasn't looking for a dog at the time. I was staying in Judy's guest house, recovering from the abusive relationship with Jack. Around that time, I was casually dating my friend Mark, who had introduced me to David, the Groomer. Mark was passionate about dog rescue, and I admired how deeply he cared for abandoned and mistreated dogs.

However, nearly every other week, Mark would ask if I could foster or adopt a dog. As much as I have always loved dogs, I had to be honest with him—I just couldn't take on that responsibility at the time. My life felt too unsettled. I traveled frequently for work, and my living situation was still in flux. Bringing a dog into my life felt unfair, both to the animal and to me.

Then one night, Mark and I were out to dinner in Malibu when he received a call about an emergency dog rescue. The story was heartbreaking. A 10-year-old boy named Patrick had been hearing soft whimpering coming from a taped box in the alley behind his house in Thousand Oaks. For three days he heard this sound. Finally, unable to ignore it any longer, Patrick opened the box. In his own words, the puppy inside "jumped out, like a *flash* of white light."

So, Patrick chased after the dog, brought him home, and named him Flash. His mother immediately told him they couldn't keep the dog and took him to the local shelter in Calabasas. When she arrived, the shelter staff informed her that they were at full capacity. Given Flash's condition—he had been strangled, beaten, taped in a box and discarded in the trash—the staff explained that he would likely be euthanized if left there because they didn't have the resources to care for him.

Somehow, Patrick's mother ended up with Mark's phone number and called him while we were at dinner. After hanging up, Mark looked at me with absolute seriousness and said, "You have to take this dog." Once again, I tried to explain my situation, pleading, "Mark, you know that I love dogs, but I just can't take one right now!"

Mark, clearly worried, told me all the grim details about how Flash had been found. His concern was written all over his face, and after a moment, I caved. "Okay, I'll watch the dog for two weeks—two weeks —until you find him a home," I said reluctantly.

That was sixteen years ago, and Flash is laying by my side as I type right now. I'm forever grateful to Patrick, the boy who found him, for naming him. Otherwise he would have ended up with something silly like Shiva, with no offense to Shiva, of course. The name, Flash, is just so much better for my little companion, and I appreciate how organically he came into my life.

Having Flash forced me to slow down, be home more often, and travel less. This shift made me confront emotions I had been able to avoid by using my busy schedule as an easy distraction from deeper feelings. With Flash, I no longer had that option—his presence grounded me, and I was finally compelled to sit with my thoughts and emotions rather than escape them.

And, as anyone with a dog can tell you, the healing they provide is unmatched. Dogs offer the purest form of unconditional love, with no judgment, expectations, or ulterior motives. Their presence alone can release oxytocin, and they greet us with love, even on our hardest days. That in itself was transformative after dealing with an emotionally abusive partner, which meant that I never knew what kind of energy would greet me when I walked in with Jack.

Because of Flash's injuries—his collapsed trachea from being strangled—I rarely used a collar or leash. He quickly became deeply attached to me, and from that point on, he was by my side on countless adventures. Whether it was hanging out at the studios I owned, accompanying me on travels, or simply being present in everyday life, Flash proved to be the perfect, easygoing companion. It has brought great joy to give him a secure, happy, and healthy life.

After everything Flash has endured, he's become very well-adjusted over time, revealing a playful, rascally personality that never fails to make me smile. He taught me that Maslow's *Hierarchy of Needs* shouldn't exclude animals. Here was this little dog, once abandoned and mistreated, who—now that his basic needs and socialization were met—began to express a hilarious, unique personality. It made me realize that animals in the wild, living in constant states of fight or flight, rarely have the opportunity to ascend Maslow's ladder to reveal their individual personalities. Similarly, humans who are homeless or victims of trauma, when stuck in survival mode, often cannot fully express their unique personalities, either.

When basic needs like food, shelter, and safety are unmet, both animals and humans focus solely on survival, leaving little room for self-expression or personal growth, let alone self-realization. This insight made me more empathetic toward people struggling with survival, reminding me that everyone's personality and potential lie beneath, waiting to emerge once they feel safe and secure.

FULL CIRCLE

In the following pages, I'll share some of the natural methods that have brought me healing, although I am currently working on a separate book that will detail this process more thoroughly. The first and most essential step is learning to slow down. Nature operates at a much slower pace than we do, and true integrated change only occurs in a state of surrendered acceptance. You may have experienced pivotal moments like I have—a-ha's, eclipses, or life-altering shifts— but those moments are just the beginning. They mark the start of a long journey, like the first step in turning a metaphorical bus around. There are many smaller, necessary actions along the way, and embracing each one with patience, consistency, and trust is key to making meaningful transformations. I always say, "I trust the laws of the universe, I do not trust the laws of man." Nature is slower and unhurried, yet we've grown fixated on rushed, artificial measures of time.

In the past, I've made the mistake of being impatient, rushing through critical phases, and not allowing the process to fully unfold. Again, transformation is not a single moment but a series of small, essential steps. When we push too hard or try to bypass parts of the journey, we risk missing the crucial lessons embedded within each phase, giving us strength to continue evolving. And more often than not, skipping ahead means we'll find ourselves back at square one the next time we shift our attention back to the process. Only by allowing the process to unfold at its *natural* pace can we achieve meaningful and lasting transformation. An orange is sweetest when it naturally ripens vs. being artificially ripened. So is your life.

This process is often uncomfortable, which is why many people tend to avoid it. However, that discomfort is essential to our growth— just as a caterpillar must struggle within the cocoon to emerge anew, as a butterfly. It is from this isolation and surrendered state, cycled with moments of tension, resistance, belief and purpose that we build the strength necessary to transform.

IT ALL STARTS IN THE GUT

The emotional intelligence of the gut is extraordinary. This connection, known as the "gut-brain axis," is a bi-directional communication pathway between the gastrointestinal tract and the central nervous system. It means that the bacteria and nerve signals in our gut can profoundly influence emotions and mood. At the same time, our thoughts and emotions influence our digestion, linking our ability to process food with our capacity to process experiences. This intricate connection highlights the importance of gut health not just for physical well-being but also for emotional and mental balance.

I started cleansing with my detox groups every weekend,

personally focusing on probiotics, colostrum, l-glutamine, bone broth, manuka honey and other herbs to help heal the linings of my intestinal tract. I started to notice immediate changes, and quickly began to feel like myself again.

Letting go of my studio and releasing the material trappings of my business had brought a profound sense of relief. Our possessions carry emotional weight, influencing how we feel and function. Just as a computer slows down when burdened with too many files, our minds and spirits become overwhelmed when we carry too much "stuff"— whether it's unresolved thoughts and emotions, or even clutter in our lives.

Attachments and distracting responsibilities act as noise, pulling our attention from what truly matters: what is naturally occurring in each moment. Simplifying isn't just about physical de-cluttering; it's a way of reclaiming your energy, too.

My home has always been a sanctuary for me, but I took it a step further by transforming it into a mini wellness retreat. It wasn't just about aesthetics or creating a peaceful environment—it was about intentionally designing a space that provided everything I needed within arm's reach. The goal was to eliminate unnecessary effort and distractions. Even something as seemingly simple as driving to a yoga studio or spa requires energy and effort. I also wanted to avoid random interactions with others, or having to shift my focus. Instead, everything essential to my well-being was easily accessible, allowing me to fully immerse myself in this cocooned transformation process. Conscious boundaries are essential in healing and in life, especially as I recovered from years of feeling under attack by hurtful and selfish people.

At the heart of this was the installation of a sauna and cold plunge in my home. I have long embraced the healing power of heat and cold contrast, knowing how it activates the body to cleanse itself physically, vibrationally, and energetically. To enhance the benefits of these sessions, I infused my sauna rituals with healing oils, particularly frankincense and castor oil. Frankincense is known for its grounding, anti-inflammatory properties, and the heat seemed to amplify the healing qualities. I incorporated castor oil as well, to protect the surface of my skin from the heat, and further enhancing my physical healing.

I continued hosting detox retreats every weekend, inviting women to stay in my guest rooms as they immersed themselves in the detox process of juice, soup and herbal cleansing, integrated with yoga, meditation and wellness treatments. My intentional home redesign created a live/work sanctuary not just for me but for others seeking renewal and healing.

The first retreat aligned with a gorgeous full moon. Unbeknownst to me, a caterpillar had built its cocoon right in my front doorway. We fittingly named her Mezuzah. On the last day of that retreat—the morning after our Full Moon Goddess Circle—the magic unfolded. We were delighted to witness the cocoon open, revealing a gorgeous butterfly had emerged into the world. It was an incredible moment to witness, as if nature itself was mirroring the process of transformation we had committed to during the retreat.

SOMATICS AND CONSISTENCY

Before *somatics* became a buzz word in the yoga industry, where it rightfully belongs, I wrote about it in my book *As I Am*, back in 2010. To be something, we have to feel it. This is why our feelings tend to dictate our experiences. Somatic awareness has always been a cornerstone of my practices, and I believe that *Consistency is the Mother of Transformation.*

Somatic prayer, as I call it, is the conscious connection of the mind, body, and spirit through breath, movement, and sensational intention. Every morning, I would sit in my sauna, the heat activating my body, and then, while in a dynamic, meditative state, I would engage in deep, intentional somatic integration to gratitude, presence, trust, and love, as it is.

A common practice that I see others do is to use this powerful state of being to infuse their desires, which if not aligned with purpose only creates more attachments that we have to clean up later on in the process of authentic being, ultimately creating more distractions and delays. This practice is about being who you are, as you are, in each moment, without your attention deviating from the sensations in your body.

Our minds regulate our experiences, serving as both a tool for survival and a gateway to higher-level thinking and awareness. It provides a space to shape how we perceive the world. However, the mind operates on cause and effect—there is no internal governing body that flags our thoughts as "right" or "wrong." Instead, we interpret thoughts as truth based on the emotions and associations we've built from our past experiences.

Knowing this, we must train our minds to be intentional, discerning and oftentimes objective. Detachment is essential, because if left unchecked, our thoughts can create patterns that limit us, reinforcing fears or assumptions rooted in past pain or habit.

Mindfulness practices, emotional regulation, somatics, and objective awareness of our thoughts allow us to guide the mind away from automatic responses into more intentionally integrated experiences. Through these consistent practices, we cultivate and re-create healthier mental and physical pathways that permeate our being, and we become who we are, naturally.

Through this immersive wellness process, I began reconnecting with the inner part of me where I have always found comfort; my dharma—my true alignment and purpose, which I had been distracted from by years of busyness. For too long, I was consumed with the daily grind: sweeping floors, managing unreliable yoga teachers, and earning my law degree the hard way—through real-life experience. But slowly, I felt my inner strength returning, and slowly the synchronicities began to reveal themselves again.

Whether it was the years of emotional abuse, the vibrational awakening of the gong, or the crushing burdens of running a yoga studio during a global pandemic, I found myself finally submitting. The relentless buffalo in me—the one that always persevered forward—took a knee at last. In that surrender, the strong shell I had built to protect myself finally and fully cracked open. I realized that these walls, meant to shield me from pain, had also kept me from experiencing true freedom. What felt like devastation was instead liberation. It was an opportunity to be born anew, and step out of the shell at last.

As I extended the personal work I was doing with others to deepen their experiences, the retreats I led were no longer just about detoxing the body or calming the mind; they were about helping people navigate their own spiritual rebirths. Just as I had walked through the ring of fire and come out stronger, I now felt equipped to guide others through the same advanced process. This wasn't just a weekend to lose a bloating belly, this was a deeply mental and emotional journey. I was teaching them how to cultivate the kind of spiritual resilience and authentic acceptance that no one can take away or gaslight.

True power doesn't come from control or success in the worldly sense. True power comes from self-mastery. It comes from the deep knowing that no matter what happens, you have everything you need within you to heal, to thrive, and to create the life you deserve—and you don't need 72 pills a day to achieve this.

As a result of my experiences that I have shared in this book, I frequently wonder where new product ideas truly originate from when I see advertisements for product launches and their marketing campaigns. I wonder who were the real creators of style and innovation throughout history. It's easy to see how ideas can get repackaged and claimed by those with more visibility or influence. Daarun, for example, promoted the theories of other authors—acting as a catalyst to bring those ideas to a larger audience, even though the thought-provoking concepts weren't originally his.

This makes me think: what if we changed the system to amplify lesser-known voices? If we created more space for hidden talents and original thinkers, we could unlock a reservoir of creativity that has the power to transform the world for good. Much of what financial investors prioritize is a proven track record, leaving little room for fresh ideas or truly visionary ideas to receive funding. The venture capital world is currently dominated by men who understandably prioritize proven, safe investments to protect their money. However, this approach often reinforces outdated business models, replicating products, systems, and problems that may no longer serve our evolving needs. How can we create space for bold, visionary thinking to be heard, nurtured, and supported in a way that fosters true innovation and progress?

I think we are just starting to do this, however, many voices remain unheard because access to platforms is limited by influence, wealth, or status. By shifting the spotlight to those whose ideas have yet to reach the surface—before they are forced to surrender their power, creativity, and intentions—we could spark meaningful change more quickly than we ever imagined. Much easier said than done, I know, but everything begins with an intention. I hope that the rich and privileged can begin to listen to more authentic stories without feeling the need to own or control them.

INDIGO CHILDREN

I realize that my beliefs and approach to life will not resonate with everyone. In fact, I've always sensed that younger generations might come to appreciate my work and writings more deeply in the future, perhaps even after I'm gone. Allow me to share one more synchronistic story that aligns with this idea.

While I was living in San Diego around 2008, I became friends with a progressive doctor named Dr. Benjo. We worked out a trade—I'd teach him Pilates, and he'd provide me with IV drips infused with glutathione and other health-enhancing supplements. One day, I arrived for an appointment and found only one other person in the waiting room: an older, white-haired woman sitting near the door to Dr. Benjo's office. I didn't make eye contact or start a conversation with her. Instead, I took a seat on the other side of the room and began scrolling on my BlackBerry.

About fifteen minutes later, Dr. Benjo opened his office door. A man exited his office while the white-haired woman stood up. "Hello, Barbara," Dr. Benjo greeted her as she entered his office, and I continued waiting outside.

After another thirty minutes or so, Dr. Benjo opened his office door again. The woman said her goodbyes and left. Once more, I didn't make any eye contact with her.

When I finally entered Dr. Benjo's office, he asked, "Do you know who that was?" Confused, I replied, "Who?" He clarified, "The woman who just left." I responded, "No, I didn't speak to her at all." Dr. Benjo smiled and said, "Well, she had a lot to say about you!" I was completely stunned.

Dr. Benjo went on to explain that Barbara was one of the world's most sought-after psychics, with a six-month waiting list of people seeking her services. He shared that she'd told him I was one of the first Indigo children to come to Earth. This both stunned me—as Barbara knew nothing about me—and intrigued me because I had a deep fascination with Indigo children that neither of them could know about.

She didn't know that I worked with children, that I was one of the first to write children's yoga books, and that I was also the first to create yoga classes and camps for kids, often to the bemusement of my community.

I remember a world-famous yoga teacher scoffing at my first children's book back in 2003, saying, "Come on, Alanna, kids can't comprehend yoga!" That is, until he became a parent himself fifteen years later, and decided to write his own—about how flexible Daddy is. That's just another example of a short-sighted mindset. If we judged less and approached people and life with a more open mind, we all could become far more creative and innovative, instead of living with fears of being or thinking differently than everyone else.

I think of that little scenario often, even though I don't take a random stranger's esoteric opinions of me too much to heart. It's the idea of it that resonates with me. I've always felt a more natural connection with children than with most adults. Children are more open-minded, less judgmental, and they haven't yet grown rigid with worldly beliefs.

I mean, I've been "Taylor Swifting" since she was just five years old —speaking my truth, calling out injustices, publishing my own content, and doing it my way, like she does so brilliantly, in my own smaller, less visible way. It's the Indigo way we see in younger generations. However, my journey included more obstacles and far less support. We all walk through doors that someone before us worked hard to break open, just as younger generations continue to rise through glass ceilings that earlier generations worked to shatter. Every day I give thanks to the women before me who sacrificed so much so that I can enjoy my freedoms today. We still have a long way to go, but we've come so far!

BE PATIENT WITH EACH OTHER

As I sit here, reflecting on all that has transpired, I can't help but feel gratitude for my journey. It hasn't been easy, and it certainly hasn't been without pain or humiliation. But I can finally say that I have come full circle. The future feels bright, not because I expect it to be without challenges, but because I now know my value, and I will fight to protect who I am when needed. Healing also relies on our willingness to confront our shadows and pain, and to trust that it is merely an energetic process of alchemy to transform darkness, not a daunting indestructible force as animated horror stories like to portray.

If you encounter someone working through their struggles in search of deeper truth and authenticity, I hope you choose to be compassionate, and maybe even to listen. Maybe they are wiggling their mind free from global gaslighting that the rest of the world is brainwashed to believe. If someone is overwhelmed by trauma and reacting from what seems like an irrational place of pain, I encourage you to respond with kindness if the situation is safe, not with judgment. Be patient—with others and with yourself. Avoid contributing to or spreading gossip, especially if you didn't witness the event or experience it firsthand. Gossip not only hurts others but can perpetuate false narratives, making healing harder for those involved.

If someone you know is labeled as "the c word," *crazy*, take a moment to reflect on what that word really means. In truth, no one is more wickedly insane than those fully invested in the artificial structures of our world—without any awareness of the spiritual or energetic dimensions of life—they might be the ones furthest from sanity. What society often dismisses as crazy can actually be the sign of someone's innate instincts resisting the constraints of our manipulated, linear systems. It could indicate that they feel trapped, their deeper awareness is clashing with the superficial expectations of modern life, and maybe they, too, are trying to escape a thick web of gaslighting.

Consider the ripple effect of all your actions on others, including the words you share online, the content you copy and paste, and the judgments you make based on gossip or misinformation. Avoid perpetuating what is untrue until you know firsthand that it is true.

It may go without saying, but it's always worth repeating: the same compassion you extend to others should also be offered to yourself. As you explore your own triggers and reactions, you'll gain deeper insight into why others behave the way they do. Learning compassion is essential if we hope to live in harmony—not just with one another, but with the natural world. Because, whether we like it or not, we are all connected. Our thoughts, actions, and behaviors ripple outward, impacting the people around us and the world we share, and vice versa.

The journey through this book has been a deep dive into the complexities and imbalances of modern human nature—unveiling the manipulations of sociopaths, the deceptive tactics of social climbers, the insecurities hidden behind the polished actions of socialites, and the dangerous allure of charmers and groomers—combined with a slice of my spiritual synchronicities, and tips for personal growth. My experiences being exploited are not unique; whether we recognize these traits or not, many people in today's world—the new age Vikings —rely on these behaviors to "succeed" in a society that rewards competition, greed, image, and manipulation.

The sheer amount of emotional and mental labor required just to exist within the dynamics of our world today is overwhelming for most people. As a society, we've lost our space to simply live; the demands to be constantly productive, and the rapid pace of technology have crowded out the moments of stillness and simplicity that are essential to our well-being. We've become conditioned to believe that value lies in doing, achieving, and accumulating rather than being. I hope this book inspires you to make profound changes—and that together we can all move toward a more intentional, ethical, and spiritual way of living that values authenticity and natural balance on a collective level.

It is essential to reiterate this core truth: you will inevitably encounter people who do not have your best interests at heart. Some will be drawn to your light, success, and authenticity, and they won't hesitate to take what isn't theirs—whether that means your ideas, creations, or even the essence of who you are. Their tactics are often subtle but destructive. Remember, their behaviors are less about you and more about them—their fears, their insecurities, their desperate need to cling to the top of a social ladder they believe defines them. And like a cheetah chasing a herd of antelope, they will always hunt what they perceive as the easiest victim. Be strong in who you are.

It's interesting how these are often the people who seem to have it all—or at least project the appearance of having access to it all. They radiate wealth, power, and status, but the deeper you venture into their world, the more you see how shallow it often is. People who are content with who they are, people who live with a natural sense of morality aren't driven by fleeting fame or excessive wealth. They find purpose and meaning beyond material success, which offers them a deeper sense of peace.

For years, I existed among these people and, to some extent, entertained partnerships with them because I sought a platform to enlighten people to these natural truths. But I quickly learned that only those willing to play by their rules—their game—get to climb the podium, so as not to disrupt the corrupted system that they control. Progress in their world requires complicity, and I was unwilling to compromise my values to participate in a system built on superficiality.

I hope you don't read my book as a tale of victimhood. Instead, I hope my story brings you a sense of relief, knowing that you are not alone in your struggles, your instincts, or your pursuit of authenticity. My greatest wish is that it instills the confidence to break free from any pressure to live in a way that isn't true to who you are, because life is just too short (even for those longevity gurus!).

I hope this message encourages you to believe in yourself, knowing that every step toward authenticity is a step toward a more meaningful, fulfilled life. Never forget that the process is not linear or immediate, and it may feel uncomfortable at times.

I've tried to weave into this book the lessons I've learned from these toxic situations, while simultaneously sharing the resonant synchronicities that seem to be woven into the fabric of my journey. These moments of alignment grounded me, even when life felt chaotic and unfair. Whether these experiences are feedback from our own consciousness, the matrix responding to each of us, a universal broadcast of frequencies resonating through all living matter, or a blend of all, I can only describe them as ecstatically miraculous and innately trustworthy. They carry a sense that we are exactly where we need to be, even when life feels uncertain. These moments remind me that there is an intricate connection between our inner world and the greater patterns unfolding around us.

From the moment the doves sang at Paisley Park, to the serendipitous appearance of the number 22 throughout my life—I was being reminded that there is a divine and mathematical plan in play, even when those synchronicities come packaged as *chocolate-covered karmas*, inviting us to confront what is unhealed within us. I feel supported in even that twisted knowing. That no matter what, without ceasing, there are forces urging us to heal and to align with greater truth and more awareness.

There were plenty of moments when I could have easily been swallowed by the negativity—the betrayal, the manipulation, and the endless gossip from insecure individuals who saw me as a threat. But every single time, these forces reminded me that I was meant for more than just surviving the silly worldly games we're all forced to play; despite these odds, I was meant to live a life far more meaningful. You are, too.

And lastly, the greatest lesson I've always known, but finally learned, is that true power comes from within—not from external validation, the approval of others, or being seen by the world, but from alignment with who I am, as I am. It means deeply knowing myself without relying on outside influences or dependencies. While it may sound rhetorical or cliché, it's a truth you can only fully grasp once you feel it. No fleeting approval, influx of "likes," or material gain can ever replace this.

TO THE CREATIVES

One of my first jobs in LA was working for an emotionally volatile literary agent. His instructions were absurdly simple: "Watch the fax machine, and if a good idea comes in, bring it to me immediately." Then, with a maniacal laugh, he added, "Because I'll knock it off!"

To every creative who has had their work stolen or copied, know this: if you were the one to cast the pebble into the pond, every ripple that spreads outward holds energy connected to you. Even if the world never acknowledges your influence, the energetic impact of your creation is real, and it flows back to you in unseen ways. Think of it like a multi-level marketing structure—your original spark is still the root of the movement, even if others try to profit from it along the way in their make believe delusion.

Hold your head high—you created something unique and you were daring and generous enough to share your ideas with the world. That takes courage. However, moving forward, be more mindful of where you cast your next pebble. Make sure your energy and creativity are directed toward places where they can thrive, be respected, and remain protected. Every idea is a precious seed and by placing it in the correct environment, you give it the best chance to grow into its full potential without being exploited or diminished.

<u>TIPS FOR CREATIVES</u>

- Collaborate Selectively and Trust Wisely.
- Copyright your work with the US Copyright Office.
- Trademark your brand name, logo, or product concept with the USPTO.
- Register your work with the Writers Guild of America.
- Ask for a *Non Disclosure Agreement* to be signed before sharing your pitches and concepts with others. If your presenting party offers you their NDA, read every word of it before signing.
- Keep detailed records of your meetings.
- Use DRM (Digital Rights Management) on your public content.
- Leverage Creative Commons Licenses.
- Secure a trustworthy literary agent and/or entertainment attorney.

PAY IT FORWARD

Perhaps, in a way, my robustly generous outreach and sharing with the rich, famous, and powerful acted as a trap or lesson for their egos— or maybe it's all just part of a greater energetic play, with each of us merely actors exerting our free will to create. After all, the first acorn seed probably isn't concerned about the entire orchard knowing where it came from.

Not every encounter ended in disappointment, as well. Over the years several celebrities did respond with kindness and grace to my outreach and ideas. A few acknowledged the value of my work and concepts, offering words of encouragement, or even referring me to someone who could be a helpful ally. These moments were a refreshing reminder that, while not everyone acts with integrity, there are individuals—despite their fame and influence—who understand the importance of supporting others.

These people know, deep down, that they didn't reach their success alone—someone, at some point, lent them a hand. It's this awareness that drives them to pay it forward, recognizing that true success isn't just about personal achievement but also about lifting others along the way. These are people who live a sense of gratitude, aware of the privilege they hold, and neither taking it for granted nor seeing themselves as superior to others.

However, to the Posers and the Fakes, understand that authenticity cannot be mimicked indefinitely. Building a life or reputation on borrowed ideas, appearances, or false accolades may grant you temporary success, but it lacks any foundation needed for long-term fulfillment. True influence doesn't come from projection or imitation— it comes from integrity and alignment with who you really are, independently and through hard work. Eventually, the truth finds its way to the surface, and the energy you've spent curating a false image could have been invested in discovering your own unique gifts and purpose.

There's power in choosing to let go of façades and engage with the world more honestly. There is also great strength in recognizing and appreciating the greatness of others, even if you can't control them or if their light makes you feel threatened. Confidence comes from lifting others without fear of losing your own worth. And perhaps most importantly, there is transformative power in apologizing for past wrongs. Owning your mistakes is not a sign of weakness—it's a courageous step toward healing, growth, and repairing lost trust. It opens the door to becoming a more honest version of yourself.

I am far from perfect, by any means, but one thing is for certain: I have never lived anyone's life but my own. I am persistent in my commitment to who I am. I am a yogi. I am a healer. I am a visionary. And, I am a woman who's light has burned through generations of darkness in one lifetime.

If you feel tempted to imitate or take shortcuts, remember this: every action you take is a thread woven into the fabric of a larger garment—one that you alone will wear. You can choose to sew someone else's story, or you can weave your own. The path that is meant for you will only reveal itself when you listen from within. But you'll never discover that path if you're too busy pretending to be someone else.

"How wild it was, to let it be." — Cheryl Strayed, *Wild*

HEALING ANCESTRAL TRAUMA

Ancestral trauma refers to the emotional and psychological wounds that are passed down through generations, often unconsciously. These inherited traumas may stem from events such as war, slavery, injustice, or family abuse. Science backs up these theories proving that trauma can indeed leave lasting effects within our DNA coding, not by altering the genetic code itself but through epigenetic changes. Epigenetics refers to modifications that affect how genes are expressed—essentially, which genes are turned "on" or "off"—without changing the DNA sequence.

Stressful or traumatic events can create these biological imprints, which can be passed down through generations, influencing how descendants respond to stress and trauma. Over time, these unhealed wounds can manifest in descendants as mental health challenges, relationship difficulties, chronic stress, or recurring patterns of abuse. Healing ancestral trauma not only liberates an individual's well-being but can also break generational cycles, and offer freedom to future generations.

Studies have found that descendants of Holocaust survivors and communities impacted by slavery or colonization often exhibit heightened stress responses, depression, or anxiety. The first step in healing ancestral trauma is awareness. It requires recognizing patterns in your life—such as anxiety, shame, fear, or a sense of not belonging—that may not align with your personal experiences but have roots in your lineage.

As a young teenager, I began sensing a dark, unsettling presence and experiencing night terrors. Even at that early age, I intuitively felt that this force was connected to the unresolved trauma carried through generations on both sides of my family. I had grown up hearing stories of abuse, hardship, and emotional pain that stretched back multiple generations, and over time, I began to recognize a pattern emerging. It became clear that these experiences weren't isolated incidents but part of a larger cycle of inherited trauma.

Though I couldn't fully comprehend what this force was or where it originated, I made a fierce commitment to overcome it—for myself and for my family. As I progressed on my healing journey, I encountered impasses and resistance from my family as I tried to evolve and inspire them in similar ways, like many people experience with their families.

Some modern day therapies often advises cutting ties and moving on from challenging family relationships, but that never felt right to me —it seemed entitled. I was given this life, connected to these people in profound ways, who I love and care for deeply, even if there was a history of deep frustrations, misunderstandings and past hurts. Breaking those bonds felt selfish.

Instead of trying to cut ties and walk away—which again, may be the right path for many—I chose to *energetically* include my family in the healing work I was doing, from a distance. Healing isn't just a personal endeavor; it ripples outward, affecting those connected to us, especially through genetic and emotional bonds.

I mentioned in *Chapter 1* that my mother is a devout Catholic, practicing her form of meditation through prayer, Adoration of the Eucharist, attending Mass, and other heart-centered rituals. What my mother may have lacked in communication skills, she made up for in prayer. As much as the younger me wished for more direct communication, understanding and guidance, I was granted a rare, more daring opportunity to figure out my life on my own terms.

Though our practices looked different on the surface—mine through meditation and somatic work, and my mother's through prayer and rosary meditations—the core principle was the same: connecting to each moment with intention, love, and presence. As each of us changed, we all changed, and as we each prayed, we all healed.

I believe there is an undeniable quantum bond between those who share DNA, connecting individuals through the same energetic resonance, regardless of distance. In these connections, the strongest resonance naturally influences the others. This is influenced by the Law of Entrainment. Over time, through an unconventional and non-verbal process, my positive yogic practices and intentions, combined with my mother's fervent prayers, began to spark subtle but meaningful shifts throughout our entire family dynamic.

The work became a shared journey, even if on a silent, unconscious level, with differing approaches. Healing can include finding new ways to hold space for connection—especially when relationships are strained in person. This approach, even though I wasn't conscious of it at the time, allowed for positive growth to occur without forcing change or creating further conflict.

I also whole-heartedly believe that the healing of ancestral trauma can benefit the spirits of those who have since passed. Several indigenous traditions, as well as certain branches of psychology and energy work, also propose that unresolved trauma can remain in a family lineage, affecting both the living and the deceased.

Everything in our existence is vibration and frequency. Time may very well be an illusion. Matter is energy in motion, oscillating at various rates. We are all vibrations resonating from within, with an accumulation of action, feedback and experience along the way. Just as each ripple in a pond causes subtle shifts in the water's surface, every action and intention we emit has the power to create change.

As we dive deeper into this process, we quickly realize that we are all interconnected, and each person's transformation benefits us all.

According to the principles of Kabbalah, individual transformation sends ripples throughout the collective. This ancient teaching suggests that personal healing uplifts not only the individual but also the entire network of existence, with the impact directly proportional to the depth of transformation achieved—like the difference between lifting a mountain vs. lifting a single leaf, as a metaphorical example.

The saying, "to whom much is given, much is expected," doesn't apply solely to blessings but to traumas as well. When someone breaks free from negative patterns, chooses not to react to suffering, or heals after experiencing trauma, those shifts contribute to the healing and evolution of everyone connected to them. Ultimately, since we are all part of this greater whole, every transformation of each individual reverberates through us all to some degree. We can make a positive difference in how we live each moment of our lives.

Even though it wasn't easy for any of us in my family, we had a stubborn, powerful, and true love for one another, and genuine intentions for each other's well-being. No matter how strained things became, this fierce kind of love refused to give up, even when circumstances might have tempted us to walk away. This love became the anchor, forcing us to face challenges and to grow, even when it wasn't comfortable or easy, or even if at a distance and in silence.

Consider how your intentions, thoughts, and energies extend beyond just yourself—how they influence your family's past, present, and future. Every interaction carries energy, and the patterns you create today can either perpetuate or break cycles that have been passed down through generations. Find a safe space to consistently resonate love, forgiveness, and healing, and consider holding your family in the same vibrational intention with you. Then, hopefully, you will shift not only your individual experiences, but also the energetic field of your family—both ancestors and descendants.

CONSCIOUS MORALITY

I believe that when we realize the power of our own actions we can quickly transform our world for the better, choosing to live with with conscious morality that doesn't rely on punishment to be upheld by the powerful few who exempt themselves from the very standards they demand of others. Far too often, people give away their power mindlessly, unaware of the immense value of their personal attention and energy they are seduced into surrendering to the power hungry vampires of our world. Only when we realize that we are all connected will we begin treating others as ourselves, as members of our vastly extended family.

AS YOU ARE

Lastly, please remember that authenticity isn't about perfection—it's about embracing your whole self, including the messy, imperfect parts, and having the courage to honor your values in every decision. This kind of life requires the ability to tune out external noise so you can listen to the wisdom within.

You must also be willing to let go of what no longer aligns with who you are. This includes outdated beliefs, toxic environments, or relationships that drain your energy. It's not easy, but the reward is priceless—a life where your actions reflect your soul's purpose, not someone else's expectations. Remember, your authenticity is your power. The world doesn't need another person following the crowd; it needs you—fully awake, unapologetic, and aligned with your truth.

I wish you the greatest journey of your Self!

PROMPTS & AFFIRMATIONS

What recurring signs, symbols, or patterns keep showing up in your life, and what might they mean to you?

....
....
....
....
....

What feelings arise when you encounter a coincidence or synchronicity? Does it stir a sense of curiosity, reassurance, or fear?

....
....
....
....
....
....

Where in your life are you resisting or ignoring subtle nudges? What might shift if you leaned into your intuitive signals instead?

....
....
....
....
....
....

As I finalized this last page in the Conclusion of this book, I am sitting here in Buffalo, with Flash, visiting my family for my father's 80th birthday. This moment of reflection also feels perfectly timed.

Happy Birthday, Pops! Here's to celebrating life, and calling things out, as they are.

Aho Mitakuye Oyasin
To All My Relations

I AM CONSCIOUSNESS

I AM the space in which all things happen. I AM consciousness. I AM the now. I AM. **- Eckhart Tolle**

For those spiritually inclined or curious, I wanted to share some of my beliefs around living in *The Dharma Zone*, as I call it in my book, *As I Am*, and why I believe that I have lived a life rich with synchronicities. At its core, this state of being resonates with the timeless wisdom shared by great spiritual teachers throughout the ages, and some of the healing lessons explored in this book ultimately circle back to the same essential truth. No matter the path or tradition, the message remains consistent: ***Be Present***.

Again, I do not claim to be puritanical by any means, nor am I bound by rigid religious dogma, but I hold a deep reverence for spirituality, and the teachings of great teachers who have come before us. Yes, I clearly have a bit of a free-spirited, hippie yogi perspective, but there's an important distinction: I'm not just trying to manifest these ideas or imitate them. I am fully living, experiencing, naturally expressing, and embodying these concepts as they unfold in real-time, organically. It's not about following a trend, replicating a practice or trying to manifest a manufactured desire—it's about being present with the patterns as they arise in the present moment of I AM.

Throughout my spiritual life, I've been drawn to a concept that Yogananda Paramahansa coined, *Christ Consciousness,* a state of being that transcends the ego, aligning our consciousness with a universal, higher self. It is the realization of the interconnectedness of all things, with the idea that the divine presence, referred to as the "I AM," exists within every person, and through inner work and personal growth, anyone can awaken to this divine essence.

As I mentioned already, this is not tied to any specific religion, but it is rooted in the teachings of Jesus Christ who was a great teacher and healer to all people. I've encountered diversely differing backgrounds and beliefs—Christians, Muslims, Hindus, Jews, and more—who also resonate with this state of being. Void of religious frameworks, it focuses instead on the embodiment of divine truth, which means aligning with and recognizing things as they are.

Over time, I've come to see my journey—and the journeys of others with whom I have shared overlapping synchronicities, interestingly enough like Prince, Tupac, Elvis—as aligning with similar, present-moment, truth-aligned broadcasts, or manifestations of consciousness. These individuals, in their own unique and imperfect ways, seemed to embody this consciousness with their ability to align with absolute truth.

I'm sure you've met people in your life with whom you just resonate—almost as if you're vibrating on the same frequency. There's an effortless connection and sense of understanding that feels natural. In the same way, there are others with whom you just don't "vibe." These individuals feel discordant, as if their energy clashes with your own and misunderstandings become common. I believe synchronicities are like energetic resonances of consciousness—ripples of harmonics emanating from a shared source.

My fascination with Prince, Tupac, and Elvis, for example, stems not only from the synchronicities I've experienced in their regard, but also from recognizing their alignment with this I AM Consciousness, reflecting their similar pursuit of authenticity, spiritual truth, and justice, likely discovered by growing disillusioned of fame.

Real artists, unlike people who seek fame, are often deeply spiritual and visionary. Many artists who reach the pinnacle of fame realize that external success cannot satisfy their deeper spiritual hunger for truth which made them artists to begin with. Like me, they've had the rare experience of seeing firsthand what typically lies behind the curtain of fame—typically it's a manipulative team of agents, stylists, marketers, propagandists, and deal-makers, not an all-powerful wizard. Those who haven't reached such heights might still believe the illusion that fame and success hold the key to freedom and fulfillment. They cling to the hope that if they keep striving, the thirst within them will one day be quenched.

But the truth is that those fearless, truth-seeking artists, like Prince, discovered firsthand that real freedom doesn't come from the applause of the world; it comes from stepping beyond the illusion and embracing the authentic self—the I AM.

When we become too attached to dogmatic ideas, rigid beliefs, or outdated patterns—without staying present to the realities unfolding in each moment—we risk missing the many, in-the-moment messengers and messages that reveal the miraculous. Visionaries are often labeled crazy by the world, but it is their conviction to a truer reality that creates new worlds, new inventions, and new ways of thinking. It is then, and only then, that the world embraces them as a genius. Trust yourself. Dare to see the world more truthfully.

As you reach the final pages of this book, my hope for you is a life aligned with your truth, refusing to be distracted by the illusions and deceptions of manufactured marketing and filtered fame. I hope that you choose consciously where to direct your attention and hard-earned dollars, knowing that every choice you make holds the potential to shape the world around you. I hope that you see through ill-intentioned people who are solely looking to profit from you in any capacity.

I encourage you to support authenticity, to take time to understand the truth and origin of matters, to exercise compassion with boundaries when necessary, to value genuine connections, and to invest in what promotes well-being, justice, and sustainability for this beautiful planet we are all blessed to experience.

With Love
~ Alanna

AFTER-THOUGHTS

After finishing this book, a couple things happened immediately after that I thought were worth sharing.

GEORGE

While gaining permissions from specific people I mentioned by name in this book, I reached out to George from the Prince-inspired yoga class. Not only did he give me permission, but he responded with this text (which I included parts of):

"I believe that my mat was purple as well," (which it was) "And btw - at that class I had no idea of any of your Prince prior experiences. In fact, in the beginning of it, I was wondering what was going on with how the class was moving. The atmosphere was unlike any class before. There was an intense calmness - if that is a thing! There was a strange buzz/hum vibration. It was fascinating to me and a little uncomfortable. It just got stronger and built and built. It was perfectly leading to something fully ecstatic in a way very different from the forced stuff in some yoga practices... And, yep, you were a bit incredulous...about my suggestion that Prince was your lover..."

RIP JACK

Unsettling and downright "bizarre"—the very moment I finished this book, I closed my computer, feeling a sense of deep relief. About twenty minutes later, I went to the local health food store to grab ingredients for a celebratory dinner. And as I was exiting the store, who should be standing there but someone I hadn't seen or thought much about in 14 years? Yup, Jack the Ripper himself. I was flooded with a mix of confusing, fearful emotions—fearful because I know firsthand the cruelty he is capable of—but I couldn't help but find the timing of seeing him, well, on par. I am happy to close that chapter once and for all. RIP.